The Perfect Match

By Sahdaish Pall

Published in 2015 by Sahdaish Pall
Copyright © Sahdaish Pall

IBSN 978-1-326-47942-8

First Edition

A CIP catalogue record for this title is available from the British Library.

To my wonderful sons Vijay and Ajay Pall. May your lives be filled with so much joy and laughter, in the same way that you have filled mine.

Prologue

Nikita Heer peeled her eyes open and they were still wet from her tears. They stung like crazy.

She didn't know how long she had been asleep but her eyelids still felt so heavy, like she'd not slept at all. She blinked trying to clear her sight, wondering where she was.

Her back ached and she was uncomfortable on the bed, but her body felt too heavy to move.

Her eyes darted around the room looking for a clock. She spotted one above the large double glazed window which told her it was twelve thirty. God, had she been asleep that long?

She was surrounded by a warm stuffy smell and her body felt clammy from the heat that had built up in the room. Her throat was dry, wanting water.

For a moment she couldn't recall where she was and she stared up at the ceiling, her head spinning when she closed her eyes. As the haze lifted from her thoughts, it all came rushing back to her. Her breath caught in her chest. Throwing back the covers, Nikita jumped out of bed. Her feet hit the floor and a sharp pain shot through her stomach and up through her chest. She fell to the ground in agony. God, it fucking hurt so much.

Tears developed at the back of her eyes and before long they spilled over her cheeks and were dripping onto her chest. She wrapped her arms around her stomach and tears rolled down her face again, the pain was unbearable. Her stomach felt swollen and sore, hurting even more if she pressed on it. She was sure that she had a cracked rib.

After a moment, too scared to move, Nikita slowly raised her head and looked around for her bag. Where was it? She was sure she had it. Panic rose in her gut before she spotted it propped up against the wall. Nikita reached over and dragged it towards her.

As she undid the zip on the bag, she was startled by a knock on the door. Nikita froze. She didn't know whether she should open it, she didn't want to open it; she didn't want to see anyone. She decided that if she didn't open the door, the person knocking would soon leave. They would think that she wasn't there. She also knew if she tried to get up, the pain in her stomach would feel like a knife slicing through her. Even breathing caused agony.

Then there was a second knock, this time more urgent. She struggled and grabbed the edge of the mattress to help pull her up. She stopped to take a deep breath and walked over to the door. Reaching out with trembling hands she turned the handle. Keeping her other hand steady on the back of the door, she opened it very slightly just so she could see the person on the other side and they could see her.

A lady was standing in the doorway. She was an older woman, probably in her late fifties, wearing traditional Indian clothes. Her silvery grey hair was tied up in a bun at the back of her head. She wore thick rimmed glasses and was carrying the scent of incense sticks and spice.

The older woman spoke in a soft voice. "How are you, Nikita? You didn't come down to the office so I thought I'd better come and check on you. My name's Sue."

Nikita rubbed her face with her numb hands without responding. She just stared without uttering a word.

Sue spoke again, "You look confused. You came to the refuge late last night with the police. They dropped you off here, do you remember?"

Nikita remembered alright. How could she forget? The events of yesterday would be imprinted on her memory forever. She would never forget how hard it was for her to escape her hell hole. She remembered how her feet burned as she forced them to carry her until she could run no further. She had developed a stitch on the left side of her stomach but she'd ignored it. She focused on placing one foot in front of the other until she reached the telephone booth. She opened the door, stepped inside and collapsed on the floor. Her breathing came in short ragged gasps. Nikita sat lifeless, for the next hour, with no energy or will power to do anything. The stench of urine was overwhelming, but she didn't have the strength to pull herself off the cold concrete floor, even though the smell was making her sick.

Nikita told herself she had to get up. She had to do this, he could be looking for her and any minute now, he may find her. It was this thought that spurred her on. She couldn't go back there, not for anyone or anything. As she recalled the events of the last few days, Nikita felt the hysterics catch hold of her insides, urging her to start screaming. She bit down on her clenched fist which muffled her scream. She had to make this phone call, yes, it was her only escape. She reached up and grabbed the shelf below the phone and prayed it held her weight as she used it as leverage to pull herself up. She lifted the receiver and dialled 999.

The lady spoke again transporting Nikita back from her thoughts. "I'd like for you to see a doctor, just to make sure that you're okay. The police want to speak to you as well, about your injuries."

Okay? Okay? What did that word even mean? Nikita hadn't been okay in such a long time and this lady had come to see if she was okay?! That was a joke, Nikita thought.

"Well, if you need anything or you want to talk to someone, come and see me downstairs in the main office, I'm on duty today," she said. Then she turned around and walked away.

Nikita shut the door behind her. She leaned her head against the door, bracing herself as pain knotted in her stomach.

Sighing, Nikita turned and looked at the room. There was a single bed in the corner, a wardrobe on the opposite side and a fridge to one side. She opened the fridge door. It was empty but clean, except for the extremely strong smell of detergent that came flooding out.

A basket sat on the floor at the foot of the bed. Slowly, step by step, she walked over to it and looked inside it. There was some soap, shampoo, toothpaste, a toothbrush and a towel in it.

She had one arm wrapped around her waist and with the other hand she picked up her own bag and tipped it out onto the bed. A couple of pairs of track suit jogging bottoms, and two t-shirts fell out with a few pieces of underwear. It was all she could fit into this small duffel bag. She concealed it under the sink before he returned home from work. She couldn't risk him finding it. Having looked in the side pocket she found her passport, her MP3 player which she hadn't realised was in there and some money. The cookie jar where she kept money for bills was the only bit of cash she had access to, so she took it. She had her debit card but she didn't dare use it, in case it gave away her location. It didn't matter anyway, as there was never much money in the account. Nikita paid for everything and as a teaching assistant she wasn't on a great salary. She earned enough to get by and now she would have to give that up as well.

Nikita picked up the MP3 player and tossed it to one side. The last thing she wanted was to think about music, even though music had always been the love of her life. It was the one thing that helped her through the day, lifting her mood no matter how she was feeling, but not today. Nothing could help her today.

Nikita stared at herself in the mirror. Feeling disgusted, she had the sudden need to have a wash. She couldn't bare it. She had to get these filthy clothes off. Her hair was tangled and greasy and she felt the urge to pull it all out. She had to get rid of his smell that lingered over her, the sweat from his hands that had touched her. His saliva on her breasts, her neck and shoulders. It was almost like she could still feel him breathing on her, and hear his voice ringing in her head.

She shuddered and she felt a shiver run up her spine.

She looked around and there was no shower in her room. There would have be one outside, somewhere.

Nikita walked over and lay the side of her head against the door. She listened. She couldn't hear any movement so she slowly pulled the door open, hoping that no one would hear her. She felt so embarrassed to be there and she didn't want anyone to see her. She looked down the long white corridor and saw other doors leading off it. Were these other rooms like hers? Did they also house women like her? God, how many were there?

The corridor seemed to go on forever and she rubbed her eyes to get a clearer look. She saw an open door opposite her bedroom and she could see a toilet. Hoping there was a bath or a shower in there, Nikita quickly grabbed all the toiletries and dashed across the corridor on tip toes into what turned out to be the shower room. She held her breath for as long as she could and grit her teeth so that she couldn't yell out at the pain. She turned and locked the door and slowly started to undress.

Her body shook with pain and yet there was a numbness that overshadowed it. Nikita looked into the mirror. Who was the person staring back at her? She had horrible frizzy hair, a pale complexion, a black eye, a cut swollen lip and a sad face. There was a large gash under the eye which had started to scab over, but it was deep and she knew that it was going to leave a scar. It was like a tattoo of his name. Every time she would look in the mirror, she would be reminded of him and everything he had put her through. Nikita looked down at herself. Black and blue marks visible on her legs, arms, her whole body.

Ashamed, she stared into the tall mirror. Her body was soft and dumpy. Her breasts large and floppy. They weren't taut the way he liked them. Her stomach was soft with a layer of fat and her thighs had dimples where cellulite had built up. It was all her fault. This was why she was never able to win him over. She held up her hands and saw that her nails were full of dirt. She noticed the wedding band on her left hand and it felt like it was strangling her. She tried to pull it off but her hands were too swollen.

Nikita turned away unable to look at herself any longer, the feeling of repulsion coursing through her. She was pathetic. Her life was a joke. She didn't understand. She had done everything she was supposed to. She followed the path her parents had decided for her. She had played the part of the honourable obedient daughter. She hadn't challenged her parents, never disobeyed them and never said no to any of their decisions. She did everything she was told to. Then why had things turned out the way they had? Why was her life not perfect, not wonderful, not blissful? Why was it full of so much pain, humiliation and sorrow?

Nikita broke down and started to cry uncontrollably. He'd ruined every part of her. Never had she dreamed that her life would come to this. There was no way out.

Standing up straight, she took a deep breath, pushing the tears back even as they tried to defy her. She opened the curtain and stepped into the shower. It felt so good to have the water running down her back. She stood for a couple of minutes lifeless, letting the water massage her body.

She grabbed the bottle of shower gel and squeezed it onto her hand. She scrubbed everywhere as hard as she could and almost until her skin became red raw, but she couldn't help it. She needed every ounce of her body to be free of his touch.

Her mind started to wonder and she thought about what had happened. How could anyone treat another person in this way? The way that he had treated her. Her life had been turned upside down.

She felt a horrible pain in her stomach, her lungs weren't taking in any air, no matter how hard she tried and her head started to spin. Collapsing on to the floor of the shower, she curled her legs up to her chest ignoring the pain and wrapped her arms around them. She buried her face in her knees and cried and cried and cried. There was nothing else left for her to do.

Nikita sat on the floor for a while longer before she managed to pick herself up. She grabbed the towel and dried herself off, being careful not to press on the bruising. After getting dressed, Nikita washed her underwear with some soap in the wash basin and she went back to the bedroom and hung her clothes on the radiator to dry.

She sighed, stepped back and sat on the bed.

How did it get to this? Even when she was young, even though her parents were strict, she was still happy. She still had her friends and family around her, but now she had no one. How was she going to cope on her own? Maybe if she'd spoken up when all this had first started, she wouldn't be here today.

Nikita could still remember the day that her auntie had called with the proposal and she could remember all too well, the events that had occurred thereafter.

Chapter 1 – The Meeting

When Nikita was little she wanted to do so many things with her life. There were many dreams and aspirations. First she wanted to be a singer, then an actress and then a dancer. She was a member of the school choir and the school brass band and always took part in school theatre productions, she absolutely loved them. She received so much joy from singing and being on stage; she could just get up in front of hundreds of people and start singing her heart out. She had nerves of steel.

She had grown up since then. Now her favourite pastime was reading and watching movies, especially the chick flicks, they made her day. Pretty Woman and Sleepless in Seattle were her most recent Hollywood favourites. She also loved watching Indian movies; they were always so romantic, with beautiful music and story lines. She could watch them again and again without getting bored.

Nikita would often day dream while watching these movies, dreaming of meeting that special person, with whom she would spend the rest of her life with. Someone who will make her go weak at the knees and her breath catch. For some people, marriage and finding someone to love, was not on their bucket list, but Nikita was a dreamer and she wanted the fairytale story. She wished that one day she will meet her handsome and charming prince like the ones in the Disney books she read as a youngster. She wanted the big wedding and to live happily ever after. Bollywood movie actors were always hunky handsome men and she'd imagine he would also be like those heroes. Or maybe he would be like one of the leading men in the books she liked to read, strong and courageous, willing to do anything for their loved ones.

At school, Nikita's girlfriends would ask her who she fancied, but the truth was that she wasn't interested in any of the boys at school. He was going to be very special and one in a million.

Reality was different. These were only dreams and Nikita knew that when the time came, she wouldn't have a choice. This was the life of an Indian girl. Her parents were very strict and placed so many restrictions on her choices and wishes, but this wasn't news to Nikita. She had known this all her life, but she never had the heart to say anything to them. Just one look from her dad would frighten the life out of her. She'd never argued with him about anything and she wasn't going to start now. What she wanted in life and what was going to happen, were two extremes of a spectrum. She always knew that she would have an arranged marriage. That was expectation. Love marriages were unheard of in her family and it wasn't something she had ever seriously contemplated because she knew it would never happen, as much as she wanted it to. In reality it was never an option.

Nikita's dad was a cheerful loving man who brought Nikita up to be a hard working, obedient, and honourable daughter. He was a courageous man that took on many challenges in life and Nikita learnt a lot from him. She was running his business for him at the age of seventeen.

When Nikita finished school at the age of sixteen, she wasn't permitted to go to college and onto university, but she never argued. She lost touch with many of her friends after she left school. They went on to study further and make new friends. She knew if she'd had the same choices, she could have made something of her life.

After she left school, she was roped into the family business and because she was the eldest and the responsibility fell to her. Her brother and sister were still at school and her mum kept on working at the bra factory to ensure there was still an income while dad was building up the business.

When Nikita turned seventeen, she started taking driving lessons and within six months, she had passed her driving test first time.

Nikita's dad bought her an old Vauxhall Corsa which was old but easy to handle. He passed her the keys as soon as she came back from the driving test. He gave her the responsibility to open up and lock up the shop and then he could get some decent rest when he needed to be up in the early hours of the morning to go to the cash and carry.

He never openly acknowledged it, but she knew her father was proud of her.

Nikita's parents loved her very much. She had no doubt about that, but her dad was very old fashioned and lived his life by his traditions and what she called ancient customary practices. He never seemed to get it. Even people in India had moved on and started living their lives more like western societies, but Indians like him, who came over to the United Kingdom twenty or thirty years ago, were still living their lives as they did then.

As soon as Nikita turned twenty one, her mum started spreading the word amongst relatives to keep an eye out for a potential husband for her. Nikita often tried to talk to her mum about it, to explain she wasn't ready yet, but her mum always said that she'd got married at the same age and it had worked out for her. Nikita felt as though she just couldn't get through to her mum.

It was a cold February evening and Nikita was watching Eastenders after locking up the store and driving home, when the telephone started ringing. Nikita answered the call. "Hello."

"Hello beta, how are you?" asked auntie. Auntie always called Nikita child in Panjabi when she was in a good mood.

"I'm fine auntie, how are you?"

"I'm good. Actually I'm great and I have some very good news for you, but first I must speak to your mum. Is she home?"

Nikita's heart started to sink into her stomach; she knew what this would be about.

"Mum, Auntie's on the phone for you," Nikita called.

She came out of the kitchen drying her hands on a towel and Nikita passed her mum the receiver. Nikita went back to watching her programme but now her focus was not on the Television.

"Hello Sindy, how are you?" Mum asked.

Auntie Sindy and Nikita's mum were first cousins and her name wasn't really Sindy, but Surinder. She preferred to be called Sindy, all her friends found it easier to pronounce and it fit better with the people she hung around with.

Nikita saw her mum's eyes light up while she was talking on the phone and she sounded very excited. Her voice was travelling up and down in excitement and Nikita's heart dropped deeper and deeper with every word. "Really? Oh my. Really? Oh my. Oh definitely Sindy, we will be there this Sunday," mum said and then she put the phone down.

"What did she say mum, are we going somewhere on Sunday?" Nikita asked, trying to keep her voice from shaking.

"Oh my God Nikita, it's your lucky day."

"What do you mean?" Nikita asked nervous.

"Your auntie Sindy has found the perfect match for you and we are going to meet him this Sunday."

Nikita's blood ran cold. She tried to protest but her mum wouldn't listen. How was it that she didn't get a say in this? Nikita sighed in resignation. There was no point in arguing, as nothing she ever said was considered in any way, shape or form. Nikita could never understand how their minds worked. How could they introduce her to someone and expect them to decide within a matter of minutes, if they wanted to spend the rest of their lives together? Compatibility or attraction didn't seem to figure in the equation. There would be no time to date, to get to know each other, to develop a relationship, a friendship or anything else for that matter. The expectation would be for a 'yes' or a 'no' and Nikita guessed that he would be the one casting the vote.

Mum had told Nikita that his name was Sam, short for Samarjeet and he was from Wolverhampton. Nikita hadn't even travelled to the West Midlands; it was so far away from Letchworth. How was she going to see her family?

Sindy told Nikita's mum about Sam and his family. Between them, they made arrangements for Sam and Nikita to meet up the coming weekend in London.

The following day Sindy called again to speak to Nikita's mum and both were getting very excited, discussing the meeting, making arrangements, planning the wedding? Nikita hadn't even met him yet, but it seemed that their minds were already made up.

Mum had been through the same situation, though maybe it had been even worse for her. She didn't even meet her husband to be, Nikita's dad, before they got married. They just saw each other on a photo as a way of introduction to, this is who you will be marrying. Crazy.

Nikita loved her culture, but she could never understand some of these traditions. She couldn't comprehend how people prepared themselves for this sort of relationship. Spending their life with a person they didn't know and possibly didn't have anything in common with. So many people from her parents' generation had been married this way and within the first year of their marriage, they had already had their first child.

This was something Nikita wasn't comfortable with.

She always thought she would only really be with someone, all heart, body and soul when she was in love with them, but sex was part and parcel of this agreement. It wasn't about making love, or fulfilling each other's desires and pleasures. It was about having sex because it was what he expected, but this wasn't what Nikita wanted. Her views on what a relationship should be, was totally different to that of her parents.

From the conversations her mum and Sindy were having, it sounded like Sam was an educated man and so Nikita guessed he had to be an open minded person.

On the morning of the meeting Nikita got up very early. She had suffered with a very restless night. The nerves were starting to get to her.

18

She didn't know what to wear, whether it should be western clothes or Asian clothes? Trousers or a skirt? Make up or no makeup? In the end Nikita decided on an Indian suit and a subtle amount of makeup. She didn't over dress because her mum always said that the boy's family would think she was too keen and that wasn't good for her reputation. All Indian girls were the image of pride and innocence.

Mum needed to go to the day time discos and see what went on there, then she would realise how innocent Indian girls really were.

As if it wasn't enough that Nikita was meeting a total stranger, she had to take all these other practices into consideration as well.

Nikita imagined what Sam would look like. Would he have big strong muscles, a beautiful face and a gorgeous smile? Actually, she realised she didn't care. As long as he wanted to be her best friend. Later she could grow to love him, she was sure.

Letchworth was only about sixty miles up the A1M from Southall in London, but they were stuck in traffic on the M4 for nearly two hours. Nikita kept wiping her hands on her trousers; she was so nervous that her palms were sweating.

Her dad sat in the passenger seat next to her. Ever since she'd passed her driving test, if her dad could get away with not driving anywhere, he would, which meant Nikita had to drive everywhere. Nikita's mum and sister were in the back seat and mum would not shut up.

"How exciting, our daughter is getting fixed up. Soon you will be a married woman."

"Mum, don't you think you're jumping the gun a bit?"

Nikita's dad shot her a scary look, which she knew meant, 'shut up'. She didn't say anything after that and mum went quiet as well. Nikita saw her mum's face contort from the rear view mirror and she dropped her head. Nobody ever spoke against dad's silent commands.

The meeting had been planned at Sindy's house, with all the family there; it was a very awkward situation.

Nikita sat in their front room with her heart beating hard and fast in her chest. Now her palms and forehead were sweating even more. God, they must have their central heating turned up high, Nikita thought. She wished she could open a window but, she didn't have the nerve, she felt like her bum was glued to the sofa.

"Shit man, this is so scary," Nikita said to her sister, Ria. She was rubbing her hands nervously.

Ria was the younger of the two. She had her life mapped out and Nikita always felt a little envious of her. She had plans to go to university, no questions were asked. Nikita had been roped in to look after the family business and she never gave her dad anything to stress about, so dad had become a lot more lenient with Ria and Nikita's younger brother Kam. He was still in primary school, so there were no expectations for him just yet.

"I don't know why you put up with it. I would never let them do this to me," said Ria.

"That's the difference between you and I Ria, I could never do anything to hurt them."

"That's why you've always been their favourite Nikita, because you're the goody two shoes and I could never live up to that."

Nikita was quite taken aback by these comments. Ria had never said anything like this before and frankly Nikita was very surprised.

Ria didn't realise that she was getting the opportunities that Nikita could only ever dream about. In a way, Nikita had sacrificed her freedom so that Ria could have hers and right now, she didn't think that Ria recognised that.

"What are you talking about? How can you say that I'm their favourite? You're the one that has all the privileges of going to university and getting an education. I would do anything to be in your shoes right now."

Ria stared at Nikita with eyes wide open. She couldn't believe what she was hearing and it made her think about what she'd just said to her big sister. Ria had never thought about how difficult it was for Nikita. To her, the business was what Nikita did.

Ria and Nikita never really saw eye to eye. Nikita hadn't realised when Ria had grown up. She could only remember her as a baby and then one day she came back from the shop with her dad and there she was, all grown up preparing for university. How did that happen?

Sindy brought in a cup of spiced tea and placed it on the coffee table in front of Nikita, with a plate full of Indian sweets. Nikita's favourite, gulab jaman and jalebi, drenched in sugary syrup. Not great in a calorie controlled diet. Nikita picked up a piece of jalebi and took a bite. They were delicious. If she'd been at home she would have heated them in the microwave for ten seconds and then they would have been perfect. She could have done the same here and on any other day she would have, but to get to Sindy's kitchen, she would have to walk through the dining room. Sam and his family were sitting there with her family. To top it off, she wasn't sure that her wobbly legs would carry her.

Nikita took a sip of tea and she could taste the cardamoms, root ginger and fennel seeds which gave it a spicy flavour. It helped to calm her nerves a little, but not for long because after a while, everyone left her in the room and sent Sam in. Before he walked in, Nikita's mum ran back in and gave her the big thumbs up and a huge smile. She was so excited; anyone would think it was her wedding. Nikita rolled her eyes.

When Sindy had called a few days before, she had described Sam to Nikita's mum as a 'Sunny Deol' lookalike. Sunny was a big Bollywood superstar who was absolutely gorgeous and he was one of Nikita's favourite actors. He had biceps the size of a woman's thighs. This made Nikita feel a little apprehensive, because she didn't consider herself to be pretty. She didn't think she was ugly, but she wasn't all that to look at either and to top it off, she didn't have the perfect 34-26-34 figure. Being a size fourteen at five foot two inches tall, she felt her figure was far from perfect. So if he looked like Sunny Deol then he could never be interested in her. She told herself it didn't matter. She just had to go through the motions and get through the day. She would talk and answer any questions. She would be polite and respectful, just like her mother had said and it would soon be over, she told herself. All she could do was to shut up and endure it. It would all be over shortly.

When Sam walked in, the first thing Nikita noticed was his stride. He seemed to float, just like the angels she had read about in some of her favourite science fiction books. He was smartly dressed, handsome and carried himself with pride. He was wearing a Hugo Boss jacket, with a pair of faded blue jeans and a crisp white t-shirt. He looked like he was about six feet tall. Nikita couldn't be sure because she was sitting down, but he couldn't be far off it. So that was the first nail on the coffin. Heels were out of the question; she wouldn't last five minutes in them.

He sat down opposite her and smiled sheepishly. To her surprise he was very polite; he spoke in a deep raspy voice. "Hi, I'm Sam," he said. His voice was so sexy that Nikita was almost salivating.

"Hello, I'm Nikita," she replied. Shit, this was very awkward. What did one say?

A long silence followed.

"So Nikita, what do you do?"

"Well, I work in the family business."

Nikita kept thinking about her mum's instructions. 'Don't talk too much, don't be cheeky, keep your head down, don't make too much eye contact,' blah, blah, blah.

"I'm training in law and planning on becoming a solicitor, I'm in my final year," he said.

Well that's it isn't it, the final nail on the coffin. There was no way that he was going to be interested in her. He was so well educated and Nikita didn't even have an A level to her name. However it didn't seem to bother him and he continued to ask her more questions. He asked about her likes and dislikes. He was ever so polite. One day he is going to make a girl very happy, Nikita thought to herself. He seemed so perfect.

"What do you like to do when you're not working? I mean do you have any hobbies?"

"I love music, reading, watching movies; they're all a passion of mine. But I don't get too much time. You know what family businesses are like; sometimes you're working around the clock. What about you?" Nikita asked.

"I enjoy football. I still play sometimes, but I like to watch it."

"My brother's a big fan of football, so I do watch it sometimes when he hogs the TV and won't let anyone else watch anything," Nikita smiled. "The problem is that no matter how many times he has explained it to me, I still don't understand the off side rule."

Sam laughed.

Shit, am I looking at him too much? She found it hard to take her eyes off him.

His smile was bright, like he'd had his teeth whitened recently. He had lips that looked like strawberries ready to eat. He had big round eyes the colour of hazelnuts. He was so gorgeous.

Nikita told herself to focus.

"Do you go out much, clubbing, drinking, socialising?"

"Not really. My dad's too strict, so I've never been to any clubs or bars. I do enjoy being around my friends though, but they normally come round to my house and I'll cook for them, but like I said, we're very busy, so I don't see them too often either."

"You cook?"

"You say that like its surprising."

"Well it's not very often you get Asian girls cooking now. They're all too busy getting educated or a career. Even my sister can't cook."

But cooking was something Nikita could do and do very well. Ever since she was young she loved cooking and was always experimenting with new ideas. Her mum taught her to cook so many different Indian dishes, from appetizers to main courses to desserts. Nikita's mum always said that she didn't want anyone to ever say she hadn't taught her daughters anything. So learning to cook was as important as learning to make a decent cup of tea, it was an essential part of an Indian girls life. Nikita didn't mind though, she enjoyed cooking and even took it up as a GCSE.

"Well you don't have to worry there, I love cooking, Sam." Oh shit, she called him by his name, mum said not to address him using his name, it was meant to be disrespectful. Nikita's mum never called her dad by his name either; she always called him Ji, which was the respectful way of addressing your partner. Oh forget it; it was too late now anyway, she thought. If he had an issue with it then too bad, she couldn't take the words back.

"My mum taught me a lot about cooking. I can cook most Indian foods, but as I've got older, I started trying dishes from other countries, like Chinese and Italian. I have a really close friend, who's mixed race, Chinese and Thai and she's given me loads of tips on Chinese recipes."

Sam smiled at Nikita and they talked for a while longer about music, movies and television. As they talked, Nikita became consciously aware of Sam's scent enveloping her, attaching itself to her clothes. He smelt gorgeous. Oh well, it's a shame she thought, but these things happen and not everyone is interested in the first person they meet.

After a short while, Sam's mum knocked on the door and walked in. "Hello," she said to Nikita.

Nikita put her hands together and greeted Sam's mum with a formal Sikh greeting, the way her parents had taught her.

"Sat Sri Akal," Nikita smiled. This means God is the ultimate truth. Sam's mum turned to him and said, "We need to be leaving now son."

"Okay," he told his mum, "I'll be right out." He looked over to Nikita and said, "Hopefully I'll see you again, soon."

"Okay," Nikita said and with that Sam left the room.

He looked like he was interested, something Nikita didn't see coming, but then again, it could just be his way of being polite. Sam was very handsome and they were right when they said he looked like Sunny Deol, he had the same drowning eyes.

Nikita stayed in the front room for the next half an hour and she could hear both families talking, saying their goodbyes and hugging each other before Sam's family left. She thought they had forgotten about her. 'Hello, I'm still here you know.' But she couldn't just waltz into the other room with all those people there; her mum would have a heart attack. She desperately wanted to see him again. Just one more peek couldn't hurt, but she lost her bottle. It wasn't worth the headache her mum would undoubtedly give her after.

When Nikita and her family left Southall, her dad was in no state to drive back. He'd had a few shots of whiskey with her uncle. An Indian shot wasn't like a shot you got in a pub. Each measure was half a glass. Nikita was already feeling sick from the whole experience and now she had to drive home. Well, at least it was over.

There was so much traffic on the M25, which agitated Nikita and to top it off, Nikita's dad fell asleep and his loud snoring was getting on her nerves. She looked over to her dad sitting in the front passenger seat and she noticed the way his heavy breathing was making his moustache shake aggressively under his nose. Nikita's mouth pulled up to one side and she felt some of her anxiety drain away.

Dad didn't ask her anything about Sam before he fell asleep because in this family, dads didn't talk to their daughters about these sorts of things. It was left up to mum to have the discussion with Nikita.

As the car was moving slowly in the traffic, Nikita wound the window down and looked out over the fields either side of the motorway. Driving through Hertfordshire and then entering Letchworth was a sight for sore eyes. She loved the smell of Letchworth; it seemed to have a scent of its own. It was a beautiful town, built within a belt of open countryside. The streets were clean and you were never scared to be out late in the evening. People were very polite and friendly.

As Nikita stared out of the window, her thoughts drifted back to the meeting. Her first impression of Sam was that he was an intelligent and handsome man. His skin was the colour of toffee and his eyes were shaped like almonds. Simply divine. He was so polite and gentlemanly, Nikita found herself feeling comfortable and at ease talking to him. The thought of spending her life with a man like that, fascinated her. However, fascination was all it could be. There was no way a man as handsome and intelligent as him, would be interested in a simple, uneducated girl like her. She was sure of it. Nikita let out a low sigh under her breath, so low that no one else noticed.

Once they arrived at home and managed to drag dad into the house half asleep, Nikita's mum started harassing her for information about the meeting. Nikita knew her mum was burning to ask in the car but she didn't want dad to overhear the conversation, even though he was asleep.

"Wasn't he handsome?" she said. "He's training to be a barrister you know. I think that you two will make the perfect match."

"Mum," Nikita said. "He's training as a solicitor not a barrister, there's a difference and don't get your hopes up, he probably won't be interested, he's too well educated."

"Oh don't talk nonsense. Men these days want a hard working and respectable wife and you are all of these and he looked very happy when he joined us after the meeting. I think he is interested." Nikita understood her mum meant well and she was only looking out for her, but Nikita couldn't help feel that her mum was getting on her nerves.

"Whatever mum," Nikita mumbled under her breath as she ran up the stairs rolling her eyes once more.

Nikita never spoke back to her parents when they annoyed her, because she knew it would upset them. She would just internalise it, until the anger and frustration would die down inside her. She was always a good daughter and they loved her for it. Sometimes she wanted to scream at them and shout at them and say, 'No, I don't want to do that,' or 'will someone listen to what I'm saying', but she never did. She would sit in her bedroom and imagine what it would feel like to rebel against them. She had some friends whose parents were a lot more westernised than her parents. These friends had cut their hair and had it

26

coloured and wore western clothes all the time. Nikita wished she could get her hair cut as well, but wouldn't dare because she knew that her dad would probably kill her. She cut her fringe a little once but only ever wore it down at school. She would pin it back once she got home so that her dad didn't see it. After a while she stopped trimming it and let it grow out because she just got sick of hiding it.

Chapter 2 - The Wedding

Four weeks later the news broke when Nikita's mum received the dreaded telephone call. The families were so happy when Sam agreed to the marriage, but Nikita didn't really have much of a say. As far as she was concerned everyone thought he was a very good catch, so they just assumed that it was okay with her. Nikita's family thought she had hit the jack pot. In their eyes this was better than winning the lottery.

Nikita felt very uneasy about the whole situation. Since the day she had met Sam, she hadn't seen or spoken to him again. It didn't make sense to her. Why did a man with such promising future prospects, want to be with a simple person like her? How could they possibly be compatible? He would be used to a completely different lifestyle. He was so handsome. She wouldn't be surprised if he had been in a number of relationships. Nikita imagined that girls probably threw themselves at him and she had no experience at all. Everything felt so wrong to her, but she couldn't argue with her parents just because she had a gut instinct. They would never listen to her.

Nikita's parents went straight into planning the wedding and before she knew it, the date was set. Nerves made pimples break out on her face and she noticed the condition of her skin deteriorating. Like most girls before their wedding, she knew she should be trying to lose weight, but she found herself overindulging in chocolate and cream cakes. Comfort eating helped her feel any better.

Nikita stood in the mirror and appraised herself. She was only twenty two and she felt like she had the body of a forty year old. She twisted and turned, staring at her thighs. Covered in cellulite and dimples, they looked horrible. She had knobbly knees and ankles that were not sexy. She looked at her stomach trying to hold it in, but when she let out her breath, it stuck out. She had big breasts but these were already heading in a south direction. Nikita lifted them and imagined what they would look like if they were firm and perky. When she let go, they dropped again, hurting her a little. It was no good. This was what God had given her. Some of her friends had said that they would kill to have boobs like hers, but they were just being polite and trying to make her feel better about herself. She knew what she was and beautiful was not a way she would describe herself. How was she ever going to have a physical relationship with a man that was so perfect?

Weeks went by and Nikita's dad wouldn't let her have any contact with Sam. She wasn't allowed to call him, or meet him and it must have been the same for him, because he hadn't contacted her either. Nikita made excuses to herself, to rationalise why there had been no contact. He was busy with his studies and wedding preparations and anyway, they would have all their lives to build on their relationship and get to know each other after they got married. She felt stupid thinking like this, because it went against everything that she believed in.

Nikita's parents planned a trip to India to buy all her wedding clothes and jewellery. It was so much cheaper than buying them here. Even taking the cost of the tickets into account, it still worked out so much better.

They travelled to Punjab which is a state in the North West region of India and was the home of both Nikita's parents. She loved visiting India. She'd been there six times before this trip and the beauty of the country never seized to amaze her. The smells, the sights, the culture, it was mind blowing.

They travelled by car from the airport to the village of Jalandhar, where her dad had recently built the family home. Luckily for them Nikita thought, it had all the mod cons of being in England, but when you stepped outside, you still got to see the culture of India. It was good to have access to a proper seated toilet, Nikita hated squatting.

The relatives in India were so happy for her.

Her parents were flaunting a photograph of Sam in front of everybody. Everyone's comments were almost the same. They kept saying, 'Oh, he is so tall, fair and handsome, he will have a good job, you will be so well off, Nikita we are so happy for you.' 'You have been a good daughter and now you will get what you deserve.' 'You know what they say, you reap what you sow.'

Nikita knew they meant well, but it was a little off putting. Everyone seemed to talk about how lucky she was, because of everything he was going to give her and provide her with. Apparently it was fate that had brought them together, they were the perfect match. But Nikita wanted for just one of them to say that Sam was lucky, that he was fortunate to have met her, but no one said anything like that. Then again, that was probably because people didn't think that she was much of a catch. What did she have to offer anyone? Nothing. Some experience running a business and that was it. She hadn't even studied any A levels.

After she got married, how would she get a job? Right now she worked with her dad, for herself. She had no experience working in any other type of environment or ever been for an interview. She didn't even have a CV.

She would have to prepare herself, for a life without her dad, the business and everything else that she was used to. Everything was going to change.

While Nikita was in India, she did most of her wedding shopping. While visiting a cousin's house in Phagwara, they travelled to the famous Bansa Bazaar on a rickshaw. Nikita felt guilty. She could see the man struggling while he cycled with three of them sitting in the carriage. He looked so frail and weak and it was hot. God only knew where he got his strength. Many people made their living in this way and it only cost Nikita thirty rupees which equated to about twenty five pence. India was a very beautiful country but there was so much poverty. The streets were full of people begging. A woman with a young child approached Nikita, holding out her hand, telling Nikita that her baby hadn't eaten all day. Nikita couldn't help but pass some money over. As soon as Nikita had placed the rupees in the lady's hand, more beggars approached. They followed Nikita until Nikita's mum shooed them away. Nikita felt sad for them, but she also knew that for many beggars, this was part of a business.

As they walked down one of the main high streets, there was a strong smell of food coming from the shops. The stores had shutters at the entrance and once they were lifted, the whole store was open for you to walk into. Nikita could smell samosas and fried bread, but she rarely ate from the shops, she didn't have a very strong stomach.

There were so many boutiques selling wedding dresses. As she walked passed each shop, the sales assistants were calling her into their store. She didn't know which way to turn; they were calling from all sides.

"Please come in madam," one said.

"We have all the latest designs," another said.

"We will do you a very good deal," a third said.

"Madam, come this way," a fourth said.

Nikita stood confused. She didn't know which shop to go into first or who had the best designs. Everything felt so crowded.

Nikita's cousin took her to the Punjab Cloth House, which was run by people that he knew and trusted. Nikita's cousin was sure that this was a shop where they weren't going to get ripped off.

As soon as Nikita and her family walked in, they were seated in front of a raised stage area and the owner was sitting barefoot on top of it. The great thing about Indians was that they knew how to be hospitable. The customer service was great. Drinks and sandwiches were ordered before Nikita had even started talking about what she was looking for.

As Nikita began to tell the owner what she wanted, the garments were already flying off the shelves. There was so much choice.

"Slow down," she told him. "Let me feel the fabric, I need to think." The owner was trying so hard to show Nikita as much variety as possible in the hope that she would pick something, but she was just getting more and more confused.

Before she came to India, Nikita had an idea of what she was looking for. Now having seen so many designs, she wasn't sure anymore.

"This colour will totally suit you," he said with a strong Indian accent.

"Let me be the judge of that," Nikita said as she rolled her eyes. "Show me that one," she pointed. "And that one."

"I think that the pink will suit your skin complexion best," he said.

"But I don't want pink, I want red."

"But."

"Are you getting married or me?" Nikita interrupted. "I want red." Now he was really starting to piss her off. Nikita bit her lip, not wanting to appear too rude. After all, these people were friends of her cousin and she didn't want to upset them.

"Okay," he said. "We have some new arrivals in the back, just been delivered, I will get those for you."

"Shaan," he shouted. "Bring the new arrivals."

They waited for Shaan to bring the dresses from the back store room and in the interim; a fresh round of Pepsi, Limca and Gold spot drinks arrived.

Nikita tried on so many different dresses. They had long tops and short tops, with an A line skirt and fish tail style skirt. Then just as Nikita was about to give up, her eyes drifted to a packed outfit. It was the right shade of. Not bright red and not maroon, but a crimson, rich deep red. "Show me that one."

"Shaan, open that one," the owner ordered. Shaan picked it up and opened the clear plastic packaging from the seal. As he pulled out the dress, Nikita's eyes widened. She had found the most beautiful wedding dress of all. It was perfect. It was made in silk with green and gold crystals. It had diamante work embellished all around the border of the full length skirt. The top was in a corset style with little cap sleeves and to finish it off, it had a beautifully embroidered heavy scarf, with the same embellishment as the skirt on all four sides.

When she tried it on, she knew that it was the one for her. It made her feel like a princess and for a little while forgetting all her worries, she felt excited. Nikita lightly stroked the dress as she stared into the mirror. It felt luxurious and elegant. She imagined what she would look like on her wedding day, when she got dressed and appeared in front of everyone. She would look beautiful shimmering under the spot lights on the dance floor, when she and Sam had their first dance.

Nikita thought back to her meeting with Sam. Those beautiful big eyes and strawberry lips. Would they taste as good as they looked? Heat started to build in her stomach and butterflies tickled a little. Nikita felt nervous as the reality of what was happening, started to sink in. She looked up in a silent prayer, asking that He make everything go well. All she wanted was to be happy. She didn't care if she didn't have the luxury holidays or flash cars. It was never a desire, but she did desire love and friendship and she looked forward to finally having that with Sam.

Nikita smiled into the mirror, happy with what she saw. She took a deep breath, turned and pulled away the changing room curtain stepping out. Everyone in the store stopped what they were doing and stared. She could tell that they all loved it, most of all her mum.

Mum was almost crying when she saw Nikita walking out of the changing room. "You look beautiful," she said, her eyes welling up. "I can't believe you're getting married. It only seems like yesterday that you were a baby and now you are leaving our family to make someone else's life a joy." Mum picked up her bag and pulled out her pocket tissues and wiped at her eyes. She almost had Nikita in tears as well.

Nikita bought matching bangles in red and white which were embedded with intricate crystals to be worn for the first time on the wedding day. She picked out a red hand bag which had gold crystals on the buckle and matching red sandals to go with the wedding dress. She tried to find the highest heals possible. Nikita knew that her feet would hurt but she had to bear it for just one day. Everything was perfect. Nikita's dad ordered the wedding cards and she picked out a gold wedding ring for Sam. She wondered if he would pick hers.

In the evenings the whole family returned to the cousin's house and they all crashed on the mobile beds on the flat roof, out in the open. May nights in India were very warm and sleeping out in the open was an experience in itself.

They would stay up half the night talking about their two different worlds. Nikita loved sitting up all night, drinking tea and chatting on the open top roof. It was a different world in India. Life just wasn't as fast paced as it was in England. People had time for each other out there.

Nikita lay on her bed, which was uncomfortable but she was getting used to it. She lay on her back, her hands resting behind her head. She stared up at the stars, the night was crystal clear. The moon was so bright and there was a warm heady smell of spice in the air. She could hear Bollywood music playing in the distance.

Nikita noticed little flashes of light and sat up to take a better look. She asked her cousin what it was.

"Those are fire flies," he told her. He got up and stood on his bed and when the next little flash of light flew passed, he cupped it in the palms of his hands being careful not to crush it. He brought it down for everyone to look at. He opened them very slightly and whole of his cupped hands were lit up. After a couple of fascinating moments, Nikita's cousin released the fire fly, and Nikita watched it fly away. It was amazing.

Two weeks wasn't a lot of time to do all the shopping and visit all the long lost relatives, but the family did what they could.

When they returned from India, Nikita slipped back into her routine of working seven days a week, but now she had something to look forward to.

Her friends would ask about Sam and probe her about the telephone calls she never received, but they didn't know that. Nikita was embarrassed that Sam never called her, so she made it up. She told them fibs about what he'd said to her. She was living out her dream even though none of it was true. They all thought it was very sweet.

Nikita asked her cousins in London to get Sam's address for her and they called her with it a week or so later. Nikita decided to try and make contact even if he couldn't. She went to the gift shop and bought a blank card so that she could write her own message in there. She wrote:

Dear Sam,
For every tear you shed, I will be there for you.
For every ounce of misery, I will be there for you.
Whatever you do that makes you feel hurt.
I will always be there for you.
For every smile you smile, I will be there for you.
For every laughter you laugh, I will be there for you.
For every joy you have, I will be there for you.
I will always be there for you.
Forever.
XXX

Nikita thought it might prompt him to contact her but she got nothing. Maybe she didn't have the correct address or maybe the card got lost in the post and he hadn't received it or maybe......... She didn't want to think anything else.

***

The wedding date came around very quickly. Six months flew by and before she'd noticed her big day was fast approaching.

It was customary for the bride to leave her family home and start a new life with her husband and his family. In Nikita's case, this meant moving two hours away to Wolverhampton. But that was okay, she could handle it. She needed to set up a new life for herself with Sam and as long as she was happy, it didn't matter where she lived.

Nikita looked forward to drowning in those dreamy eyes, and getting to know Sam.

Nikita was still shopping up until a few days before the wedding. She couldn't get out during the day, so she'd go to the twenty four hour supermarket in the middle of the night with her cousin, while her dad was asleep. She made excuses to her mum about things she needed to get.

Mum didn't argue much because she knew she only had a few days left with her daughter and she didn't want to upset her.

Nikita's cousin Suki was like a sister to her. She was six months older than Nikita, but she had plans for her future. Marriage was a long way away. She was midway through a part-time university degree in Film and Media Studies and loved it. She had always wanted to take up a degree in this subject but her parents hadn't agreed. Suki worried that if she told her dad that she was studying a non-academic subject, he wouldn't let her attend. In the end she decided to lie to her parents. They thought she was studying economics. They would find out in the end, but Suki didn't care. By that time her degree would be complete and nobody could take it away from her.

"What you going to get today?" Suki asked.

"I still need to get some underwear."

"But you've bought loads already, you don't need anymore."

"I do. I need some Bridget Jones pants."

"Errrrr, why do you need those? You don't want to be wearing those after the wedding."

"Listen Missy, every month when I get my waterfalls, do you really think that those knickers which are literally a scrap of material are going to help me?" Nikita replied. "I don't think so."

"Why don't you just use tampons?"

"I can't. I've never even, you know... done it, so how can I shove something up there? I'm too scared," Nikita whispered. "Maybe later I might feel comfortable, but right now, I think I'm fine as I am, thank you." They both giggled as they walked around the store which felt more like a morgue rather than a supermarket.

"So what do you think it will feel like when you kiss him?" Suki asked.

"Well, I don't know," Nikita said shyly.

"Are you going to let him tongue you the first time?"

"Suki, why do you have to be so vile about these sorts of things all the time? You always make it sound so dirty."

"I'm only asking," she said exasperated. "What about sleeping with him? Are you going to have sex with him the first night you sleep with him?"

"Suki!" Nikita said.

"Okay, okay. Sorry I asked."

Suki annoyed Nikita at times, but maybe this time she had a point. Nikita had pushed thoughts about sex to the back of her mind, but these thoughts may be real issues for her in a few days or so. So how was she going to handle it? That was something she was going to have to think about and think about quick fast.

Nikita and Suki strolled in at two in the morning but her mum didn't say anything, even though she waited up for them to return.

The wedding ran over three days and in the beginning, Nikita was too busy to think about the butterflies in her stomach. That was until the morning of the wedding day. She was so nervous; it made her feel physically ill. Spots appeared on her face and she had bags under her eyes. She put it down to the nerves and the lack of sleep. It had been days since Nikita had had a good night's rest.

There were so many traditional little customs that had to be followed. Nikita enjoyed taking part and watching the others do things like draw out patterns in the garden using flour and coloured powder. She had 'Mayan' which was made from gram flour and oil, rubbed all over her body. In India they believe this homemade body rub will bring about a glow in the bride's complexion and make her look beautiful and radiant on her wedding day. That's what they told Nikita, anyway. Although often Nikita wished she wasn't born into an Asian family, she actually loved some of the customs and practices. She loved the vibrant colours, the traditions, the little games, the family gatherings, the food, everything. Panjabi people were renowned for being party animals and music and dance was believed to be in their blood. The sound of the dhol which was like a big drum was the signature instrument present in all Punjabi music. The sound was so infectious that you couldn't help but move your feet.

Nikita really enjoyed the build up to the wedding day. It was so exciting and nerve racking at the same time.

Sam and Nikita got married with a traditional Sikh ceremony. They circled around the Guru Granth Sahib, the Sikh holy book, four times while the sacred prayers were read out loud for everyone to hear. The prayers were symbolised the four stages of love and married life and represented the holy union of two souls. By agreeing to get married in this way, showed commitment and loyalty to the marriage. The reason the wedding took place in front of the Granth was so that the Sikh Gurus could bear witness to the marriage. This was followed by the singing of religious hymns. Some of these were quite chirpy and Nikita felt her knee bop up and down to the rhythm of the music. Ouch! She felt her mum pinch her from behind. Her mum had given her strict instructions to behave herself, but she couldn't help it. The excitement and adrenaline was running through her body. It made her want to dance.

Nikita tried not to look over at Sam. He sat next to her, his eyes fixed to the front. He wore a cream and gold traditional Indian suit made in silk, a pink turban and had grown his beard. Although Nikita kept her head down, as her mum had ordered, she tried to peak out of the side of her eye. Sam was sitting cross legged and she noticed their knees were almost touching. His hands were resting on his legs, the palms orange with henna. Nikita stared at his feet for a moment which looked fresh and free from dry skin. That was another tick in Nikita's box. At least he was clean, she thought.

Nikita looked down at her hands which also had henna on them. However, her palms were intricately patterned which was quite expensive to get done. Her feet were also painted with henna and decorated with toe rings and ankle jewellery with little bells on them.

It was a long day and the wedding dress was very heavy, weighing her down. Nikita felt like she had fifteen kilos of weights strapped to her body. The scarf was very heavy as well and it was pinned to Nikita's hair so that it wouldn't come off. But even if she could take it off, her mum would never have let her.

Nikita had to maintain dignity and respect which meant that she couldn't walk around and investigate what was going on. If it was up to her, she would have greeted all the guests, welcomed them and thanked them for attending and being part of such a special day. But this was considered unacceptable and inappropriate behaviour by her mum and who was she to argue? Nikita contemplated that not being able to welcome people was rude. She tried to look around because she wanted to see what Sam was doing, but her mum quickly put a stop to that.

"Do you want everyone to think that we haven't taught our daughter any manners? Keep your eyes down, people will say our daughter has no shame," her mum whispered angrily through gritted teeth.

In the end Nikita had to make do with Ria and Suki giving her regular updates on who was drunk and who was making a fool of themselves on the dance floor. Apparently Nikita's father in law was so drunk that he was dancing up close to Nikita's mother in law. Ria was cringing as she relayed these titbits of information to Nikita.

After a couple of songs, the wedding band made a request for the bride and groom to come onto the dance floor for their first dance. Ria and Suki helped Nikita up and walked her to the centre of the dance area. Nikita saw people pushing Sam to the front. He still had a shot of what looked like whiskey in his hand. Nikita saw the way he gulped it down and she silently wished to God that this wasn't an everyday occurrence. She wasn't a huge fan of alcohol. She'd seen too many times the effect it had on people. Ria and Suki left Nikita and walked back to the edge of the dance floor. Nikita noticed people getting off their seats and joining Suki and Ria.

Sam walked towards Nikita and the guests started cheering. The music started to play and he picked up Nikita's hands, threaded his fingers through hers and started to sway. He moved in closer to Nikita and she felt heat rise up her face. It sent a tingling feeling up her arm and she had the urge to giggle, but she didn't. The zing that ran through her fingers, made her feel like she wanted to pull her hands away and wipe them against her dress, but again she didn't. As the band started singing, Nikita felt more comfortable holding Sam's hand and they both started to dance with a little more confidence. Nikita stared up into Sam's face. Wow those dreamy eyes. She looked forward to getting to know this gorgeous man and to fall in love with such a beautiful person. She imagined what it would feel like to kiss those strawberry lips and those hands that held her hands in a tight grip, what would it feel like to have them run over her body? The thought sent a shiver up her spine and she knew she had to stop thinking about it. Nikita blushed more as Sam moved in even closer.

His chest was pressed up against hers and for a moment, Nikita forgot about everyone surrounding them. The top two buttons on Sam's shirt were open and she could see a smattering of dark hair across his solid taut chest. She stared up at his face. He had shaved, no longer carrying the beard that he had grown to go along with his turban. He wasn't wearing the turban or the Indian suit either, but a grey Armani suit and he looked stunning. Nikita was never one for the rugged, hairy man. She preferred clean shaven, well groomed men and Sam looked beautiful.

Nikita moved slowly to the music, looking much taller than she actually was. The heels were hurting her feet now, but she didn't care. In height she reached Sam's shoulder and she was happy about that.

Before long all the family and friends were holding hands in a huge circle around Sam and Nikita and were cheering them on. People clapped their hands and shouted words of endearment to the happy couple.

Nikita's mum came over and gave Nikita a hug and tears flowed from her eyes. They were happy tears. This was followed by all Nikita's aunties stepping forward and gathering her in an embrace. Before the end of the song, everyone was back on the dance floor and Nikita had been pulled away by her sister and cousins and Sam's family had pulled him away to dance with them. Nikita stayed on the dance floor a little longer but after a couple of songs her feet were hurting so much, she needed to sit down.

Everyone enjoyed the reception party. Everything had gone to plan and at six o'clock Nikita was ready to head back to her home for the last time. The next time she visited, it was no longer going to be her home, but her parent's home and her home was going to be with Sam in Wolverhampton.

The saddest part of the day was still to come. This was the ritual of Doli, which signified the bride leaving her father's family to become part of the in-laws family. For that reason, some people were almost mourning. Nikita could understand that it was upsetting, but had seen some women react excessively and start howling. She couldn't stand that.

Nikita left the reception party before Sam did and made her way home. Many of the guests were still on the dance floor, but her cousins and close family left with her.

As they turned into the cul-de-sac, a lump caught in Nikita's throat. This was it. This was finally it. The time she dreaded most was here and there was nothing she could do about it. She was a married woman now and she had to do what was expected of her. Move to her husband's home, make him happy, and support him in his dreams and aspirations. Build a life with him; build a home with him, live to fulfil his wishes. Nikita's mum had taught her a lot, but never talked about how she had squashed her own dreams so that Nikita's dad could live out his. Nikita had aspirations too, even if she didn't know what they were just yet. Sam was an educated man, so he couldn't have the

41

same mentality as the others. Education taught equality and tolerance, didn't it? Nikita decided that when the time was right and she was comfortable with him, she would talk to him about it. With luck, he would understand.

When she arrived back home, she took each step leading up to the front door with a heavy heart. She felt a pull from behind that was trying to stop her from going in. She knew that once she was inside, she would be leaving her home.

When she passed the threshold of the door, she looked around for the last time. She took a deep breath and the scent took her back to her childhood. Everything that had felt, warm, comfortable and safe, was all about to change. She'd decorated this home herself. She had chosen a warm terracotta colour for the walls and a beige and gold border. The floor was laminated in a light oak and she was very proud of the finished look.

Nikita could see her mum's eyes welling up and she wanted to hold her but she was ushered upstairs by her auntie. She was told to wait there until she was asked to come down.

Sam wasn't there yet, so she assumed they were waiting for him to arrive.

She was in her parent's bedroom at the front of the house, sitting on their bed and she could see the road outside from there. Nikita looked up at Margaret's house. I'm really going to miss her she thought.

When Nikita was little, she would go and play in Margaret's garden which was like the secret garden in the story book. Nikita had to walk through an arch made of ivy and climbing roses which led into the most beautiful garden she had ever seen. In the summer it was over-grown with lavender, tulips and blue bells. When Margaret's mum, Mrs. Cook came to stay; she knitted Ria and Nikita a jumper for Christmas. They were such lovely people. Uncle and auntie, an elderly couple lived two doors away from Margaret. Nikita wondered who was going to help them when they needed a doctor's appointment, or help them with paying the bills.

Next door were Josy and Alex, a couple from Goa, Nikita was going to miss them too.

Nikita's thoughts returned to the people downstairs. She could hear the women singing traditional Punjabi folk songs. These had beautiful lyrics and harmonies, but were very sad. Nikita listened.

Please don't send me away dad.
Let me hug my sisters
You can love me or be angry with me
But please don't send me away
Please don't send me away mum
Just for another day
Let me hold my dad's hand
Just like the way I used to

Nikita felt her heart break as she heard the next folk song.

Who bore her and who will take her away?
Dad, from your palace your dear one has become a stranger.
Mothers and daughters meet and they hold each other with a special connection.
The brother sends his sister on her way.
The henna goes on the hands of the married one.
Her heart starts to shake as she leaves her mum and dad.
They brought her up just to hand her over to become a stranger.

Nikita felt her composure crack and she let out a low sob. Tears rolled down her face and she quickly wiped them away. She pulled a tissue out of its holder and patted it along her cheek and under her eyes. She took in a deep breath and looked out of the window again.

As Nikita looked up the road, she spotted Sam's car driving down. He'd hired a Rolls Royce for the wedding and she was going to be travelling back with him to Wolverhampton in this.

Nikita felt anxiety twist in her stomach. She was worried because Sam hadn't spoken to her all day but she put it down to nerves. After all, he'd spent most of his time during the reception party on the dance floor with his friends, so he must have been happy. He looked happy.

Nikita's heart started doing somersaults in her chest. She knew this was it. She was leaving her life behind to build a new one with her new family. Tears stung at the back of her eyes again and she couldn't hold them back. They poured out and over her cheeks, almost ruining her makeup. It was a good job she was wearing waterproof mascara.

Nikita's brother Kam came upstairs to get her. He took her by the hand and walked her to the top of the stairs. The tears were streaming down her face now and she could hardly see where she was going. Kam held on tight and Nikita could see the camera man standing at the bottom of the stairs to film the whole episode. She wanted to tell him to move out of her face, but again she just let it be. They got to the bottom of the stairs and Kam walked Nikita into the living room, to an empty chair that was placed next to where Sam was seated. She was told to hold out a corner of her scarf in front of her and her mum placed handfuls of rice into it. Mum put her hand on Nikita's head to give her a blessing and placed some money in Nikita's hand. Mum started crying and gave Nikita a huge hug. Everyone around Nikita was crying their eyes out. One by one all the family, the aunties, uncles and her cousins came over and put some money in her hand and then gave her a hug and cried on her shoulder.

Sam sat there very quietly. What was he thinking? Would he have known to expect this sort of reaction?

Nikita saw her dad approach, his eyes red from the tears he was fighting back. He gifted Nikita money and placed his hands on her head. Nikita grabbed him from around his stomach and buried her head into it. She could just about reach around her dad's padded belly and she didn't want to let go. She wanted to tell him that she loved him; she'd never told him that before. She had spent so much time over the last few years with him, more than any other member of her family and they had built up a real bond. They went to work together, they came home together, they ate together and they had become really close.

After a few long seconds, Nikita felt someone's hand break her hold from around her dad and pull her arms away, but she didn't want to let go, she didn't want to leave. She wasn't ready yet so she fought back to hold on. It was no use, they pulled her hands away. Nikita looked up at her dad and he looked back at her for a second. He had tears streaming down his face. Then he turned and walked away. Nikita had only ever seen her dad cry once before this. It was a time when he was really drunk and he was talking about his mum who died when Nikita was six, but that was years ago. How was he going to cope without her? He relied on her for a lot. Nikita knew he had never told her but she was sure that he was going to miss her, more than anyone else. Then Nikita's auntie came over and asked her and Sam to stand and she led them to the front door.

Nikita was told to grab handfuls of the rice that was still in the scarf and throw it backwards and sideways over people that were following her. Sam stepped out of the front door, followed by Nikita and he led her to the Rolls. Sam climbed in the front passenger seat still not saying a word and Nikita climbed in the back. The Rolls was luxurious and spacious and Nikita's cousin's wife Bhabs, jumped in next to her. Nikita was allowed to take one relative with her for the first night and it was a relief to her because at least she would know one person there.

It was very quiet in the car as they drove up the M1 and then the M6. Sam still didn't say anything much. He must have been tired, Nikita thought. Bhabs was already asleep next to her; it had been a long day. Nikita kicked off her red sandals and sat back in the comfortable leather seats. She thought she should get some rest while she could. She didn't know what to expect when she got to her in-law's house.

When they arrived at Sam's parents' house, there were still some customs that had to be completed and although Nikita could have fallen asleep where she was sitting, she took part and did what she was told to do.

That night she slept in Sam's sister's bedroom, because in her family the bride didn't spend the first night with her husband. She and Bhabs slept in the same bed talking about the day and slowly they both fell asleep.

Chapter 3 – The Beginning

Nikita woke early the next morning, feeling slightly numb. Her sleep hadn't been comfortable, she'd only managed to get a few hours of shut eye.

She couldn't believe she had been married the day before. Was she meant to feel any different? She didn't? Accept for the nerves, they seemed to be flying high.

She sat up and looked around. It was definitely a girly room. There were teddy bears everywhere; Sam's sister obviously collected them. In the corner of the room was a book shelf stacked full of fictional novels. Nikita climbed out of bed and walked over to take a look at the titles. Wow, it was a really good collection, but not all in Nikita's favourite genre, Science fiction and romance. None of her favourite authors either, but at least she had something in common with her sister in law. Hopefully this would make a good talking point between the two.

There was a knock on the door and Nikita asked whoever it was to come in. It was one of Sam's cousins.

Nikita was escorted to and from the bathroom and back to the bedroom. Her mother in law brought Bhabs and Nikita some tea and toast and some Indian sweets. Nikita was expecting Full English with sausages, egg, bacon, with baked beans and lots of HP sauce poured over it. Mmm... Her mouth was watering just thinking about it. Nikita's stomach rumbled. She hadn't eaten properly in days and it was catching up with her. She tried to hide her disappointment and smiled at her mother in law regardless.

Sam's mum gave Nikita a beautiful pink dress and told her that she would be wearing it for the day. It had a full length skirt with a short top, all made in pure silk with gold sequenze embroidery but it had a chiffon scarf. Chiffon was a very light material, which was much more comfortable than the heavy embroidered dress she wore the day before. Nikita felt relieved she didn't have to suffer with a headache today. She gave Nikita eight twenty four carat gold bangles as a gift for the wedding and asked her to put them on. Nikita was shocked when she saw them. They must have cost thousands of pounds and she put them on with pride.

Sam's family had organised a gathering in a small community centre near their home. Nikita's family had also been invited. This day was a much less formal day than the wedding. Nikita was able to relax a little and meet the family that she was going to be part of from now on. All these unfamiliar faces staring at her. It made her feel a little uncomfortable; she wasn't used to so much attention. She smiled all the same, at people she didn't know. Little kids came over and pointed the finger at her, whispering in each other's ears.

Bhabs had joined Sam's family and was deep in conversation.

Nikita sat separate from the rest of the family, on a table that had been especially set up for her. An empty seat sat next to her, which was probably for Sam, but he was nowhere to be seen. Nikita hadn't seen him all morning. Her mother in law had told her that he had gone to set up the hall, but Nikita couldn't see him anywhere.

The DJ had set up his system and the music had been turned up to very loud. The lights flashed in Nikita's eyes and she wished the DJ would slow it down a little. She still felt very tired and tender from the long wedding day.

Nikita's mum and dad arrived with only their close family members. Her sister and cousins pulled chairs over to sit with her. Ria started teasing Nikita about the night before. Nikita felt the heat creep up her neck and into her cheeks. She quietly explained to Ria that it didn't work that way and that she'd spent the night with Bhabs.

Nikita was very quiet for the next few moments, deep in thought. Although nothing had happened the night before, she was dreading tonight. She would be expected to spend the night with Sam and she wasn't ready, she still didn't know him. She never imagined she would have to sleep with a total stranger, someone she didn't love. She tried hard to push the thought to the back of her mind; he would understand she told herself. He's an educated man, she was sure he had the same views as her.

The family gathering turned into a party. Everyone was dancing and for the first time Nikita saw her dad joining in as well. He looked relaxed and carefree. It a sight she saw very often.

People ate the delicious food, drank until their hearts were content and danced the day away.

By six o'clock, Nikita was ready to collapse. She was so tired, she needed her bed. The lack of sleep over the last few days was starting to get on top of her. Her shoulders and neck ached through to her core and she still had to get through the evening.

As the evening drew in, Nikita became more anxious. In a few hours she would be sleeping next to a stranger. The thought sent chills up her spine. She couldn't do this.

As the party drew to a close, it was time for Nikita's family to leave. This time she would be left on her own. There weren't as many tears as yesterday but it didn't stop Nikita's mum becoming emotional again. The most surprising thing was that Ria became hysterical and no matter what anyone did, she wouldn't calm down. Nikita and Ria weren't best friends but they had always been there for each other, even when they weren't talking. Nikita never realised just how much she meant to Ria and how much she was going to miss her. Nikita's cousin Ram got very drunk and became quite emotional. He started telling her that he loved her and if she ever needed anything then he was just a phone call away. Nikita's cousins were her brothers; they were very close to each other because they'd all grown up together.

Ram approached Sam, slowly walking over to him while trying to keep his balance. Nikita's heart started beating hard. She knew that her cousin often put his foot in it and seeing as he was drunk; the likelihood of that happening had just increased ten folds.

"Look after her Sam, I know my sister and she's a hundred percent good, take care of her."

Nikita couldn't read Sam's face; he didn't seem to respond to what was being said. She watched from a distance. What was he thinking? Oh God, he probably thought Ram was a moron. Nikita knew that Ram loved her like a sister, but there was a time and place for these conversations. Now was not one of those times. Especially when emotions were running high and Ram was drunk legless.

Nikita watched in silence. After a few long seconds, Nikita saw Sam's lips break into a straight smile and he hugged Ram. Nikita let out a breath, she hadn't even realised she had been holding.

Nikita's family left that evening including Bhabs and she watched them drive away. All three cars disappeared down the road, leaving her with a bunch of complete strangers. Nikita looked around nervous and awkward, but this was the life of an Indian girl. She just had to bare it.

Sam's family drove them back to his house. Nikita's new home wasn't far from his parent's house; her mother in law had told her it was only a ten minute walk away.

Sam had already bought a house for them and they were moving in straight away, which was a relief. Nikita had heard so many horror stories about mother in laws. She was glad not to be living in the same house, but that didn't mean that she wouldn't behave like the dutiful daughter in law. She made a conscious decision she would always be good and look after her in laws as much as she could. There were also many horror stories about bitchy daughter in laws and Nikita promised herself she was never going to become one of them.

Before they went inside, Sam's mum poured drops of mustard oil on each side of the front door entering the house. Traditionally mustard oil was poured when welcoming an important person for the first time. Nikita guessed that meant she was an important person and she liked the feeling. Sam's mum blessed both Sam and Nikita as they entered the threshold of the house. Nikita walked in.

As she breathed in, she noted the different scent of this house. She became overwhelmed, knowing that this was her house. A house that she would soon make a home. As she walked through the hallway and into the living room, she looked around. The décor wasn't to her taste, as a matter of fact, it was horrible, but that was okay because she could change it. This was going to be her first real home.

Sam's family stayed for a little while longer. They made some tea and put their feet up. His mum was gossiping about a relative.

"Did you see the gifts that she brought? I swear it must have been lying around in her loft for years. These people have no shame. They turn up for the free food and drink and they can't even be bothered to give a decent wedding present. I feel like chucking it back in her face."

Leila responded. "Tell me about it mum. Did you see the suit auntie Gejo gave me? It was disgusting. I wouldn't even use the material to wipe shit off my shoe."

Nikita watched the banter between mother and daughter for a little while longer.

Leila was Sam's sister. She was being very friendly and Nikita smiled and nodded in conversation. Leila was studying at a university in Leeds. She had only just completed her first year with two more to go. Nikita wouldn't be seeing much of her once she returned to university, but she hoped that one day they would become good friends. She showed Nikita around the house.

Leila showed Nikita the kitchen, which had decent enough units but she had to change that cooker. Having walked through the kitchen they headed for the back of the house. The bathroom was downstairs, but that was okay, Nikita was used to it. Then they headed upstairs and first Leila showed Nikita the spare room which just had a double bed and a wardrobe, but was totally bare otherwise. The window looked quite dusty so Nikita made a mental note to clean up in there.

After this, Nikita was led through to her bedroom. There was a big four poster bed which was decorated with rose petals and candles were lit and placed along the fireplace. It was an old Victorian style house. Although it had central heating and double glazing, it still had some of its old features, like the fireplaces in the bedrooms and high ceilings.

Nikita felt extremely nervous seeing the decorated bed. As she put her vanity case down on the dressing table, she caught a glimpse of herself in the mirror and she could almost see the dread on her face. Calm down, it will be okay, he'll understand, she told herself.

After an hour, everyone left. Sam and Nikita were left in the house alone.

She sat nervously on the sofa, looking around at the four walls, then at the henna patterns on her hands and then the bangles that she had been gifted. Sam didn't say anything. He went straight to the fridge and pulled out a cold beer.

Nikita's suit case had been taken upstairs so she went up and pulled out her pyjamas and slipped them on. It felt so good to take all that weight off her body. She took the pins out of her hair and let it drop down over her shoulders. God that felt good. She sat at the dressing table and pulled out her hair brush from the vanity case and brushed out the tangles. She sat staring at her reflection in the mirror and removed the bindi's from her forehead and placed them back in her case. Next she took out her disposable makeup remover wipes and wiped away all her makeup. She felt much better in herself, but the nerves were still doing somersaults in her stomach. Nikita didn't know what to do next. Should she stay upstairs and wait for Sam to come up, or should she go back down and wait to come back up with him? She hovered around for a few minutes and then decided she'd use the toilet as an excuse to go down and then she'd assess the situation.

Slowly she walked down the stairs. They were very steep and added to how tired she was feeling, she worried that she might fall down them. The stairs led straight into the living room. Sam was still sitting on the sofa with his feet up on the coffee table. Nikita knew this was something that would annoy her. It was so unhygienic. Sam still had a bottle of beer in his hand, except this time there was an empty one on the table next to his feet. She hadn't asked him if he liked drinking when they met, but she supposed now she didn't need to.

Nikita popped to the bathroom, washed her face and then hovered in there for a short moment, thinking about how to break the silence. She felt annoyed with Sam. Why wasn't he making more of an effort? It was difficult for them both, not only him.

Nikita sighed. Calm down, she told herself. He must see her as a stranger as well and she felt some comfort because hopefully that would mean he felt just as awkward as she did. Nikita took a deep breath and walked back to the living room.

"It's been a long few days hasn't it?" she said casually, trying not to reveal her uneasiness.

"Yes it has," he replied. "Go and grab some sleep, you're probably tired," he said.

Nikita smiled at him and made her way up the stairs. She was so relieved that he didn't look like he was going to try anything and that helped her to relax. But it also worried her a little, as he didn't seem to want to talk either and she wouldn't have minded a bit more conversation than the two lines he had spoken. Was he not happy with the marriage? She pushed the thought to the back of her mind as she climbed the stairs.

Nikita collected up all the rose petals in her hand, then placing them onto the bedside cabinet before climbing into bed. Obviously it was going to feel different, because it wasn't her bed, but she would get used to it. She lay there staring up at the ceiling. She could hear the traffic outside on the main road and it wasn't something that she was used to. Her parent's home was in a cul-de-sac, so it was always very quiet.

She lay thinking about the last few weeks, the last two days and her dad's face. It brought tears to her eyes again. She wondered how he would be feeling, how he was going to cope without her. Running a business with no support was so difficult and there were things he relied on Nikita to do, never having to worry about them himself. Now he would have to take on all the responsibility, and even though Nikita knew it wasn't her fault, she felt a tinge of guilt.

Just then she heard footsteps coming up the stairs. Worried, she quickly shut her eyes tight, pretending she had fallen asleep. Her heart started beating really hard in her chest. Nikita could hear Sam getting changed in the dark, the sound of clothes being stripped from his body and then he climbed into bed without saying anything. Then without touching her, he turned his face the other way and went to sleep. She felt a little offended, she knew she didn't want him to try anything but he could have at least said something, a good night. He could have held her hand, or given her a hug; she wouldn't have minded that, but nothing. Before long she could hear his light snore and she realised he was asleep. It didn't take long for Nikita to fall asleep, but then she kept tossing and turning. Sleeping next to a stranger in a strange bed was horrible. Anxiety stopped her from falling into a deep resting sleep.

Nikita got up around seven o'clock the next morning and quickly had a shower before Sam could wake up. It took her ten minutes just to work out how to use the system. She made herself a cup of tea and sat down on the sofa. She looked around the living room, which was quite plain; it definitely needed a woman's touch. She was already making plans and writing up a list of things to do in her head. The hideous wall paper needed changing and the carpet was a light russet colour which looked like vomit, so that had to go as well. There was a television in the corner and a small dining table against the opposite wall. The room had a very big oak fireplace and a large gold framed mirror above it and that was it.

Nikita put the television on to watch the news. She had been so out of touch for the last week that World War Three could have broken out and she wouldn't have had a clue. She spent around half an hour watching the news and then she got bored. She looked around to see what else she could do. Breakfast. Nikita went into the kitchen and looked in the fridge to see what she could find. There wasn't much, but some milk, bread and eggs, so she decided to make some omelettes. There was a small stereo on top of the kitchen work surface and although she wasn't familiar with any of the local radio channels, she tuned it until she found some Indian music. She turned the music up, not too loud but so that she could enjoy it. She bopped around the kitchen singing along with some of the songs. She finished making the omelettes and covered them up with foil and set them to one side. This only took her another twenty minutes and then she sat there twiddling her thumbs again. What to do now, it was still only eight o'clock.

Sam came down around half an hour later looking very tired.

"Morning," Nikita said in a cheerful voice, "I've made breakfast".

"I can't stop," he replied. "I have to see a friend who needs me to look at some papers for him," he continued as he walked into the bathroom.

Nikita's face dropped. This was meant to be their first day together and she had so many questions that she wanted to ask him and so many things she wanted to say, but he was on his way out. Maybe his friend really did need him, so she lifted her chin up and waited for Sam to come out of the bathroom.

Sam walked straight towards the front door and without looking back at Nikita he shouted as he headed out, "See you later."

She didn't have the chance to respond.

Nikita was expecting that Sam would take some time off work, but he didn't. Every evening there was a work function, meetings with clients, board meetings and every night Sam came home late.

Nikita made sure the dinner was hot and served as soon as he got in. This was followed by Sam taking a quick shower and then to bed. She didn't get a chance to get to know him, he was always so busy.

Weeks went by and it was the same routine every day. Nikita worried that Sam was having a relationship with someone else because he sure wasn't making an effort with her. People visited and Nikita made excuses that he was at work, or he was studying, or he was doing a favour for a friend and helping them out. She never really knew what his job involved because Sam never talked to her about it. He was never there.

Nikita's mum called to check on her. As usual Nikita lied and said she was fine and that Sam was working late. Nikita felt so ashamed. It was only a few weeks into her marriage and she hadn't managed to make anything work. At first she didn't let it bother her, because she understood he was also finding it hard. However, they hadn't even managed to develop a friendship; they were still living like strangers. Nikita's heart sank when she answered the phone. "How's dad?" she asked.

"He's fine, he really misses you, though he won't say," mum replied.

"I miss you guys too," Nikita said. Tears were prickling at the back of her eyes but she was trying hard not to let them flow. Mum would have realised that something was wrong. Nikita tried hard to keep her voice level.

"Do you remember when sometimes your dad would park his car down the road because there wouldn't be anywhere to park outside the house and when a space became available he would ask you to move his car up?"

"Yeh, I remember mum. He used to be such a pain," Nikita laughed, remembering how annoyed she used to get. "Sometimes I would be in my pyjamas but he would still make me go out."

"Well, last night he parked the car down the road as usual and then he kept looking out the window until there was space. Then he walked over to the hallway and shouted up the stairs, 'Nikki, come down and move the car'."

"But I'm not there mum," she said quietly, a lump developing in her throat. Nikita's eyes welled up.

"I know," she said. "I called out and asked him, who are you calling? She's not here. For an instance he forgot that you weren't upstairs. I know he doesn't say it but he really does miss you. I see it in his eyes. He was quiet all evening after that."

Nikita felt like crying, it made her heart ache. She really missed her dad as well and no matter how much she wished that she hadn't got married, there was no going back. She had made her bed and now she had to lie in it.

Nikita realised that she should have spoken up when she first met Sam, but she couldn't, it would have broken her mum and dad's heart. Now if she told them it wasn't working out, they would be devastated. They were so proud of her. To hear that their eldest daughter couldn't make her marriage work, they would never be able to look anyone in the face.

Days turned into weeks and weeks turned into months, but things never changed. Nikita tried everything. She turned the house into a home, she tried romantic candlelit meals, she tried booking into restaurants, she tried dressing up and making an effort but he didn't seem to notice anything. He would come home, eat and then watch TV or go out. They hardly talked.

Nikita managed to get a job as a teaching assistant at a local primary school, which she enjoyed very much. It was hard work but very rewarding. She spent four days at the school and one day studying at college. She was working and training at the same time. Sometimes to break the ice with Sam, she tried talking about her day. "You know what?" No response. "Something really amazing happened today." Still no response. "Little Ben was struggling with reading and I've been supporting him over the last few weeks and he's already started to read sentences, isn't that amazing?" Nikita voice carried so much excitement. She expected to get a response of some sort, may be a smile, even a small grin, she'd helplessly built her hopes up. All Sam had to respond with was a murmur. He mumbled something under his breath, too low for Nikita to hear. He hardly acknowledged what she had just said. As time went on Nikita slowly stopped talking to Sam about work as well.

Chapter 4 - The First Time

It was cold outside. Winter had descended. It felt like it was colder up North compared to what Nikita was used to in Letchworth. Or maybe it was just a colder winter this year. Nikita enjoyed the winter months. She always felt it was a romantic season. Opportunities to snuggle up, drink hot cups of cocoa with whipped cream with cream and marshmallows, or take walks in the local park, with your feet crunching on the frosted grass.

It also meant Christmas, Nikita's favourite time of year. She loved to make a fuss celebrating the festive season. Even though her family were strict Sikhs, Nikita went to a Church of England primary school. It had its own church and all the Christian festivals were celebrated there. That's how Nikita got involved in the school choir and at Christmas she loved singing carols for the local community. Nikita remembered how the school celebrated Harvest festival and how they decorated the church with food that was donated by the children. After the service was over, the children made hampers with the food and handed them out to the elderly people living in bungalows situated close to the church.

Feeling good, Nikita decided she was going to take the leap and initiate something to take her and her husband to first base. She had to try something. If she left things the way they were, she was never going to get to know him. That's when plan B kicked into action. Nikita cooked a nice meal, bought some candles and set the table. She bought an artificial Christmas tree which she decorated and stood it to one side of the fire place. She didn't switch the lights on yet. She wanted to wait for Sam to get home so they could switch them on together. It was going to be romantic.

The plan was to talk to him, to discuss what had been going on. At first she thought he didn't want to pressurize her but now her concerns had gone beyond that. She'd thought it through and today was about showing him that she was serious about their relationship and she was ready to move things on. She wasn't ready for sex exactly, he was still a stranger to her, but she wouldn't mind getting close.

Nikita heard the car pull up and she felt a little jolt of excitement. It was silly really, because she knew this may not work, but she couldn't help but feel optimistic. Something had to work, so why not this? She felt her heart beat quicken and the nerves made her tremble a little. When Sam got in the door, Nikita took his bag and jacket and put it away. "Hi Sam, how was your day?" she asked.

Sam mumbled something about it being the same as usual. He went straight to the fridge and grabbed a beer, poured himself some dinner and went and sat on the sofa in front of the TV. He ignored her candlelit table and the Christmas tree, but she wasn't going to let it dishearten her. She was determined and she had to know what was going on. Her heart was pounding and she felt a little lightheaded but she had to ask the question. She took a deep breath. "Sam is everything okay, have I done something wrong?"

He didn't respond.

She sat down on the sofa next to him and spoke in a low voice. "Since we've been married, you haven't even looked at me. Is it because you don't find me attractive, or is there someone else? Please talk to me." Nikita tried to swallow but her throat had become dry. However, she had started now so she had to get everything out of her system. She had to let him know how she was feeling. "This won't work if we don't communicate and I for one want it to work. How can we get through the rest of our lives like this? The least we can do is become friends, but if we don't talk, then how can we get to know each other?" Nikita sounded desperate but she didn't care. This wasn't a game to her, she was in it for the long haul and so she needed answers.

Sam looked at her, his face unreadable and put his plate down. He took her by the hand and led her up the stairs. It was the first time he'd held her hand since the wedding day and she felt a tingling sensation trickle up her arm. She felt a little excited and a lot nervous. Butterflies fluttered deep in her stomach and her body began to shake. Sam took her into the bedroom and sat on the bed. Nikita felt a surge of excitement race through her veins. Sam pulled her towards him. Nikita put her arms around his shoulders and she moved in closer to him, placing herself between his legs. Sam started to run his hands up Nikita's leg and she giggled as it tickled.

Was this the key? She just needed to talk to him and let him know what she was thinking. She should have done this long ago. Finally Nikita felt a small sense of relief, like today could be the first day of the rest of their lives.

She leaned in closer and let her weight sag against Sam's chest. She lay her head against his shoulder. It felt so warm to be close to him and she felt some of the anxiety release from her body. Maybe now they could start building on their relationship. Nikita hugged Sam for a long few seconds. His hands started to climb higher up her skirt and then tugged at her knickers. Nikita tried to push him away.

"What are you doing Sam?"

"This is what you want isn't it?"

"No Sam, I don't. I'm sorry if I gave you that impression but I want us to talk. I want us to get closer and yes we can take things further, but only when I feel ready, not like this," she told him.

Sam got up and turned Nikita around. He pushed her back onto the bed with one swift movement which took her by surprise. He was much bigger than she was. She couldn't release herself from his grip.

"What are you doing Sam? I told you I don't want to," she grimaced. Nikita pushed at him again.

Sam started to nuzzle in the arch of her neck and at first it tickled. She asked him to stop. She thought he was just playing with her. But then he got rougher and he wouldn't let her hands go. She tried to get up but he was too strong. Using his body weight, he held her hands above her head and he pressed his body up against the length of her. He pulled down her knickers with his other hand. Her excitement was quickly replaced with the feeling of dread which now rushed through every part of her body.

"No," she screamed, "No!"

Nikita tried to fight back, she tried to kick her legs but she couldn't move them. Her skin burned on her wrists, where he held her so tightly.

She felt so embarrassed, so ashamed. She hadn't removed her clothes in front of anyone since she was a little girl and in a matter of seconds she was half naked. Nikita stared at his face. She couldn't read what was in his eyes but it frightened her.

"Stop it Sam please, I asked you to stop," she pleaded with rivulets of tears running down her face.

But he didn't. She was pinned to the bed and he used his legs to push between her thighs. She clenched and tightened her muscles as she felt his hardness rubbing against her legs. She could feel his heavy breath on her face and neck and the weight of his body was crushing her. The smell of his aftershave that she had always adored, now repulsed her, she couldn't stand to feel it around her. Nikita screamed for mercy again but Sam didn't listen. It was like he was seeing red. She pushed and pushed as hard as she could, but it was no good. She couldn't force him off. Before she could stop him he had dropped all his weight on top of her and almost knocked the wind out of her. She turned her face away from him, she knew what was coming. Right there, she wished she was dead. Her emotions had gone haywire. The humiliation, embarrassment and pain were all too much for her. She tried one last time without success to push against his chest and then she gave up.

Realising Nikita's defeat, Sam pushed his hardness into her.

Nikita screamed in pain. It felt like someone had taken a knife and cut her in half. Tears run down the sides of her face and she let out a low sob but that didn't stop Sam. She managed to free her hands as he thrust himself into her emotionlessly, but it didn't help. She tried to hit him across his face and shoulders, but he grabbed both hands again and pinned them against the bed. She couldn't believe that this was happening to her. It hurt so much.

He wasn't gentle like she had imagined, he was rough and he didn't care about how she was feeling. He didn't even look at her. His breath came in ragged gasps, only mumbling foul language under his breath. He moved in close to her ear. "This is what you wanted remember? You came onto me. It was what you were desperate for, wasn't it and you like it," he said in a low gruff voice.

She felt him stiffen and then he groaned. When he finished, he lifted himself off her, pulled his trousers up. "You deserved that," he said in a low voice. He walked away, panting with sweat across his brow.

Nikita lay there, tears streaming down her face, her legs limp and hanging off the end of the bed. Pain thrust through her lower stomach and she felt a sharp throbbing between her legs. She tugged at her skirt to pull it down from around her waist. Nikita rolled off the bed and fell to the floor. She sat there for the next few hours, too scared to move in case it hurt even more.

All her dreams were in tatters.

She hated him. She didn't want to do this and he'd forced her to. People called it love making, Nikita called it brutality.

Sam had a wash, got changed and climbed into bed. He didn't even seem to notice her sitting on the floor. She heard the low rumble of his snore and she looked back at him. Nikita stared at his face. She watched him, the way he slept in such peace after leaving her so sore. She felt her heavy heart throb.

She realised for the first time that he wasn't a man but an animal who had no conscience. How could he fall asleep so easily after what he had just done to her?

Nikita slowly descended the stairs, to head to the bathroom and filled the bath. She poured, shampoo, shower gel, Dettol, anything she could get her hands on into the running water and sat in it for a long while. She felt dirty and violated, she needed to wash it all off. She used a bar of soap and scrubbed until her skin felt numb. Her mind raced over what had just happened and with every thought came a sharp stabbing pain. Nikita sobbed in the bath for the next few hours. The water turned cold but her body was so numb, that she didn't seem to realise.

She was a fool. A stupid, stupid fool. She had dreamed so many times about the first time. How wonderful it was going to be. Sending butterflies fluttering in her stomach and her pulse racing. It was going to be the most beautiful night of her life. But in reality it was the most traumatic experience ever.

From this day on, Nikita knew never to ask Sam for anything again. She realised the response she would get, would be violation, embarrassment and degradation.

Nikita's life changed from that day on. Sam forced himself onto her every night and she cried herself to sleep, every night. Slowly she got used to it. It became part and parcel of a daily routine. She learnt to switch off when they did it, because to her it was nothing more than sex. Dirty, unloving, humiliating, sex. He forced Nikita do things which made her feel repulsed but slowly she learnt to detach her heart and mind from her body, so that emotionally it didn't hurt so much anymore. Sometimes when she had her period, she would lie even when the cycle had ended. Nikita's period normally only lasted four days, but she made out it lasted for a whole week. She'd wear a sanitary towel when she didn't need to, just so she could drag it out as long as she could. It was silly really. She actually felt lucky he didn't like to have sex while she was on her period. She'd heard that it didn't bother some people but at least she got a reprieve for a short while. He cursed her throughout her period cycle.

Sometimes Nikita would think about other ways to stop him coming near her. What could she do to make him detest her and not want to touch her? What if she didn't wash? He wouldn't come near her then. But she had to wash, because she had to work, she couldn't go into the school smelling, so that wasn't an option. What if she ate loads and put on lots of weight, then he wouldn't want to be near her, she would repulse him. She'd come to realise very quickly that he hated big women. He described to her how much he loathed her figure and he made sure she was on a constant diet.

Sometimes Sam's friends would visit and Nikita would always make an effort. She didn't want to give him an excuse to hurt her anymore so she dressed well, put on her makeup and smiled. She cooked nice meals to keep Sam and his friends happy. His friends often commented on how tasty the food was but compliments were something she never got from Sam.

Darren and Sam were really good friends. They had both been to the same university and the last time Darren visited, he had asked Nikita to make him some chilli chicken. Darren lived away from home and missed his mum's home cooking. "Sure", Nikita had told him. Darren was a very friendly down to earth type of guy and he reminded Nikita of her brother. He would make her laugh with his silly little jokes just like Kam used to.

Sam told Nikita that Darren was coming over after work. "Great," she said with a hint of sarcasm. As much as she liked Darren, she was tired of keeping up the pretence. "The last time he was here, he asked me to make him chilli chicken. I'll pick up the chicken on my way home from work and get started as soon as I get in."

Sam didn't bother to respond and left for work.

He was working in a legal firm now. He got to deal with the smaller cases and was guided and mentored by the more experienced solicitors. Nikita continued to work at the school where she made some good friends. It was the only place that she got some real conversation and she was grateful for that.

After work Nikita popped into her local butchers and picked up some boneless chicken thigh meat. She had all the spices at home. Her mum had spent years teaching her how she should always have dry ingredients in her cupboard. If she ever had any unannounced visitors, she would be able to throw something together without any trouble. It was good advice.

Once Nikita arrived home, she threw her bag on the sofa, washed her hands and popped on her apron. She knew Sam and Darren would be home in an hour, so she spiced up the chicken, coated it with corn flour, ketchup and soya sauce and put it in the fridge to marinate. After thirty minutes, she fried off the chicken in some oil and placed it to one side. In a separate pan she poured in a little oil and threw in the chopped garlic, ginger and chillies and once they were browned she through in some tinned chopped tomatoes. In went the spicy seasoning and then she added the chopped red onions and peppers. After a few minutes she added the already cooked chicken and her dish was almost ready. She would add the chopped coriander when she was ready to serve. The fragrance was mouth watering.

Darren often came round to watch the football with Sam and there was a big match on tonight. Chelsea v Manchester United. Nikita knew it would be a loud evening with lots of screaming and shouting and nerves being tossed all over the place.

They arrived home at around six thirty and tossed their briefcases in the front room. They took off their jackets and went straight to the sofa in front of the TV. Nikita came out of the kitchen to greet them both.

"Hi Sam, did you have a good day?"

"Same as usual," he mumbled.

"What about you Darren, how was your day?"

"Oh, it was good thanks Nikita." Darren looked up at Nikita and smiled his dazzling smile. "You look nice," he said. "You've done something different with your hair."

"Ah, thanks Darren," Nikita smiled. "I thought I'd try something different. You like?"

"Yeh, definitely. It looks great."

Sam shot Nikita a hard look.

She ignored him.

"What can I get you both to drink?"

"Beer," Sam replied in a cold voice. He didn't look at her as he said it. Nikita tried to ignore him and pretended it didn't bother her. But it did. He always managed to make her feel so small and insignificant with just a few words. She kept her cool and didn't respond. It wasn't worth the hassle she knew she would receive afterwards. That was hard for Nikita. She had never been treated this way. Her confidence was taking a hammering and she could almost feel it withering away, inch by inch, day by day.

Nikita quickly went to the kitchen and took two beers out of the fridge.

"Your chicken is almost ready; I can bring it in if you're both ready to eat?"

Sam shot her that look again. "Can you shut up now, the match is about to start."

Nikita just stared at his face for a long few seconds and when he didn't lower his glare she dropped her eyes in disbelief. She knew what sort of man he was but she was always shocked when he degraded her in this way in front of others.

Her eyes welled up and she quickly turned her face and walked back to the kitchen. She was trying so hard not to make it obvious to anyone. She put on an act so that people wouldn't talk about them, wouldn't shun her for not being able to make her marriage work, but he made everything so difficult.

"What's your problem?" Darren asked.

"The match is about to start and she just keeps barking and barking," Sam said.

"Sam," Darren said, "How can you talk about her like that? She's your wife for God's sake."

Sam didn't respond.

Nikita leaned over the kitchen sink and grabbed onto the front of it trying to fight back the tears. She squeezed the edge so hard that it made her nails hurt. She couldn't let a guest see her like this, what would he think?

After ten minutes or so, Nikita took the chicken out of the oven where she was keeping it warm and added the chopped coriander. It looked delicious. In a separate dish she placed some fries. She wiped away her tears, straightened her face and had a quick look in the mirror. She took a deep breath and walked into the living room placing both serving dishes on the table in front of Sam and Darren. She returned to the kitchen to get the dinner plates and placed these on the table as well. They could help themselves.

Nikita stayed in the kitchen for most of the evening. She didn't mind though, it gave her the opportunity to do something she loved, reading. She'd bought P.S I Love You to read because she'd watched the film in the cinema with some friends and really enjoyed it. It was such a sad film, she had cried most of the way through it. One of her friends had told her that she should read the book, as often the books were way better than the movie, so Nikita thought that she should try it. Nikita was reading for about half an hour when she heard Sam shouting, "Beer." Nikita quickly went to the fridge and took out two more beers. She didn't want Sam coming in the kitchen and catching her reading, especially not this book. He would think it was a waste of time, but she liked reading. It took her away from reality and made her pain a little less. To be able to drown herself into someone else's world, kept her sane. One of Nikita's favourite authors was Catherine Anderson and she loved her romantic novels, even though they did seem to be a little exaggerated. Did the heroes from her novels really exist? Were there men like that out there? Nikita didn't think so. Reality had hit her hard. Like she had walked into a brick wall. It appeared from nowhere without warning, and there was no getting away from it.

Nikita hurried into the living room and placed the opened bottles of beer on the table and quickly headed back to the kitchen to continue reading. After a while she heard Darren shout. "Nikita, come and watch the penalty shoot out."

She put her book down and walked into the living room. She looked around and Sam wasn't there. "Where's Sam gone?" she asked Darren.

"Oh, he's just popped out to take a phone call."

Nikita sat down next to Darren and started to watch the penalty shoot out. It reminded her of the times her brother would fight her for the remote control just so he could watch his football match. She didn't have a TV in her bedroom, so she would have to sit and watch the game with him.

"Oh no", Darren shouted as Chelsea missed a penalty shot.

Nikita heard Sam's footsteps as he came down the stairs. He took one look at her and turned his face. She could see that he was not happy with her. She got up, picked up the dirty dishes and empty beer bottles and went back to the kitchen. After the match was over, Darren left quite quickly. He popped his head in the kitchen and thanked Nikita for the enjoyable evening and the food. "It's okay," she said. "I'm glad you liked it."

"Liked it? I loved the chicken. They always say that no one can cook better than your mum, but I have to say that your cooking comes damn close."

"I'll take that as a compliment," Nikita said as she smiled.

Nikita continued washing up and as she stared out of her kitchen window, she thought about Darren and how much he reminded her of Kam. She missed her brother so much. After all, she'd help to raise him. Tears prickled at the back of her eyes but she suppressed them just like everything else in her life.

Nikita was jerked back from her thoughts by Sam entering the kitchen. She tried not to look at him; she knew he was angry. He stood by the kitchen units staring at her. She was scared to even look at him, but she was also frightened in case he thought he was being ignored. Nikita's heart beat fast in her chest and she felt her throat tighten. She kept her eyes peeled to the dishes in her hand. She coughed to clear her throat.

"Good match was it?" she asked trying to keep her voice from shaking. He didn't respond. "I'm glad Darren liked the chicken, did you like it?" As soon as Nikita had mentioned Darren's name, she knew she'd made a grave mistake. She looked at Sam from the corner of her eyes and she could see the anger seething from him. His forehead was creased and he was breathing heavily. This frightened her even more. Before she could turn to face him, Sam charged over to her and started screaming in her face.

"If you ever, ever embarrass me like that again, I will kill you," he screamed through gritted teeth.

Nikita threw her wet hands up in defence. "What did I do Sam? Why are you so angry?"

He grabbed her by the hair and pulled her head back. She was sure he was going to have a clump of hair in his hands when he let go.

"Do you know how embarrassing it is to see your wife coming onto your friends like that?"

She could smell the alcohol on his breath and he spit in her face as he spoke.

"But I wasn't," she tried to tell him. "You're being stupid and you're hurting me, let go," she shrieked.

"Oh, so now I'm the stupid one, am I? You uneducated fat bitch. Don't you ever go anywhere near my mates again, you got that?"

Nikita didn't answer as she struggled.

"You got that?" he yelled again.

"Yes, yes, yes," she screamed.

"Yes, yes, yes," he repeated in a high pitched voice, mimicking her. He let go of her hair and she stood holding her head without looking up. She tried to walk passed him, but he grabbed her with such rage that she knew her arms were going to bruise. He pushed her back with great force, slamming her into the sink unit and she felt a sharp pain in her back. It took the wind out of her and she worried that it may have done some internal damage. She fell to the ground unable to stand and circled her arms around her stomach. Her back burned and the pain shot down her torso and along her thighs. Her vision became blurred; she could see black spots dart in front of her eyes and for a short moment Nikita felt like she was going to pass out.

No matter how strict Nikita's dad had been, he had never laid a hand on her and here she was, receiving the first beating of her life time, from a man that was meant to be her best friend.

She didn't see him leave the kitchen but she heard his footsteps charging up the stairs. Her head was pounding. She tried so hard to control her crying in case he heard her and came back down. She tried to hold it in, but the tears still poured down her face.

How could he say those things to her? He was her husband. Fat bitch, fat bitch, fat bitch, it just kept running through her head. Did she repulse him that much? She sat on the floor for what seemed like hours. The tap was still running in the sink and the water started to over flow. She quickly got up and turned it off, biting her lip to stop her from screaming out at the pain. She stood up and felt the overwhelming pain in her heart and in her stomach and she burst into tears again. She wanted to yell and scream but she couldn't. She wanted to smash the dishes and punch the walls. She wanted to pull her hair out and scratch her face, anything to take away the overwhelming pain in her heart. She couldn't understand it. Why was he treating her like this? He didn't talk to her; he didn't try and get to know her and now this. What had she done to deserve this? Nikita stood in the kitchen for a while longer and then tried to compose herself. She finished washing the dishes, her hands still shaking. She washed everything, not thinking, or concentrating, she was almost in a zombie like state. Slowly the pain lessoned to a throb and she was able to breathe a little easier. She was scared and wondered if she should go upstairs or not. She stayed downstairs watching the time tick over and then decided after a while that he must have fallen asleep by then, especially as he'd had that beer, so she went upstairs and quietly climbed into bed.

Chapter 5 - Walking On Egg Shells

After that day Nikita came home from work as quickly as possible. She became a robot. She got up, went to work, came home, cooked and went to bed. It became Groundhog Day, every day, except there was nothing that she could do to change it. Or rather, there was nothing that she would dare do to change it.

Her only respite came from reading her books before Sam came home. She enjoyed reading novels so much but she only had enough time to get through a few pages before he stepped in the door. She didn't want him getting angry at her again so she steered clear of doing things that would upset him. She hid her books from him. Every evening she put the dinner on and sat on the breakfast table and read a few pages. She'd listen for the front door opening and as soon as she heard the key turning, she would quickly shut her book and hide it in the cupboard under the sink, behind her collection of detergents. Sometimes she would hear a noise and she'd quickly shut the book and hide it. She'd rush to the stove and start to stir the pot. She'd wait a few seconds but then realise that she was mistaken. Then she would relax.

This was no way for her to live her life.

He was always in a bad mood. Always looking to kick off an argument and she was continuously walking on egg shells. There wasn't much communication between them at all now, not that there had been much before. They were strangers living under one roof. It didn't even feel like her home anymore. There was an atmosphere in the house that frightened her. The smell of the house made her body tingle nervously. Your home was meant to be a place of peace and tranquillity and after a hard day's work, a place where you felt comfortable and safe, but Nikita didn't feel safe anymore.

She kept wishing and hoping that things would get better but they never did.

She dreamt that maybe one day she would wake up and all of this would just have been one long nightmare, but that never happened either. This was her life, it was her reality.

Nikita's mum, would phone to see how she was and Nikita always put on a false, happy voice. Mum would ask how they were getting on and Nikita said they were very happy but they were both busy with work. Mum was so proud of her. As much as she wanted to, Nikita could never tell her mum the truth because she knew it would break her mum's heart.

***

Nikita dreaded the phone call she was expecting. Her cousin was turning twenty one and she knew his family would be hosting a party in her home town and she would be expected to attend. Nikita wanted to go. She hadn't seen any of her family in such a long time and she missed them desperately, but she knew that it wouldn't be good for her. She knew they would be expecting her to come with her in-laws as well. Nikita stressed for days and then one evening it happened. Nikita's mum's sister, her aunt called. Nikita swallowed hard as she answered the phone and heard her auntie's voice. "Hello auntie, how are you?" she asked trying not to let her aunt hear the anxiety in her voice.

"I'm fine Nikita, how are you? You don't even phone these days. I feel like you've forgotten all your old family now that you've settled into your new life."

Nikita let out a fake low laugh. "I'm good, I've just been really busy with work and you know Sam's got a big family. Every weekend there's something going on," she lied.

"I know, we have to get used to it don't we? You have your own life now. Well at least you're happy," she said.

Nikita felt like crying. Her auntie was like her mum. When Nikita was younger, she spent just as much time at her aunt's home as she did her own. Never did a week go by when Nikita hadn't seen her. Even on Mother's Day, Nikita would always buy her Maasi a Mother's day card and flowers.

"Well, you know its Baljinder's twenty first birthday next month. We're having a party in the local community centre and you have to come okay?" she demanded. "Make sure you come with Sam and bring your mum as well."

Nikita wished that she could make up an excuse but she knew it would upset her auntie.

"Okay auntie we'll be there, don't worry."

"That's great my dear. I'm so looking forward to seeing you there. It's been a long time. Anyway I'd better go; I need to make some more calls."

"Okay auntie, I'll see you soon," Nikita promised as she put the phone down.

Nikita dreaded telling Sam about the party so she told her mother in law and let her speak to him. His mum made arrangements with him to attend, but he wasn't happy about going.

The party date came around so quickly and Sam argued with Nikita all morning. He was going to make sure that she didn't enjoy the party. Every dress that Nikita put on, he didn't like. She lost count of how many times she had to change.

"Why do we have to go to this stupid party? I don't get it. Why should I sit with them bastards? I don't even know who they are," he moaned.

Nikita's desired response ran through her mind. 'Well, if you made more of an effort maybe you would get to know them and they're not bastards. They're much better human beings than you and the only bastard around here is you,' Nikita thought but couldn't say out loud. The important thing was that he was going to the party and if she said anything, he would start arguing again and this would give him an excuse not to attend.

Nikita didn't hear her mother in law coming upstairs. Her mother in law had a front door key and let herself in. She heard Sam shouting at Nikita and she knocked on the bedroom door. Sam opened it and just walked passed her heading downstairs. Nikita didn't look at her mother in law because she knew the sorrow in her eyes would be obvious. His mum walked over and sat on the bed. Nikita carried on applying her makeup, over the top of the makeup she had already put on.

"Why is he angry? Has something happened between the two of you?" his mother asked.

Nikita felt like telling her everything. 'When is something not wrong between the two of us? When has it ever been right between the two of us?' But she couldn't say it. "He's angry about going to the party and he keeps arguing with me about it," Nikita told her.

"I heard what he was saying. I thought that he would be different to his father, but he's just the same," she told Nikita.

Nikita looked up at her in surprise.

Her mother in law saw the question in her eyes but she didn't say much else.

It made Nikita really angry because if she knew what her son was like, then why didn't she speak against him? Why didn't she say that she would to talk to him?

"You're strong," his mum said. "If he's anything like his father, then I would have given up by now. I would have been distraught, but I can see that you're handling it. You've got a big heart," she continued. "Indian girls these days, pack their bags very quickly and give up, but you haven't. I'm glad that you're sticking it out."

Nikita was shocked. She wanted to scream at her mother in law. Did she think that this was going to make her feel better? Did she think that it made her feel brave to be handling the situation? Nikita wanted to tell her mother in law that she hated Sam, that he had broken her heart in every way possible, that she was scared of him, that she hated her life, that she was miserable, but she just couldn't say it. Nikita's mouth felt dry, her voice wasn't coming out. She came to the realisation that she was in this alone. There was not going to be a hero who was going to whisk her away from it all. Her heart sank to the pit of her stomach and she controlled the tears building at the back of her eyes.

Getting through the party was such hard work for Nikita. She was smiling in front of everyone, but inside she felt like crying. Luckily Sam was putting on an act as well. Somehow he'd managed to charm everyone and even Nikita's mum was running around, fussing over him. Then suddenly the DJ dedicated a song to Sam and Nikita. She looked over to her cousin and he stuck his thumbs up at her. Kam had made the request. It was their wedding song. It had been almost a year since the wedding and this was her families way of celebrating the anniversary.

Everyone started pushing Nikita towards the dance floor and Sam was already standing there, continuing with the charade no doubt. He grabbed Nikita's hands and smiled at her. A cold shiver ran up her spine and although she probably always knew it, for the first time she allowed herself to think, this man was complete evil.

Nikita put on a fake smile and forced her feet to move to the rhythm of the music.

Sam behaved as though the last year had never happened, like she'd dreamt it all. He held her hands as they slowly swayed to the music. He pulled her close, smiling all the time. To onlookers Sam and Nikita looked like they were very much in love.

She couldn't hear the music; she just knew that she needed to move.

Everybody stared at them, smiling, clapping along with the song and cheering as they danced. Sam's hands dropped to Nikita's waist and she shuddered as she felt his touch. He pulled her closer and she felt her face start to burn. The top few buttons of his shirt were undone, he'd lost his tie somewhere and Nikita became very conscious when he pushed his chest against her face. Her family started whistling and cheering but Nikita's heart was screaming.

When the song ended, relief rushed through Nikita's body. Now she could hide again. She looked at her mother in law but her mum was too busy hugging her. Nikita knew she had been watching.

Towards the end of the party Nikita's mum started insisting that they all visit home before heading back to Wolverhampton. Heading back to the hell hole, Nikita thought. Nikita didn't want to visit home, but she couldn't come up with an excuse good enough not to. She hadn't visited since she'd got married and now that they were in Letchworth, she had to pass through.

They got to the house and Nikita made herself busy in the kitchen. There was lots of washing up to do from earlier on in the day, so she got started. She didn't want to talk to anyone. She knew they would be asking her questions and she would have to lie to them. In the party she found it easy to avoid the questions, the music was so loud.

After ten minutes or so, Sam came in the kitchen. He put his hands on her waist and leaned in close. She could feel his breath on the back of her neck. Anybody watching would think that he was whispering romantic words of endearment into her ear. She could smell the heavy scent of booze.

"I want to go," he mumbled. He was slurring his words.

Before Nikita could respond, he spoke again. "Didn't take you long, did it?"

"What are you talking about?" Nikita asked.

"You come to your parent's home and you can't wait to take off your wedding rings can you?" he mumbled.

Nikita didn't know what he was talking about. "Sam, I don't understand, what are you saying?"

"That's what you think of our marriage isn't it. You wish you never married me don't you?"

Nikita could tell that he was talking through gritted teeth. Then he pointed at the two rings lying on the window sill above the sink. A plain gold band and a gold cluster ring similar to hers. They were her sister's.

"You're a selfish bitch aren't you? You don't care what people will think throwing your wedding rings around like that. Then you wonder why I get pissed off. Can you blame me when you behave like this?" he said in a low voice only she could hear.

"Those are Ria's rings," Nikita told him and she pulled her hand out of the soapy water to prove that she still had her rings on.

"Does the bitch have to copy everything that you do?" Nikita felt a jolt of anger rush through her. How dare he speak of her sister in that way? Yet she said nothing. She ignored his question and her mum walked into the kitchen. Sam walked out.

She had to fight to hold back the tears. Her heart was thumping in her chest uncontrollably and she just wanted to get out of there. Nikita pretended that she got washing up liquid in her eyes, which made her eyes water.

Luckily Nikita's mother in law suggested they should leave and she couldn't have said it sooner.

Nikita's cousins wanted to get another bottle of whiskey out to drink with Sam, but Nikita insisted they had to leave. Her cousins were flocked around him like flies hovering around shit. That was Nikita's analogy of him. They were laughing and joking with him. They were so impressed by him, his job and his status. It was a shame they didn't really know what he was about. They didn't know what a horrible, cold, cruel bastard he was and Nikita didn't have the heart to tell them. They really thought that he was a wonderful person. Sam had everyone fooled.

Nikita was so glad when the day was over. She'd never felt so much relief getting into the car and driving back to her nightmare. Sam was too drunk to drive, but she was glad, because he slept for most of the journey. Nikita's mother in law didn't say much either, except for a few comments about Nikita's mum and how she had looked after her throughout the party.

When they got back, Nikita dragged Sam into the house. His mum didn't stop and walked straight home. That's when she realised that she truly was on her own. Even though his mum knew what her son was like and what he was doing to Nikita, his mum wasn't going to do anything to help or support her. Nikita tried to drag Sam up the stairs but he pushed her away, so she just followed him up and he dropped onto the mattress. Nikita took off his shoes and socks and lifted his legs onto the bed and placed the duvet on top of him.

She got changed out of her party clothes and jewellery and put her pyjamas on. She was about to leave the bedroom when he spoke.

"Get into bed," he moaned.

Nikita's heart sank. She hated him touching her. It made her feel dirty and violated and she couldn't stand it, but she didn't have the guts to refuse either.

The curtains were still open and the moonlight shone through the window. The street lamp lit up the bedroom, so Nikita drew the curtains. She wanted it to be pitch black, then she wouldn't have to look at him.

Nikita slowly climbed into bed. He took his top off and pushed up against her. He tugged on her top. She had already removed her bra when she got changed and he groped her aggressively. She felt her nipples harden and she hated that her body responded to him in that way. He climbed on top, pushed her legs open with his thighs and she felt him enter. She was tense and didn't move, but this made it more enjoyable for him and she hated that he received more pleasure because she couldn't relax. She could tell that the more she tensed, the more he enjoyed it. She could hear it in the way he groaned and she found it harder and harder to block him out. She felt him tense and stiffen and then his weight dropped onto her, almost winding her. All the while her face was turned away from him. After a few moments he rolled back over and went to sleep. He didn't kiss her, he never had. He never made love to her, it was just sex and she despised herself for letting him do this to her.

Nikita got out of bed and grabbed some fresh clothes. She went back down to have a wash. She sat in the bath for over an hour scrubbing her body, crying and washing. She wanted everything to be over.

Chapter 6 - The End

Months went by since Nikita had seen to her mum and dad. Sam had refused to drive her down since the birthday party and he wouldn't let her go on her own.

When Nikita's parents arranged a religious prayer ceremony in celebration of her brother's birthday, she planned to go. Sam wasn't happy about attending but somehow she managed to get him to agree. She knew she'd probably end up paying for it afterwards, but it was worth it if she got to see her family and her little brother, whom she adored and loved so much. She was looking forward to seeing everyone.

The morning woke Nikita with little bursts of sunlight coming through the opening in the drawn curtain. It made her smile as she stretched her aching limbs. She was so excited about attending. She picked out a peacock green trouser suit, with green and ruby coloured stones along with Sam's Polo shirt and ironed them. Nikita did everything she could to keep Sam happy. She didn't want to give him any opportunity to make an excuse not to attend. Sam came into the bedroom while she was ironing.

"I'm not going," he said.

Nikita looked at him in horror. "What, why? You said it was okay for us to go, you agreed," she said, her voice almost a shrill.

"Yeh, well I've changed my mind. I'm going out with some mates."

"But I've already told mum that we're coming, what am I going to say to her now?"

"Say what you want. Do you really think I give a shit?" His face was smug.

"You've done this on purpose haven't you; you never had any intention of going in the first place, did you?"

Sam smiled and walked away. Nikita fell onto her bed and let out a low sob. He was playing her and he was enjoying it. He liked playing these games with her; it made him feel like he was in control.

Her life had become a long river of tears and heartache. Life just wasn't what she had imagined it to be.

She pressed her fists against her forehead trying to stop herself from crying but it was useless. It just made her angrier. She hated that she was powerless to do anything else. How much longer could she put up with this? She had to tell someone. But who? He was never going to change. Even if he could, she would never be able to forgive him. She was a generous and caring person, but she couldn't forgive him. Not for what he had done to her. She had spent too many sleepless nights, crying on her pillow, suffering with nightmares, curling up in pain and hating herself for letting him do this to her. She needed to get out!

Dialling her mother's number from the phone upstairs, Nikita wiped at her tears. Mum could tell that something was wrong. She could hear it in Nikita's voice. Nikita lied to her again and told her that she had gone to sleep with a very bad headache and that she had woken up with the flu. Her nose was running and her voice sounded deep from crying and to her mum it sounded as though she had a very badly blocked nose. She gave her mum a bullshit story about having a temperature and how she was going to take some pain killers and go to sleep. Nikita's mum told her to rest and promised that she would call her later.

Nikita didn't attend the ceremony. She stayed in bed for most of the day.

Sam returned later that evening and as usual, there was no conversation between husband and wife.

That night the phone rang. Nikita knew that it would be her mum. She was checking to see how her daughter was feeling and she would want to know when she was going to be visiting. Nikita kept trying to make excuses but mum kept insisting. Nikita could see that Sam was starting to get angry. She could see his temper starting to flare and she could feel her heart thumping. It was making her breathless. Nikita made an excuse about someone being at the front door and put the phone down.

Sam went in the kitchen and got a bottle of beer.

Nikita could feel the trouble crackling in the air, but what could she do? She decided that she was not going to respond to anything he said and hopefully he would shut up after a while and there wouldn't be an argument.

She was watching a reality show, except she wasn't really watching it but just pretending to keep herself occupied. She couldn't go upstairs because he would call her lazy. She couldn't sit and read in the kitchen, because he'd probably rip up her book, so she sat downstairs, always watching and hoping he wouldn't start on her. Later that night, as Nikita had predicted he started.

"Why are you always watching these stupid programmes? What do you see in them?" he moaned. "They're not going to give you any more brain cells, are they?"

Nikita didn't respond. She was determined not to engage but she thought about all the things that she wanted to say to him. 'I hate you, you fucking bastard. You're so full of shit it's unbelievable.' Nikita smiled inwardly thinking about the satisfaction she would have if she could bring herself to say those things and the consequences would be worth it just to see his face.

"Is that all your parents have taught you? How to sit on your fat arse and watch television."

Nikita still kept quiet.

"These illiterate animals. If they can't teach their children anything but watching these stupid programmes then they shouldn't get their children married."

Rage started to build like a fire ball deep down inside her. How could she stay quiet? He infuriated her. What had her parents ever done to him but show him love and respect?

"My parents have nothing to do with this? Leave them out of it. You can say what you want to me, but you have no right to say anything about them," she said.

Sam glared at Nikita, fury raging in his eyes. "Why shouldn't I bring that bitch into this? She really gets on my fucking nerves, always interfering. Doesn't she know that you're married now and that you've got duties to fulfil? Phoning here every day, sticking her nose in where it's not wanted and insisting that you go down to that shitty so called town of yours. You think I don't know that you're always talking about me. Cussing me!"

The room started to spin. Nikita couldn't believe it. He called her mum a bitch. It infuriated her so much and something snapped inside her. The contained anger erupted. Nikita stood up and glared at Sam. "Don't you dare say anything about my mum. Don't talk about her with that filthy mouth of yours, do you hear me?" she screamed, her face red with anger. She had never answered Sam back, let alone shout at him.

His long strides came calm and collected and the next thing she realised, she was on the floor, her cheek throbbing. She didn't see the fist coming in her direction. Nikita reached up and touched her face. There was a slick wetness. She pulled her hand away and looked at it; she had blood on her fingers. There was a sharp sting under her eye and she knew that she would be off work for days.

"I hate you, I hate you," she screamed at him.

Pulling her by the hair, Sam yanked her up and into the hallway, shoving her up the stairs. As she resisted, Sam pushed her down on the steps and wrapped his thick sweaty fingers around her neck.

"Think you're some big hot shot? Think you can speak to me like that and get away with it? You're lucky you got me, you fucking bitch," he screamed in her face. "I never wanted anything to do with you, but they wouldn't listen would they? My life has been fucked since you came along."

Nikita tried to fight him off, trying to push her hands under his to break his grip from around her throat, but she couldn't. The strength in her arms had left her. Her head started to spin and her arms and legs became heavy. Black dots darted around in front of her eyes. She couldn't keep them open, she couldn't breathe. She was struggling, trying to gasp for any little bit of air that she could squeeze through his hold but she didn't have the strength to keep trying. Her head was spinning and his face started to become blurred. The darkness started to envelope her. She was being pushed into a tunnel with no light and it was getting darker and darker.

So this is what dying felt like she thought. What will my mum think? What will my dad think? This is going to crush them. She never expected it would end like this. She thought about everything she had dreamed of doing, but she hadn't done anything worth remembering. No around the world trips, or having a family of her own, becoming a mother. That wasn't going to happen now. She wasn't going to have the chance to say goodbye to anyone. Everything had been taken away from her. First he took her dignity and pride and now he was taking her life. But without those things, life wasn't worth living anyway.

Her thoughts became muddled. Will he get arrested? Will he get done for murder? Will they find her body? Nikita's thoughts started to drift away.

She couldn't fight it anymore. Darkness descended and her body relaxed. The life drifted out of her, leaving her limp and powerless. Her thoughts disappeared but at least it was over for her. Everything went black.

She didn't have to feel anymore embarrassment, shame, or pain and people would find out what he was really like, without her having to tell them...............

Chapter 7 – Run for your life

Nikita's stomach hurt, face hurt and her eyes hurt. Swelling on her eyes made it difficult for them to open and they were sore. Her eyes flickered open slightly and the four walls spun around and around.

Pain shot through her torso. She didn't think you were meant to feel any pain once you were dead. Nikita's thoughts became muddled as they mingled with flash backs of the day before. Maybe she was in hell.

She didn't know why, but her life had been so miserable, that she knew it had to have been a punishment, but for what? She'd never deliberately hurt anyone, stolen anything or cheated anyone. So why was her life so dejected?

Nikita shook her head to clear it. She blinked and felt around. She realised she was in her bed. She sat up and as she moved, she felt a sharp pain in her ribs. Her cheek felt stiff so she reached up to touch it, running her fingers over a knobbly thick line below her eye. The cut had scabbed over and the blood had dried against her cheek. Nikita held her head in her hands. It throbbed like crazy and her throat felt like someone had rubbed sandpaper on the inside of it. It was dry and gritty. Her stomach was very tender and painful when she moved.

The only sound in the room was of the clock ticking and the cars driving by the house. She looked over to the clock on her bedside cabinet, trying to focus her eyes. It was 10am. The curtains were still drawn and the room felt hot and smelt very stuffy.

She stared down at herself and realised she was still in the same clothes she had worn the night before. The flash backs returned and she remembered the punch to her face, the struggle on the stairs, the tightness around her throat and not being able to breathe. Her hand automatically rose to her neck and she rubbed it unconsciously again.

Climbing slowly out of bed and walking over to the wardrobe, Nikita looked in the mirror. Her hair was tangled. She had a very big purple bruise on her face below her eye and she looked like shit. Her eyelids looked tender and swollen, one more than the other and there was dry blood on her face. Her clothes were torn and her eyes were red and blood shot. Nikita's ears hurt every time she tried to swallow and she could see finger marks around her neck.

She stepped backwards and sat back down on the bed letting out a low sob. What had she become? She used to be happy, even with her parent's restrictions, she still loved being alive but now she didn't even recognise the face in the mirror. It wasn't her.

Nikita wished that she was dead. At least then it would have been over. Death had to be better than the everyday pain and the lying to her family and friends. Anything was better than the humiliation that she was made to feel.

She hated Sam so much. He could never do anything properly. He was never a proper friend or husband and now he couldn't even finish her off properly. She held her stomach; he had brought her to this, to a point in her life where she wished she was dead.

There was no way she could stay there anymore. He had tried to kill her. She slowly opened the bedroom door and stood there for a while listening for any movement. It was very quiet in the house. Where was he? She listened for any movement downstairs but she couldn't hear anything. She slowly walked downstairs and headed straight for the front door. She turned the handle, but it was locked. She looked for her keys but couldn't find them anywhere. She couldn't find her handbag so she went and checked the back door and it too was locked. Nikita went to the kitchen cupboard where the spare backdoor key was kept, but that wasn't in its normal place either. The windows were always kept locked and she didn't have a key. The realisation dawned on her, he had locked her in the house. There was no way for her to get out, no way to escape. She needed to call the police so she went to pick up the telephone, but it wasn't there. Even the lead had been taken out of the socket. He didn't want her to contact anyone either, she was trapped.

She waited all day. Nobody came to the door and she didn't know if anyone had tried to call her.

Her mind went over it and over it again. She spent all day thinking about what to do. She didn't eat anything, even a cup of tea made her throat sting. She sat in silence.

Nikita looked at the time and realised it was heading towards six o'clock. Her heart started to sink into her stomach; she didn't know what to do. She was so frightened that there would be a repeat of what had happened yesterday and there was no way that she could handle it again.

Nikita sighed; she knew what she had to do. She would behave as normal as possible so that he would let his guard down; it was the only way she was going to get out. She would put up with whatever he put her through to save herself.

She needed her keys and some money to get away.

Nikita put her passport and a change of clothes, some toiletries and took the money from the cookie jar, which she kept for bills, into a bag and hid it under the sink. He wouldn't look there. He rarely spent any time in the kitchen.

"The kitchen is a place for women," he would always say. Nikita needed to behave as normal as possible so she went in the kitchen and made some dinner. She put it in the oven to keep it warm.

She forced herself to eat a can of chicken soup. If she was to escape she would need the energy and it was the only thing she had in her cupboard that would cause her the least bit of discomfort.

Every step she took caused her excruciating pain in her stomach; maybe she had cracked a rib. When she went to the toilet, she noticed blood in her urine. What damage had he done? She could only hope it was nothing serious, but then again she wasn't surprised after what had happened the night before.

Nikita had a bath, brushed her hair and tried to bring about a normal expression to her face which was almost impossible. She looked like she had gone ten rounds in a boxing ring with Mohammed Ali. Wetting a small face flannel, she slowly washed off the blood on her cheek and it revealed a long gash under her eye. It was definitely going to scar. He'd left a reminder of himself for the rest of her life. Every time she would look in the mirror, she would be reminded of him.

At seven o'clock she heard the front door open and she froze. She was sitting at the breakfast table in the kitchen.

Sam walked in and she heard him run up the stairs. Maybe he went to see if she was dead. Then she heard him running down the stairs, jumping the last few steps and he raced into the kitchen. He saw her sitting there, his expression nonchalance.

He looked at Nikita and then spoke. "Look, last night it got a bit out of hand. I shouldn't have hurt you but you made me so angry."

Nikita stared at him.

"You know not to push my buttons. If you behave then there won't be a repeat of yesterday. Bear that in mind and let's move on."

Nikita nodded in agreement. She felt numb. She didn't even have the emotions to feel shocked anymore. The way he had passed off last night's incident as though it was her fault, she had brought it upon herself? He made her sick. If he had experienced the same as her from someone else, the police would be involved. His whole family would be around him, praying for his full and quick recovery and he wanted to forget about it and move on? Things had got a bit out of hand, he'd said. The conversation he'd just had was ridiculous. How could he brush it off just like that? He must have seen the bruising on her face, her neck, her black eyes and all these had occurred because things had just got out of hand? Sam went to the fridge and got out a bottle of beer.

He took his food out of the oven and returned back to the living room. Nikita stayed in the kitchen for the next couple of hours while he watched the TV. He was behaving like today was just another day in the miserable life of Nikita. He didn't speak a word after that, but that wasn't unusual; he barely spoke to her anyway.

Nikita's stomach was hurting even more now. Sitting up on the wooden dining chair wasn't doing it any good. She needed to lie down. She took two paracetamols tablets to help and then went through the lounge and headed for the bedroom. Nikita discreetly looked around to see if she could see his keys anywhere and they were on top of the fire place. Sam was watching the news and didn't even look at her.

Nikita slowly climbed the stairs taking one step at a time, breathing in for as long she could to help stem the pain. She hoped the medicine would kick in soon; she didn't know how much more of this she could take.

Lying down on the bed, she tossed and turned to lie in different positions to get as comfortable as possible and then she heard footsteps. He was coming.

Nikita felt like her heart had stopped beating. She couldn't breathe. She angled her body, facing away from his side of the bed and pretended that she was asleep.

Once he was asleep, she was going to make a run for it. She had to get away.

She could hear him, taking his clothes off in the dark and even being in the same room as him disgusted her. She hated him so much, like she'd never hated any other person before in her life. She couldn't bear the thought of him lying next to her, but she knew that if she wanted to escape, she would have to bare it.

Sam got into bed and she heard him yawn. She continued to listen for the low snoring noise. She waited and waited and waited.

After around thirty minutes she felt something touch her leg. Was she dreaming? It felt so real. It was real. It was him. Nikita froze. She didn't know what to do. If she fought him, she would never get out, but she couldn't bear to let him touch her either. What was she going to do? She felt sick, she was in pain, she wanted to scream and she wished she was dead. What sort of sick bastard was he? After everything he had put her through, he thought he could still do what he wanted with her? No, no, no. Please for God's sake, don't do this to me, she screamed in her head. Her body was shaking. The weight of him, his hands running over her bare skin underneath her clothes, she thought she was going to be physically sick.

The next few minutes were a blur. Her brain must have switched off or maybe she passed out, but she didn't feel anything. She heard no sounds, she felt numb. Tears ran down her face, droplets trickling into her ears. She made no sound herself. Her throat had contracted to a point where she couldn't even breathe.

When Sam had finished, he rolled off and went downstairs to use the bathroom.

Nikita stared up at the ceiling for a few moments, her body as still as a corpse. She let out a low squeal. She didn't know what was more painful, the pain in her body or the pain in her heart. She was never going to forgive this man for what he had done to her. Never!

Then she heard him coming back up the stairs and she quickly wiped her face and pretended again that she was asleep.

Think, think. This was her only opportunity to get away. She had to focus.

Before long he had fallen asleep and she waited for another short while to make sure he was in a deep sleep.

She had only one chance and she had to be absolutely certain that he wouldn't awake. If he did, this time she wouldn't make it another day and she knew it.

She climbed out of bed as quietly as she could and slowly walked towards the stairs. She bit her lower lip, she was in agony, but she held it together. She slowly tip toed down the stairs and through the living room. She was careful not to make any noise. She looked over to the fireplace and his keys were still there in front of the white wooden mantel clock which she'd received as a wedding gift from a friend. Something else she would be leaving behind. She let out a big sigh of relief and picked up the keys trying not to make a sound. She held them tight, a bunch in the palm of her hand. She grabbed her backpack from under the sink and then headed towards the front door. She froze. She thought she'd heard something.

Her instincts told her to run!

But she couldn't. She couldn't move. She stood still for what felt like hours, but could only have been minutes, listening, but it wasn't him.

Her sandals were by the front door, she slipped them on. It was wet outside but she didn't want to risk looking for a proper pair of shoes. She hadn't thought to prepare her trainers or any closed toe shoes. They were all on the shoe rack in her bedroom, so these would have to do.

She took another step towards the door and reached out with the keys in her hand. She put the key in the key hole, her heart thumping in terror. The sound was deafening to her ears.

If she runs, will he come looking for her, will he kill her? What will people say? They'll all be whispering behind her back. What if she gets forced to get back with him? She'll get labelled as a slag; they'll say she's run away with another man, she knows they will. They always blame the girl. It's never the man's fault.

Nikita shook her head. She couldn't think that way. Listening to other people, always doing what other people wanted was what had landed her in this situation in the first place. Why should she care about what anyone else thinks? She realised that if she didn't leave now she'd probably end up dead.

Nikita turned the key as quietly as she could and then turned the handle on the door. The door opened. She left the keys in the door and stepped outside; looking in both directions to make sure that there was no one around. The road looked so long. Will she make it to the end without anyone seeing her? She felt the cool breeze on her face which soothed the burning feeling of her bruises. She didn't turn around because she didn't want to look back. She shut the door as quietly as she could and walked out of the front gate. Nikita held her backpack tight and started to walk quickly down the road. When she was clear of the house she started to run. Even though it was killing her, she ran and ran and ran. Her feet became wet having stepped in puddles as her legs carried her.

A couple of cars drove passed and she turned her face away from the road to ensure no one would recognise her. Oh my God, is that a Ford Mondeo heading towards her? Fuck, what if it's him? What is she going to do? But it didn't stop. She saw a lady walking towards her and her heart sank. Would she recognise her? Nikita lowered her head letting her dark brown hair tumble over her face, but the lady didn't look at her. Nikita's heart was thumping in her chest and she started running again. She felt a stitch developing under her ribs but she couldn't stop. Even though the tablets had kicked in, she knew she would regret it in the morning, if she made it through the night.

It was cold and wet and it had started raining again. Nikita hated Spring and after today she was never going to forget it. Her feet were frozen in her open toe sandals. Her clothes clung to her body as they became more and more wet. As the cold air hit her wet clothes, her body started trembling. Nikita wanted nothing more than to collapse on the floor and gather herself together but she knew she couldn't take the risk. If she stopped now, he might catch her and she couldn't go back to that hell hole.

In the distance she could see a phone booth. She wiped at her face and tried to gauge the distance. If she could just make it there. She walked the last few steps reaching the booth and stood for a long moment trying to catch her breath. She stepped inside and collapsed on the floor. She sat there for sometime before she managed to stand again. Talking herself into picking up the receiver, Nikita called the police. She didn't know what to say to them, she just needed help. Her mouth felt frozen with the cold wet weather. "Help," was all she could say and then she put the phone down. After a few moments she realised she hadn't told them where she was. Would she have to call them again? Nikita stepped outside the booth, thinking no one was coming to help, when she saw a blue light in the distance. She squinted to focus her eyes and she felt the tight tug against her eye where the scab had formed. Without thinking she raised her hand and touched the scab again. For the second time she thought about how she was going to have to live with this scar, a reminder of her nightmare for the rest of her life.

The flashing blue light became brighter as it came closer and the white car pulled up beside her. Two police men got out. Nikita stood shaking in her wet clothes and the officer ushered her into the back seat.

Once she had arrived at the police station, she was asked to go into a room and a female officer brought her a cup of tea. The officer threw a warm blanket over Nikita. She was shivering. Her clothes were soaked through to her underwear and she felt dirty. Nikita stared at the cup of tea, holding it in both hands, trying to warm them. The cold that had reached her core, caused her teeth to chatter. Her whole body trembled with fear.

The officer encouraged her to drink her tea. The room was bare, with dirty cream walls and it was cold. The officer saw the bruising on Nikita's face and asked her what had happened, but Nikita couldn't answer them. Nikita's brain was screaming in response to the questions, but her mouth couldn't form the words.

The police officer told Nikita she needed to take some photos of her. Nikita didn't want to, but she just didn't have the strength to say no.

The officer was very patient. She spoke to in a very calm voice they would keep the pictures on file in case she ever wanted to press charges.

This surprised Nikita. She hadn't told them anything so how did they know what had happened?

The officer took pictures of Nikita's face and neck and asked her if she had any other bruising. Nikita didn't answer. She couldn't, she felt like she was living someone else's life. This wasn't meant to happen to her. She was always good, she didn't deserve this.

The officer lifted up Nikita's arm to see if there was any other bruising.

Nikita squinted from the pain near her stomach.

The officer asked Nikita to lift up her top but Nikita just stared at her, so she leaned in and placed one hand on Nikita's hand. "It's okay. You're away from it now. He can't hurt you anymore. You have to let me help you; I need to take some photos of the bruising on your stomach. I won't hurt you, I promise."

Nikita lifted up her top and the officer quickly took the photo.

She started asking Nikita questions about how long it had been going on? Was this the first time it had happened? Had he done anything else to her? The questions were not registering in Nikita's brain. She just burst into tears. She couldn't answer. Even when she tried to speak, nothing was coming out and she couldn't form any sentences.

The officer advised Nikita to go to the hospital, but Nikita didn't want to go. She didn't want to do anything, she just wanted to fall into a deep sleep and forget the world. She wanted everything and everyone to just go away.

The officer told Nikita she was going to take her somewhere safe for the night and she could stay there for as long as she wanted. She also recommended that Nikita see a doctor the following day.

Nikita looked at her through tear filled eyes and just nodded. Nikita stood, her body trembling with pain and decided at that point that she would never let anyone control her life again.

Chapter 8 – Nightmares

It wasn't long before the police came to speak to Nikita at the refuge. They told her that Sam had filed a missing person report and that he was distraught with worry.

The thought of Sam finding her made Nikita's heart fill with terror. She broke out into a cold sweat, her body trembling with fear. "I don't want to see him. Please don't tell him where I am, please." Her voice was shaking in panic.

The terror in Nikita's eyes was evident and no matter how many times the officers had dealt with cases like this, it didn't make it any easier.

They often came across these domestic cases. The officer couldn't understand why they termed it domestic, because the word itself made light of the incident. If someone was attacked and beaten or raped by a stranger, it was made into a huge issue, how it should be. But if someone was beaten or raped by their husband or partner it was seen to be acceptable and people started to make excuses for the perpetrator.

PC Hyde still couldn't understand this. He had dealt with some serious cases in his time as a police officer, but they still shocked him. This poor girl, she seemed so timid, so frightened, and fragile. Why would anyone want to hurt her? In his opinion, this psycho needed to be locked up. He had physically abused this girl until she must have passed out. He couldn't help but stare at her pale face full of fright. He found himself thinking, if it wasn't for the fact that she looked so broken, bruised and scared, she would be very beautiful. There were men out there, good humble men who would do anything to be with such a lovely young lady and yet this evil man had turned her into a punching bag.

The officers were very understanding. At first Nikita couldn't make eye contact, but PC Hyde assured her they would not tell anyone where she was. He said they would only let Sam know that she was safe and well. They urged Nikita to press charges but she told them she would think about it.

PC Hyde knew that in most cases like this, women didn't press charges and the perpetrator would get away scot free. However, he couldn't force her to do anything. It was her choice. PC Hyde felt so sorry for Nikita but knew he could do no more.

The officer walked over to Nikita and put his hand out to shake. Nikita didn't take it. Un-offended, he put his hand in his pocket and pulled out a card with his name and phone number on it asking her to contact him if she needed anything.

Sue was with Nikita when the police officers visited. She felt sorry for her. She looked at her for a moment and thought about how Nikita reminded her of her daughter.

Sue was a wrinkly grey old lady, looking forward to retirement in the next few months. Nikita liked her a lot. Sue was older than Nikita's mum, but she spoke brilliant English which wasn't that common. Nikita didn't know many Asian women at Sue's age that could speak English as good as she could. Nikita felt comfortable around her. Some of the other staff sometimes came across as being over bearing but Sue was very approachable and although Nikita didn't talk about her past much, when she did feel comfortable in talking about anything, it was only with Sue.

They spent a lot of time together. Sometimes in the evenings when it was quieter, they sat in the office for hours at a time. Nikita watched Sue work, tapping away on the computer. Nikita longed to feel valued again and sitting in the refuge with nothing to do made her feel useless.

Sue asked Nikita if she wanted to get in touch with her mum, but Nikita said she didn't. She didn't want anything to do with anyone in her past, not yet anyway. She didn't have the strength to deal with all the shit that would be thrown in her direction at the moment.

Nikita knew what the rumours would be and she didn't have the heart to hear her dad say she wasn't his daughter anymore.

Sue saw how it upset Nikita when she mentioned her family and she apologised, saying she wouldn't talk about it again. Not until Nikita said she was ready to discuss it.

When Nikita looked in the mirror, she could still see the scars on her face. She detested the remains of the cut on her lip and gash under her eye, which was healing now. It was left as a reminder of the life she had once lived. She reached up and touched the tender red cut, running her finger along it. As strict as her dad had always been, he had never laid a finger on her. Yet here she was looking like she had gone ten rounds in a boxing ring. Nikita stared into her own eyes, and emptiness stared back at her. A deep nothingness.

As time went on, Nikita became more comfortable talking about her past and she started to tell Sue about what had happened with Sam. Nikita struggled to relay the details of the horrendous events which had tainted her life with painful memories. Going over everything was like picking at a wound which had scabbed over and was now bleeding again.

Sue realised this, so she invited Nikita to the office. "Sit down," she said, pointing towards the small sofa.

She handed Nikita a book. It was called, 'My Voice'.

"What's this?" Nikita asked her.

"This is a Voice Book. It's a new idea we have introduced and I think it will be good for you."

"What do you mean? What am I going to do with it?" Nikita asked.

"Well, in the last few months I've got to know you quite well and I can see how hard it is for you to talk openly about your experiences. I thought this book might be a good way to express yourself. You don't have to talk about your trauma out loud, but you can get it out of your system by writing it down."

"Sue, I don't think I can, it's not me."

Nikita stared out of the big bay window at the front of the refuge. She felt so ashamed of herself. She understood why the staff tried to get her to face the reality of what had happened. If she didn't, how could she move on with her life? She got that. Knowing this, she still couldn't talk about it. Everything was held deep down in her heart, under lock and key and just the thought of unleashing all those feelings and emotions, frightened her.

"Nikita, take it with you and keep it in your room. If you feel like writing in it, then use it and if you don't feel like writing in it, then don't," Sue shrugged casually. "There's no harm in you keeping it in your room is there?"

"Okay," Nikita said in a low voice, "but don't expect me to use it," she grimaced as she walked out of the office.

It was Sunday and Nikita awoke early. She was still suffering with nightmares. They always seemed to be about her being chased by people she didn't recognise and sometimes, they looked like evil spirits trying to attach themselves to her. She'd be running and hiding but they would keep finding her. Sometimes she was trying to run but her legs felt heavy and she wasn't getting anywhere. Her brain would be sending signals to her legs but they wouldn't respond. The nightmares frightened her a lot and she'd wake up sweaty and breathless.

Nikita kept tossing and turning, but she couldn't get back to sleep, so she sat up. She rubbed her eyes and face and then stared at her almost bare room. In her bedroom at her parent's home, she had a whole collection of cuddly toys and bright pink fluffy cushions thrown on her bed. She loved pink, but here, it was all so plain and dull.

Nikita saw the voice book in the corner of her room, where she'd thrown it when she had come upstairs the day before. She climbed out of bed and picked it up. There was a pen on her bedside table. She opened the book and put the pen to paper and started to write.

Why why why why why why why why
bastard bastard bastard bastard bastard
Why did he do this to me?

Because I'm ugly
Because I'm stupid
He never loved me
I am useless
I am worthless

Nikita threw the book in the corner. It just made her feel so bad and she didn't want to write in it anymore.

Fuck, how was she going to get through life? At the moment she was taking it day by day, she couldn't see beyond that. All her dreams, all her aspirations, nothing seemed to exist inside her anymore, she felt empty.

Nikita didn't want to listen to music, she hated watching chick flick movies and she never wanted to read another novel again. Everything was drained from her, including the person that she used to be. There was nothing of her personality left inside.

If Nikita's parents had nurtured and encouraged her when she was younger, maybe she would have been a musician now, or attended drama school and become something in her life. She could have been on stage, in the West End, singing her heart out, or maybe playing in the Orchestra at the Symphony Hall. How much would she have loved it, but now she'd even forgotten how to read music. Dreams never came true; she'd learnt that the hard way.

But she guessed her parents did what they thought was right and she couldn't blame them for that, they truly believed in what they were doing.

Nikita grabbed her tooth brush, tooth paste and her towel and went into the bathroom.

She had learnt very quickly not to leave any toiletries in the bathroom because you wouldn't find them there the following day.

Once she'd had a wash, she went to the communal kitchen and made a cup of tea.

It was still very early and none of the other residents were up so she went back to the bedroom. Setting her mug aside on the dressing table, she picked up the voice book again. She closed her eyes and took a deep breath, and began to write.

Why did you say the things that you said to me?
You said I made a mistake, but I didn't do it purposely
You blamed me for the strain in your life
I only ever tried to be a good wife
You said that I remind you of the bad times you live
But you, I will never be able to forgive
I wanted to give you my love so strong
But in time it has just turned into a sad song
The tears have dried up and I'm feeling hollow
I would never have done it if I'd known what would follow

When I'd lie in bed awake at night
I'd wish for once you'd hold me tight
But it never happened and you turned your back
It's over now and I've to come to terms with that
The ache in my heart is ever so strong
It's been ripped to shreds, now that is wrong
I don't deserve to be treated like this
One day, I will be the one that you miss

Nikita put the pen down and stared at what she'd just written. She read it back to herself. Maybe Sue was right; she was good at writing her feelings down.

Nikita decided that she was going to try this again, but later. She felt exhausted.

Living in the refuge wasn't easy. Everyone wanted to know your business and Nikita didn't like talking about hers.

There were many other women at the refuge, some had children and although Nikita felt bad for them, it was good to know that she wasn't the only one this had happened to. In the evenings, all the women would sit together in the lounge and watch TV as they talked about their own experiences.

A new lady had arrived at the refuge, her name was Naina. She had only been there a couple of days and Nikita hadn't really spoken to her. She was a large, chunky lady, probably in her early thirties Nikita thought and she was wearing a black head scarf. She sat next to Nikita in the lounge, staring at her. Feeling a little awkward, Nikita smiled at her.

"Hi," Nikita said. She didn't want to be rude.

"Hello," Naina replied. "Why are you here?" she asked.

Nikita found this question quite intrusive. This lady didn't know her, so why did she think Nikita would answer? "I don't like to talk about it," was all Nikita said.

Naina started crying and Nikita didn't know what to do. She shouldn't have got that upset, just because Nikita didn't want to answer her question. Nikita felt bad and there was no one else in the lounge that Nikita could call upon for help, so she put her arm around Naina and started to stroke her back, slowly trying to sooth her. She pulled out a tissue from the box on the coffee table in front of them and passed it to Naina. Nikita didn't know what to say. What do you say in situations like these? Nikita noticed the bandages on Naina's arms but felt it would be rude to ask about them. After all, she didn't like talking about her past.

"My husband was beating me for more than two years" Naina began. "It started from the day I had arrived in the country. I was only twenty when I married and he was forty."

Nikita quickly did the maths; she couldn't have been more that twenty three years old, but she looked so much older.

"When I'd had enough, I tried to call my family in Pakistan to tell them what was going on but my husband caught me. He was fuming. He said I was bringing shame on him and his family and as punishment, he said he was going to cut off my hands so that I wouldn't be able to use the phone anymore."

Nikita stared down at Naina's hands and the bandages once again. Her arms were wrapped from around the wrists, up her elbows and upper arms.

"He chased me around the house with a knife and I thought he was going to kill me. He slashed my arms and I was screaming. I begged him to stop and I promised I would never do it again but he wouldn't listen. Thanks to Allah, the neighbours heard the screaming and called the police straight away. They had to break down the front door and they caught my husband with the huge butcher's knife in his hand. They arrested him straight away." Naina broke down in tears.

Nikita didn't know what to say to her, but she continued to rub her back slowly, hoping it would help her a little.

Naina had ended up in hospital because of her injuries and that's where she told the interpreter what had happened and how long it had been going on. She didn't go home after that; they brought her straight to the refuge.

Nikita was hearing different stories everyday and they were all horrendous. Even though Nikita had been through so much herself, it didn't make it any easier to listen to anyone else's pain. All the women would ask her why she was there, but Nikita couldn't bring herself to talk to them about it.

The refuge was a good place to be, it gave Nikita time to think and gather her thoughts. Sometimes she felt like she was going mad and staying there gave her the opportunity to work things out in her head.

The staff members were extremely helpful; they told Nikita about all her options.

Sometimes, when she was having a low day, Nikita felt like she just wanted to end everything and other times she just wanted to curl up in her bedroom and never come out.

At first she couldn't see a way out for herself but then the staff members encouraged her and helped her to realise she could live her own life.

She never thought she'd meet any one like Jazz. Nikita liked her. She was quiet most of the time and she kept herself to herself. Jazz was like Nikita, they had the same sense of humour and they got along really well.

One evening when Jazz broke down in tears and told Nikita why she was at the refuge, Nikita cried with her. Jazz had everything before she'd met Max. She was daddy's little girl, and when Max came into her life, her parents weren't happy. They didn't want anything to do with her, but Jazz believed Max would look after her forever. They had a whirl wind romance and an even quicker wedding. The first few years were bliss and they were planning on having a baby. Jazz said she didn't remember at which point it went wrong. It was all such a blur. She had loved him so much, and left her family for him.

Jazz was comfortable with Nikita. She was so easy to talk to and something inside her, told her that she could trust Nikita. Her heart believed she could share what she wanted with Nikita and that Nikita would never judge her.

A few months together and it felt as though they'd known each other for a long time. Nikita couldn't believe they had only just met.

After six months of being at the refuge and when Nikita felt she was ready to move on, she and Jazz decided they would look at moving into a flat together.

The prospect of moving into a property on her own was very frightening and Jazz didn't want to live on her own either, so it made sense for them to house share.

Chapter 9 - My Home

Nikita lay in her bed and stretched every muscle in her body.

The ticking of the clock and the engines of the cars driving by her flat were the only sounds that filled the silence in her bedroom.

No nightmares, thank God. Slowly they had become fewer and she wasn't having as many restless nights as she used to. There were nights when she just couldn't sleep and she'd spent much of the last year with dark puffy eyes, walking around like a zombie. No energy, no strength, no appetite, but she was starting to feel a little better now with the absence of the regular nightmares.

It was Thursday morning and she had a million and one things to do.

Job hunting was at the top of her list. She'd been out of work now for so long that she didn't know if she had it in her to hold down a job, but she knew she needed to start somewhere. Nikita had been living on welfare benefits for nearly two years and she hated it.

When Jazz and Nikita moved in, they hardly had any money between them to furnish their two bedroom flat. All they had was some money from a community care grant and some money from the gold earrings that Nikita had pawned. They managed to buy second hand mismatched furniture. It was enough to get them started, but living on benefits was very hard and even harder to save every week to purchase kitchen utensils and other household items.

Her confidence levels were at an all time low and Nikita was starting to lose her nerve as well. She knew she had to look for a job, not only so that she could start to live some quality of life but to help build up her self-esteem which she could feel diminishing on a daily basis.

This was what he had brought her down to. She'd never spent so much time in her life doing nothing and being too scared to venture outside. Nikita only left the house once a week to do her shopping and withdraw some money from the local cash point. She would spend as little time as she could in public and return home to the safe comfort of her flat, behind closed doors.

Nikita didn't always have these fears. She used to love spending time with people and had always enjoyed her work. Even when she was at school, if she wasn't attending her day to day lessons, she was attending gymnastics, or country dancing, playing the recorder, practicing for the brass band or singing in the choir. She'd get bored so she took up different extracurricular activities throughout her school life. She was so confident when she was younger that on a Monday morning when the teachers would ask if anyone wanted to share with other pupils, what they had done over the weekend, Nikita would be the first to put her hand up. She would stand in front of the whole class and sing a song she had learnt from the latest Bollywood movie that she had watched that weekend. She knew no fear. When she went camping with the school, her teachers made her sing Indian songs around the camp fire and she tried to get everyone to join in. The teachers were fascinated by her. But that memory seemed like it was from another life and she could never dream of doing that now.

As she grew older, her dad acquired a number of different businesses and she was always busy in them. She was the face of her dad's grocery store, meeting people, providing excellent customer service and building up a community of regular customers. She made sure she was polite and welcoming, helpful and a good listener. People that had come to know her, learnt to trust and confide in her about their personal lives. She had made many friends and locally people adored her. Since she'd left school she had always worked and right now she felt like she was living off charity and it made her feel uneasy.

Nikita needed to pick up the Thursday's paper to to read through the jobs pages to see if she could find anything of interest. She was also planning on going to the library to check on the internet. A computer was a luxury her benefits didn't afford her. She looked over to the clock and it was only seven thirty. It didn't really matter what day of the week it was, she rarely slept passed eight o'clock anyway.

She pulled her cheap cotton sheets to one side and got out of bed. She walked over to the window to see what sort of day it was, but all she could see was a river of fresh rain on road. She sighed. She hoped the weather would get better throughout the day. There were trickles of water on her window sill which had fallen as droplets caused by the condensation on her window. Nikita made a mental note to wipe it down.

Autumn was her favourite season of the year. Not just because her birthday was in September but she just loved the rich reds, yellows, greens and browns and when she walked through the park, it was like walking through a river of leaves, kicking them as she swam through them. They were crisp and crunchy under her feet and she loved the smell, but today it felt more like Spring than Autumn.

Letchworth was so beautiful in the Autumn, it was like something out of a landscape painting. It was a photographers dream. Of course she hadn't been back there for nearly two years and Birmingham just wasn't the same. Still this was her home now.

Nikita was glad she had moved in with Jazz, she would never have coped on her own. Before her marriage, she had friends and family over for dinner all the time; they used to have such a laugh. Her cousins practically lived around her house and they were there most evenings and weekends. Nikita's life was filled with so much happiness and now she had nothing.

Her family didn't want to know her since she had left Sam and her cousins all thought that the sun shined out of his backside. Sam had obviously made up stories to get her family on side but it really upset Nikita to think that she had to explain her reasons for leaving. They should have trusted her.

She hadn't been in touch with any of them either, including mum and dad; she knew what they were going to say.

But she had Jazz now and she was Nikita's best friend and her sister. They shared everything. She was the only one who knew Nikita's history completely. When they met in the refuge, she really liked Jazz because she was like a free spirit. She was a little crazy and she made Nikita laugh. They got on so well, it was like they had known each other for years. Jazz was quiet at first, but as she got to know Nikita and began to trust her, she started to show Nikita her true colours and boy did she have a wild side.

Jazz had a story of her own, just like every other woman who had come through the refuge. Her husband had abused her too. Unlike Nikita though, she'd had a love marriage and her parents were against the relationship from the start but she had rebelled and married him anyway.

Jazz had said that her husband Max had got involved with the wrong crowd and started taking drugs. He would come back late at night and then he wouldn't get up for work in the morning. He would sleep all day and no matter what she tried, she couldn't help him. She tried her hardest to persuade him, but he was hooked and he frightened her. He had a great job as an accountant with a well established firm, but after giving him a few chances, the company wouldn't put up with it anymore. They disciplined him for his lack of attendance and they dismissed him. That's when Max started stealing from Jazz. When she refused to fund the habit, he would beat her. She tried to stick it out for as long as she could but the violence got worse day by day.

The last straw was when her husband brought home one of his drug-ridden friends and the friend had paid Max one hundred pounds to have sex with Jazz. Max had taken the money without a second thought. When Max brought the man home and told Jazz what to do, she thought he couldn't be serious so she agreed. Thinking this could be her last chance to get him to kick the habit, she was willing to allow this man to touch her, for the sake of her husband. She didn't plan to allow this disgusting human being to have sex with her. She thought Max would put a stop to it.

After everything Max had put her through, she still had faith in him. She thought his love for her would awaken and he would stop all this madness. Until that day, deep down Jazz still thought that Max loved her. When the time came, she realised that whatever was left of their loving relationship, was now buried somewhere deep, in a place where no one could reach it. The man raped Jazz and her screams did nothing for her husband's conscience. He was too high to even notice. That's when she decided she had to leave.

Max had stripped her down until she valued herself even less than the insects people trampled on under their feet. She hated life and thought about ending it several times, but couldn't bring herself to attempt it.

Jazz had given up her family for this man, who in turn had ruined her life. She couldn't turn to them because they told her from the first day that if she married her boyfriend, she was dead to them. Her mum never called her, even though she knew her daughter's marriage had broken down.

Jazz turned to drink and cigarettes to help her deal with her pain. It was the only way she could keep herself from going insane. Nikita tried to persuade Jazz to stop, because she knew that at some point it would start to affect her health. Sometimes Nikita would pick up leaflets for her which promoted services that helped people with smoking and alcohol problems and she'd leave them lying around the flat. But Nikita also knew that this was the only thing keeping Jazz from going over the edge and if she persuaded her to give it up, then she would probably breakdown. When the time is right she will get it under control, Nikita thought.

Nikita flicked through the job section pages of the local paper and circled a couple of jobs as she enjoyed her cup of spiced tea, but she wasn't holding her breath. Cafeteria worker, cleaner, gardener, shop assistant. None of these appealed to her. The library was a bit better as she was able to email some agencies and now all she had to do was sit back and wait to see if she got an interview.

After Nikita finished her day of job hunting, grocery shopping and bought a copy of the TV magazine, she was home to have another early night.

"Let's go out," Jazz said.

"What now, don't you think it's a bit late?"

"When it comes to clubbing, I say the later we go the better," she said in a cheeky voice.

"I don't know Jazz. I've never been clubbing before and I don't know what to expect. I've never been in that sort of environment. I don't want to go out to watch people snogging and getting it on with each other, it will make me want to vomit." The closest Nikita had got to clubbing was when she watched the music channels on the free view box and it just wasn't her scene.

"It's not like that everywhere you know. People go out to enjoy themselves. Not everyone's out on the pull," Jazz pleaded.

"I don't know."

"Oh, come on. Experience some real life. Enjoy yourself for once, let your hair down. Come on, you'll love it," she begged. "Please, please, please?"

Nikita looked at her unsure.

"Look Nikita, you've been cooped up in this flat, hardly going out to do anything but the shopping. You have to move on with your life and stop thinking about that bastard."

Nikita winced at the reminder but didn't respond.

"Look, if anyone tries it on or you start to feel uncomfortable, we'll jump in a taxi and we'll come home straight away, okay? You can't say fairer than that."

Nikita sighed, "Okay," she replied.

The next two hours were a blur of makeup, curlers, and clothes.

Jazz wasn't too impressed with Nikita's choice of apparel, airing her disapproval. She made Nikita change three times because she wanted her to wear something with a low cut neck, or something short above her knees, but

Nikita didn't feel comfortable in either. In the end, Jazz just gave up.

"You look like a granny," she said moaning, before stomping off.

Nikita ignored her and ordered the taxi.

When Nikita lived in Letchworth, there weren't many clubs to go to and even if there had been, it wasn't like she was going to be visiting them anyway. In a small town like that, with so few Indian families, everyone knew everyone. No doubt if she had gone, she would have run into an uncle or someone that knew her dad and before she would have got back home her dad would have received this information, and she would be dead meat. Then after she got married, she didn't dare think about going to a club.

Sam was very clear about what he thought of the girls that visited bars and clubs. They were all slags, as far as he was concerned. "They're just going there for one thing and they deserve everything that's coming to them," he would say.

A shiver ran up Nikita's spine as she remembered his face. Don't think about him, it will ruin your evening she thought; she was going to try and enjoy herself like normal people.

The taxi arrived quickly and it dropped them off on the main high street, by the bars and restaurants. They jumped out and Nikita followed Jazz. Even though it wasn't very late, it was already quite busy. Nikita looked around and saw that people were dressed daringly, wearing pieces of material in some cases. Then she looked at her reflection in the glass frontage of a bar and she felt uneasy at the way that she was dressed. She worried that some of these young people walking around may take the piss out of her, for being out clubbing at her age, but there was nothing she could do about it now.

Jazz walked into the bar looking as stunning as she always did. She had large breasts, a tiny waist and a plump round bottom. Her dress accentuated her beautiful figure even more. Nikita always thought of Jessica Rabbit from the cartoon, Jazz was a spitting image of her. Women didn't look this good. Wherever Jazz went, she made heads turn, and although Nikita loved her, Nikita couldn't help but feel a little envious. She wished she could be as confident as Jazz.

As they walked into the bar, Jazz ordered them both a drink. "Two Malibus' and coke," she asked the barman.

"Jazz, you know I don't drink alcohol."

"Babe, live a little, try it, you'll like the flavour of this."

Nikita sighed. Why not, she was there now. It wasn't like anyone was watching anyway and she did always wonder what it felt like to be drunk. She picked up the drink from the bar and took a sip through the little black straw. It was very tasty. Nikita really liked the coconut flavour and before she'd realised, Jazz had ordered two more.

Nikita had never liked the taste of alcohol. She found the smell revolting.

The Malibu and coke however was very sweet and tasty, the sort of drink that she could get used to.

Jazz ordered Nikita another drink. This time it was an Archers and lemonade and Nikita liked the taste of this as well.

By now the bar was getting very busy and more and more people were joining the dance floor.

Nikita grabbed her bottle of WKD and feeling brave she bounced over to the dancing area as Jazz followed. The DJ was playing Justine Timberlake and 'Rock your body.'

Nikita had not felt like dancing in such a long time. Ever since she was young, music had always been a big part of her life. It made her feel good, no matter how the day was going, but her dad never liked her listening to music, especially Indian Bollywood music. Nikita and her sister would put on their Bollywood movies and copy the dance routines and she would imagine that she was a dancer on stage or in theatre. That's where one of her dreams developed from.

Nikita loved music so much that she lived and breathed music until she'd got married. She'd go to sleep with music ringing in her ears, she'd wake up and music would be ringing in her ears, she'd hear music in her head all the time.

She had a little radio which she kept hidden in her bedroom under her bed and late at night when everyone had gone to sleep, she would switch it on and put it against her ear, listening with very low volume so that no one else could hear it. She would search for the Indian radio channels and sometimes she would even fall asleep listening to it. Luckily her dad never found it.

Nikita could feel tears prickling at the back of her eyes, She missed her mum and dad immensely. It had been nearly two years since she'd even spoken to either of them. Her mum had her number because Nikita had texted it to her sister Ria and Ria had sent mum's number to her. Nikita had saved the number on her phone but couldn't bring herself to dial it. She'd searched for it in her contact list so many times that she had lost count but every time Nikita would press the cancel button, not having the guts to make the call.

Jazz shook Nikita by the shoulders. "Where have you drifted off to?" she shouted in her ear.

"Nowhere, I just remembered something," Nikita answered. She pushed a smile onto her lips and continued dancing.

Nikita found herself enjoying the evening, but her head was starting to spin.

Before long, she realised that they were crowded by a group of young men and the one behind Nikita, kept coming up to her and rubbing himself against her. She turned around and gave him a dirty look. She wanted to let him know that she didn't like it and she wasn't interested. Nikita turned back around and carried on dancing, swinging her hips. The man ignored Nikita's silent protest and this time he grabbed her by the hips trying to dance along with her.

Nikita's thoughts became fuzzier and she liked the light headed feeling. She knew she was upset, but for a moment she couldn't remember why. The man, who was probably a few years younger than her, put his arms around her and pulled her closer. Nikita wasn't used to this type of attention, especially not from such a young male. Actually, she wasn't used to attention from men at all. Nikita turned and looked at the sweet faced mousey haired young man. A lot taller than her, he had broad shoulders, and his muscles stood out under his fitted Ed Hardy T-shirt. He wore faded grey jeans and had an eyebrow piercing which Nikita found quite sexy. He whispered in Nikita's ear, but the music was so loud, she couldn't hear what he said. She turned around again and pushed up against him. He nuzzled his face in her hair and neck and Nikita moved her head to one side, giving him more access to the sensitive area under her ear. She felt the slight suction of his lips against her skin and it sent tingles through her body. He brushed her hair aside giving him better access to her neck and back. Nikita had become overly warm on the dance floor so she had undone the buttons on her light cardigan which revealed a crisp white vest and freckles at the top of her breasts.

The young man turned Nikita around and asked if he could get her a drink. At this point she knew she'd had too many but she wanted more. She asked him to surprise her and he grabbed her hand and walked her over to the bar area ordering her a drink. He passed her a cocktail glass with a creamy light brown liquid. Nikita looked at it in confusion. "What is it?"

"It's called a cheeky monkey."

Nikita took a sip and it tasted divine.

The young man introduced himself as Michael who was in the final year of his Sports Science degree. Nikita looked him over thinking no wonder he had such a fit body and she almost blushed at the naughty thought. She sat on the stool close to the bar while Michael stood next to her. Their heads were level, making it easier to talk. Michael asked Nikita about what she did, where she lived, what she liked. Nikita answered with mostly the truth, but not wanting to get into any sort of detail.

"Does that taste good?" Michael asked smiling.

"It's gorgeous," Nikita answered. "Would you like to try some?" she said as she took a sip.

Michael nodded and leaned in and kissed her. "Mmm, you're right. It does taste good," he said, having licked the flavour from her lips.

Nikita flushed. She had never been kissed before and she couldn't help but run her tongue over her lips where he had touched her. She didn't mean to, but she saw that he had noticed. He was staring at her lips intently and she knew he was going to try it again. Before he could, Nikita grabbed his hand and pulled him back onto the dance floor. She moved seductively around Michael and before long he was pressed up against her back again and she could feel the aroused hardness on her back. Nikita's head started to spin and her footsteps became uncoordinated. The dance floor was near the entrance to the bar and as more people entered and the door opened, a breeze of clarity rushed over her. She started feeling uncomfortable and she pushed Michael's hands away from her.

"Hey, what happened babe?" he shouted.

"I'm not your babe!" Nikita said in a loud stern voice.

"Hey, calm down," he said, holding his hands up.

Nikita took in a deep breath and sighed. "Look, I'm sorry," she said. "I'm not good news."

"Why don't you let me be the judge of that?" he grinned.

"I'm sorry, I can't" she said again. "I have to go."

"Hey!" he shouted, but Nikita didn't turn back.

Nikita looked around for Jazz and felt a pang of relief when she saw Jazz wasn't that far. Nikita quickly walked over and grabbed Jazz pulling her towards the front entrance. Nikita told her she wanted to go home. Now!

"No, wait a bit longer, we're having so much fun," she screamed over the loud music.

"No, I want to go home now," Nikita screamed back. "If you want to stay, then you stay, but I'm leaving."

Jazz could tell that Nikita was serious.

She started walking towards the entrance door, not looking back to see if Jazz was following or not. Nikita started to feel dizzy again and she couldn't see clearly, she needed to get some air. The club was full of smoke and there was a funny smell. Jazz had said it smelt like weed. Nikita didn't care what it was; she just knew it was going straight to her head.

Nikita pushed against the crowds of people, their faces just a blur and headed for the street. She stumbled and twisted her ankle in her heels, but she didn't stop. She had to get out of there.

Jazz wasn't very happy about it, but she followed Nikita out and left the bar to look for a taxi.

Nikita's body started shaking and she felt cold. She pulled her cardigan closed but didn't have the co-ordination to button herself up. They had to walk down the road to the taxi rank because they couldn't see any other cabs.

Jazz grabbed hold of Nikita's arm helping her to walk straight as they approached the queue for the taxis.

The alcohol overwhelmed Nikita and she felt it take hold of her emotions and stir things up.

She thought back to Sam remembering their nonexistent relationship and the way he had treated her. She didn't want to remember, but the memories kept popping up in the forefront of her mind.

They jumped in the taxi and Jazz gave their home address to the driver.

Nikita closed her eyes and pushed back the memories but it was no use, the images raced across her mind. "Jazz, why did he do this to me? Was it because of something I did?" Nikita couldn't stop the tears from rolling now.

"Honey, it wasn't your fault. He's just a bastard."

"But what did I do to deserve this? People always say, you reap what you sow. Does that mean I'm a bad person and I'm getting what I deserve?"

"Honey, don't say that. You are not a bad person and don't let anyone make you think otherwise. We're just unlucky. Sometimes this is the life of an Indian girl."

Jazz put her arm around her friend and Nikita leaned her head onto Jazz's shoulder.

The tears poured down Nikita's face and she noticed the taxi driver was looking at her through his rear view mirror.

Nikita pulled her head back and stared back at him. "That's right, have good look at the freak," she glared. "You think this is a fucking show or something. Drive the fucking taxi." Nikita saw the driver's eyes widen.

Jazz quickly stepped in and apologised. "I'm sorry Mr. Driver. She's just a little upset, that's all." The driver didn't say anything.

Nikita was about to protest but Jazz squeezed her hand, the message was clear, keep quiet.

Nikita leaned up against the window and the vibrations against her head made her feel sick.

"Jazz, I think I'm going to be sick."

"Madam, they'll be an extra forty pound charge to pay to have the cab cleaned if your friend is sick. So I'd advise that she holds it," said the driver.

Jazz opened the window of the taxi and it helped Nikita feel a little better.

When they got home, Jazz helped Nikita to her bedroom and she fell onto her pillow still crying.

She couldn't fight it anymore, as her eye lids became heavy and she let them close and her body relax................... Nikita didn't have any energy left and her thoughts disappeared but at least it was over for her.

She didn't have to feel anymore embarrassment, shame, or pain and people would find out what he was really like ....

Nikita woke, gasping for air, sweating and she realised it was just a dream. It was too much to ask not to have any nightmares two nights in a row.

She lifted a hand to her head, trying to stem the pounding feeling. Her stomach also hurt and she felt ill.

She didn't remember much else about coming back home and as she looked down at herself she realised she was still in the clothes she'd worn the night before.

Never again.

Chapter 10 – Job search

Nikita had signed up with a number of recruitment agencies around the city. She desperately wanted to work. However, the aspiration to work was lined with an undercurrent of concern about meeting new people. She hadn't spent any time with anyone other than Jazz, so her social skills were a little rusty to say the least.

The playful cheerful girl from her teen years, no longer existed. Now she felt like a nervous wreck, that oozed self consciousness, had a lack of self esteem and no confidence what so ever.

The Customer First Recruitment Agency called and asked Nikita to come in to the office. She had applied for receptionist, P.A. and administrative type roles, because she thought it would be something easy to start off with. She didn't want to go into a role where she had to deal with lots of people, not to start off with anyway.

She was so chuffed with herself having managed to get an interview, but she also felt nervous. How was she going to get through an interview, she was so out of practice?

To celebrate for getting the interview, Nikita decided to cook her and Jazz a slap up meal. Whether she got through the interview, she didn't know but she felt like celebrating. As small as it was, at least it was a step in the right direction.

Nikita picked up the ingredients for chicken curry and naan and made her way home to prepare.

She sifted the flour and removed her rings, placing them on the window sill before she started to make the dough. She stared at the rings sitting on top of the white wall tiles and it took her back to the time when Sam made trouble with her for just this reason.

Often small things would remind her of all the sad events in her life. It still gave her a gut wrenching feeling like someone had stabbed her in the stomach and was now twisting and turning the knife.

Her breath came in short and she felt so lightheaded, she had to sit down. After five minutes she took in a deep breath and got back up. She had to control herself. These memories were enough to last her a life time, but she couldn't live the rest of her life like this. She was still allowing him to control her and she had vowed that she wouldn't. She put the radio on, turned the volume right up, trying to drown out the thoughts in her mind.

Nikita was so nervous on the morning of the interview. Her heart was pounding and she had a tingling feeling running all over her body. She left early without having any breakfast because she felt so sick. Her appointment was with a lady called Tabitha at ten o'clock.

The bus was twenty minutes to the main office which was based in the Birmingham City centre.

Nikita had come to enjoy living in Birmingham. Everything was only a bus ride away and regardless of what people thought of England's second city, there were some beautiful sights to be seen. It had museums, gardens and canals, great for walking along on a sunny day and a fabulous shopping centre. Of course Nikita could only afford window shopping but hopefully things were about to change.

Once Nikita arrived at the office, she sat outside in the reception area. The company was based in newly built offices which had apple green and cream walls with black leather furniture. It was quite comfy actually. There was a framed poster on the wall which read, **I'm not afraid of storms, for I'm learning to sail my ship, Louisa May Alcott.** This was where Nikita needed to be. Her life had been through such a storm and she was still very frightened. Getting a job would help stabilise her, just like the ship mentioned in the painting. Oh God, how she wanted to move on with her life.

Nikita was early so she had to wait for another candidate to finish. The office was so busy, she felt queasy. Her tummy started grumbling, and she realised she should have eaten a little something.

Thinking about all the complicated questions they would ask her, sweat started to build on her brow,. Her palms were damp and she started to wipe them on her skirt, not wanting them to feel sticky when she shook hands with Tabitha. Nikita pulled a tissue out of her handbag and slowly wiped her forehead and hands. She felt hot and sticky. She sat trying to recall if she had sprayed deodorant on. She couldn't remember. What if she started smelling halfway through the interview? She was pretty sure that personal hygiene would be a requirement of the job. Of any job. While no one was watching, Nikita sneaked a quick whiff. She pretended that she was trying to scratch an itch on her back and as she did, she turned her head to one side and had a quick smell. Dry linen. It's okay, panic over, she was wearing deodorant.

A beautiful blonde haired woman came round the corner and walked towards Nikita. She couldn't have been older than around thirty. Her makeup was immaculate and she was wearing a very short, smart black skirt with a pretty blouse, and heels that Nikita would never dare to wear. The shoes were bright red to match the bright red belt around her petite waist.

As she walked over she held out her hand and Nikita reluctantly shook it, hoping she wouldn't realise how clammy Nikita's hands were.

"Hello Nikita Heer, great to put a face to the voice," she smiled.

Nikita had spoken to Tabitha on a number of occasions when she was interviewed over the phone.

"If you'd just like to follow me to my office. Can I get you a tea, coffee or anything else?"

Yeh, a paper bag would be nice to hide my face, Nikita thought. Nikita bit her lip to stop her saying anything sarcastic when Tabitha asked, so she asked for a glass of water. She could feel her throat drying up.

Nikita walked into the office and it was quite an informal setting, just like the reception area, with a couple of tub chairs and a low level office table.

Tabitha picked up her writing pad and made a few notes. What was she writing because she hadn't asked Nikita anything yet? Then there was a knock on the door and another woman walked in, a shorter, older woman. She had a glass of water. She smiled at Nikita and put the water in front of her on the table and then left.

"Right," said Tabitha. "Did you have any difficulty in finding the office?"

"No, it was fine. I called in at reception yesterday and got the directions and I left home early just in case I did get lost, it gave me some time to find the office."

"That's good, it shows that you plan ahead and I like people that are punctual. You wouldn't believe how many people turn up late for their interview. The way that I see it is, if they can't be bothered to turn up on time at an interview, how can they be trusted to turn up to work on time? Trust me, I'm not very impressed and we put our customers first, hence the title of our agency and it's the company motto."

Nikita smiled. "I'd rather arrive early than late. That's one thing you will find with me Tabitha, I am very punctual," Nikita said.

"That's good to know. Right, I'm going to ask you a number of questions as part of your interview and I'm going to be making notes as I go along, because I'll need to keep a record of your answers. Is that okay?" she asked.

Nikita just nodded and smiled.

Her heart started thumping in her chest; she just prayed that Tabitha couldn't hear it.

"If there's anything that you don't understand or want to go back to at the end of the interview then just say so and if you want me to repeat a question, just ask."

"Okay," Nikita said, trying to generate as much confidence as she could from the bottom of her stomach. She didn't want Tabitha to see that she was nervous although she was pretty sure that it wouldn't take her too long to realise. Nikita started to wonder how long it would take for Tabitha to figure her out. Would she be able to see Nikita's history by looking at her face? Would she be able to read that she had been labelled useless, worthless and pathetic in her past?

These weren't very good skills to have noted on your CV. Maybe Tabitha would realise and Nikita was wasting her time here in this interview.

"Shall we start?" asked Tabitha, breaking into Nikita's chain of thought.

"Yes," Nikita replied and took a deep breath.

Tabitha started with her questions.

Thirty minutes later, Nikita had finished the interview questions and she could feel a big grin developing on her face. She was proud of her answers.

Tabitha put her pad down, but she had a blank expression on her face. She wasn't giving anything away. Nikita's heart started racing again. She couldn't stand any rejection right now and she wasn't sure if she had done enough to be taken on with the agency. They probably had much better candidates than her, but she was also sure that there will be no one more committed than her.

Nikita decided that it was important for her to be open and honest about her past. She would tell Tabitha about her history. She didn't have to give her the gory details, just the basics.

"Tabitha, there's something I need to talk to you about."

"Okay, what is it?" she asked, picking her note pad back up.

Nikita took a deep breath. "I was married once and he hurt me, physically and emotionally, so I left him and disappeared for a little while. I'm now living with one of my girl friends and this is the first job I've applied for since. It was difficult for me to look for work at first because I just didn't feel up to it and that's why there's a gap on my CV, but I feel I am ready now. A new job will help me to move on with my life."

At first Tabitha didn't say anything and Nikita wondered what she was thinking. Tabitha was staring at Nikita blankly; thinking about what to say.

"I'm really sorry Nikita, I had no idea," she said.

"It's okay Tabitha, you have nothing to be sorry for, and why would you have any idea? I just wanted you to know so that you could understand why I'm so nervous today, but I also want you to understand that I really do want to start re-building my life. I will put everything into any job you find me."

Tabitha smiled. "I'm sure you'll make a wonderful and competent candidate for our agency. I'm glad you were upfront and honest."

"One of my friends is experiencing something similar. Her boyfriend is a football hooligan and is in and out of prison regularly. He keeps telling her that he has changed but he'll get into another fight and then end up back behind bars. At first she didn't tell us what was going on, but recently on a night out she got a bit drunk. She started to cry and she told us that he was hitting her. I knew that something was wrong quite some time ago but she wouldn't admit it. I knew it all along, once a bully always a bully. Sometimes he would cause fights and was so aggressive, but then again what more could you expect from him. Once he came out with her and he was so nice, a real gentleman, nobody could have guessed that he was such a mad man. I mean, what else could you call him? My friend kept telling us that he would change, but we knew that he wouldn't. I can't understand what sort of hold he has over her, how can she stay with a man like that?"

Nikita could have explained that leaving a violent partner wasn't a matter of choice. There were so many other factors to take into account, like worrying about what to tell the family or the community. The impact of something like this on your parents could be devastating. The perceived humiliation they would suffer because you decided to leave the relationship could be seen as dishonourable. That's why she stayed, but also to try and make it work. Jazz loved her husband. Their relationship was like a fairy tale and when things went wrong, she tried so hard to make them right again. She couldn't bring herself to leave until things got really bad and it was either her sanity, or him. Thank God she made the right decision. But Nikita didn't say any of this to Tabitha. In a way she was glad Tabitha had some sort of experience, maybe it would help her to understand what Nikita had been through.

"Anyway Nikita, enough about my friend. What we need now is for you to take a photo so that we can get an ID badge made for you and then all you have to do is wait for us to call you with a placement," she said.

Is that it? Am I in? Nikita felt a big smile on her face, she was so happy; she could feel that finally her life really was going to move on.

She almost skipped out of the office, she was that happy with herself.

It didn't take long for Tabitha to call Nikita. "Hello," she answered.

"Hi Nikita, it's Tabitha here."

"Hey Tabitha, how are you?" Nikita asked being polite. She wanted to make a good impression.

"I'm doing well, thanks Nikita. The reason I'm calling you is to let you know I have a job offer for you."

"Okay, that's great," Nikita said trying to keep her voice level. She felt like jumping up and down and waving her hands in the air. But she decided that she would wait until after she put the phone down.

"You're the first person I'm offering it to, because I wanted to give you the opportunity. It is going to be quite hard work, because it's a P.A./secretarial position for a person who is in the arts industry, an actor."

Mmmm, someone famous.

"Well, he's an up and coming actor and his P.A. has just left him for another job and he needs someone quite urgently, so he contacted us. The contract is for a couple of months until he can organise something more permanent. The tasks will include taking telephone calls, recording messages, booking meetings and he attends a lot of events and functions so you may have to assist him to these appointments as well. You up for it?"

"Absolutely," Nikita said definitively. "Sounds like just what I wanted."

"I'm glad you feel that way. My only concern is that the employer is a man and I wasn't sure how you would feel about that, considering what you've been through I mean."

"I appreciate your concern Tabitha, but I can't hide away from men forever and no matter where I work, I'm always going to come into contact with men, aren't I? I'm sure I'll be fine," and anyway Nikita desperately wanted this job.

"Well, if you're sure, the job is yours."

"I'm absolutely sure," she responded quickly.

"Okay, now, this is a very important client and I am taking a bit of a risk by placing a new candidate with him, so please don't let me down," she said.

Even Tabitha sounded a little nervous today.

"I won't let you down Tabitha, I promise."

Tabitha gave Nikita all the contact details for the client and the timetable. She had to start the following day so she needed to sort out some clothes. Nikita went through her wardrobe but she couldn't really find anything to wear, nothing smart at least. She decided to pop to the local supermarket. They always had good deals on clothes and all she needed was a black pair of trousers or skirt and a nice blouse. Nikita couldn't afford to go to the High Street stores; they were too expensive for a person living on benefits, which reminded her, that she needed to visit the job centre to inform them of her new job.

She could borrow shoes from Jazz. Their shoe size was another thing they had in common.

She was so excited about the job but she still felt apprehensive. It had been nearly two years since she'd worked and she didn't know if she would be able to manage it. Nikita sighed, she needed to have trust in herself and she knew that she could do anything she wanted to, when she put her mind to it, so why should this be any different?

Nikita inhaled deeply and then breathed out long and hard. This was it, there was no going back.

She made a list of things she needed to do and needed to get. She grabbed her keys and off she went to start working through her list. It made her feel really good to be doing something constructive and meaningful with her life.

Nikita had always told herself that she would never claim benefits. She saw it as something quite embarrassing, degrading even, and she hated telling people that she was on the dole. But at the time she couldn't help it, she wasn't in the right frame of mind to be working and she needed time to get her head together so she could decide what she wanted to do. It didn't matter now anyway. For two years she was stuck where she was and now Tabitha had thrown her a life line. Nikita had no intention of letting herself or the agency down.

On her first day at work she got up extra early. She got washed, straightened her hair and got dressed. She looked at herself in the mirror, first left, then right. She was wearing the five pound white blouse and seven pound black pencil line skirt that she'd bought from the supermarket. It looked smart and professional which is what she wanted, but she really did need to invest in some decent clothes when she got her first pay packet. Nikita borrowed a pair of red shoes from Jazz which finished off her look. She looked in the mirror again but there was something missing. Maybe it was her face, it was still too bare. Nikita put on some crimson red lipstick and rubbed her lips together. Luscious and plump, just the way she liked them. They also matched the shoes and now she was ready.

Tabitha had passed on the address for the placement and Nikita had arrived early. She wondered if she was at the right place. It was a block of apartments, albeit very nice apartments in a developing area of the city. Nikita looked around but there was no one she could ask. Maybe it was too early for people to be up.

Chapter 11 - Left in the Lurch

Jai stretched looking out of his seventh floor apartment. His arms felt heavy and tired. He had to keep himself in shape, it was important for his career. Half an hour of running on the treadmill then fifteen minutes of bicep curls every day, twice a day, kept the oxygen pumping around his body. As much as it tired him out, he loved the exercise; it always made him feel so alive.

His hair was curly and wet from the shower. He ran his hand through the brown locks to push them back.

Jai loved his apartment. It belonged to him. No mortgage, no rent and at the age of thirty, he had paid cash for it.

He didn't know why, but today he felt alone. He thought about his mum and what she would have thought of his small stylish apartment. Would she have liked it? She would have been proud of him if she was still alive. He would have persuaded her to move in with him. It had been a dream to look after her, but now that would never happen.

After she died, Jai set his mind to his school books. He hated being at home and wanted out. He also knew the only way he would manage that, would be to educate himself and pursue a career.

Later when he started going to college, one of his friends introduced him to his dad, who worked in a London Asian woman's magazine. His friend's dad liked what he saw. Jai was only eighteen but he was well built and had a handsome face. An offer was made to him, to model sherwanis' and men's suits in this wedding magazine and by the time Jai had finished college, he was performing on stage in theatres. Not long after, he was offered his first role in a movie and he hasn't looked back since then.

Jai sighed and turned around to stare at the mess on his desk. What the fuck was going on here?

She's left me in such a mess, stupid cow. She could have at least given me a bit more notice, he thought. Jai tried sorting through his pile of paperwork, invoices and receipts. Problem was, he didn't know where anything went, how the information was stored on his computer or anywhere else. His P.A. had left without giving him any notice and so there was no time for any handover. Jai just didn't have a clue.

I hope the agency sends me a good candidate he thought. He didn't have time to advertise, he needed someone immediately.

Semee had worked for him for more than a year. She was always very professional. Well dressed, smart, intelligent and efficient and something nice to look at as well.

Semee's family came from Lithuania and she moved here around ten years ago. She was very hard working and made Jai's life so much easier. He was going to miss her even though she had left him in the lurch. She took up a job with an acclaimed actor and come to think of it, if Jai was in her shoes, he probably would have done the same, so he couldn't blame her. She was a sight for sore eyes on some days, not that he looked at her in that way. No way, Jai would never look at another woman like that because he already had a gorgeous girlfriend.

Tina was out of this world beautiful.

They first met at a club about a year ago. She was out celebrating a friend's birthday and she caught his eye. She was stunning. She wore a short black dress with pink tights and black high heeled sandals and she looked hot.

She was sitting with her girl friends having a drink. Jai was with his friends; one of them was getting married so they were out celebrating.

She noticed him looking over and seemed to like what she saw as well. She had a beautiful smile and when she looked over, Jai held up his bottle of corona beer to her as if to say cheers and she smiled back at him. Before Jai left the bar, he wrote his number on a piece of paper, walking over to her. "You'll need this when you want to call me later," he said and he left the number with her and walked away.

The following day she called him. His pick up line had worked. Ever since then they'd been dating. Even though it had only been a year since the first time they'd met, things weren't the same. The cracks were already starting to form. At first, they seemed to be so much in love. She was beautiful, confident and career minded, all the qualities he loved in a woman. But as they got to know each other on a deeper level, she wasn't the person he thought she was. She came from a very privileged background, a totally different world to Jai's. She was the sort of person that always looked to the future and talked about moving on in life. It wasn't that easy for Jai. He never told her too much about his past, but when they did talk; she didn't seem to be interested. She didn't understand. "Let's not talk about the past," she would say. "Forget about it, we can't go back and change it, so there's no point in stressing over it, we have to look to the future."

The problem was that she didn't realise, that if you hadn't dealt with your past, you wouldn't be able to move forward.

Tabitha called from the agency and informed Jai she had found him the perfect replacement for his P.A. She told him her name was Nikita.

As long she could sort out his life, he didn't care what her name was.

Jai wondered what she looked like. Semee was beautiful. She was tall, very slim and a bit skinny for his liking but still very stunning. Jai liked a girl with a figure, size zero type girls never appealed to him. He liked women with smooth skin and feminine softness.

The buzzer sounded in the apartment. Great she's here. He pressed the release button and it opened the door downstairs to let her in. He put his apartment door on the latch so that she could let herself in.

Jai hoped that she was as good as Tabitha had made out. I need someone that's fast and efficient, that picks up things quickly, he thought. Jai took a glance at his watch and it was five to nine, well at least she was punctual so that was a good start.

Nikita punched in the apartment number on the intercom system and waited. No one spoke but the buzzer went on the door and she figured it had been opened for her.

She pushed the heavy door open and walked through the corridor towards the lift. She noticed the CCTV cameras in the corners of the reception area. This was a first. Never had she seen monitoring like this in a block of flats. It was clean and well maintained, like the lobby of a nice hotel. She was impressed. Nikita jumped in the lift as it pinged open and pushed the button for the seventh floor. The lift was clean, unlike the one where she lived. Hers was full of graffiti and most of the time it didn't work anyway. She never used it, because she never knew when it might break down.

Nikita's stomach cramped with anxiety and she could feel the nerves getting the better of her.

'You can do it, you can do it, you can do it,' she chanted in her head.

She had to make this work. She saw herself in the mirror on the back wall of the lift and noticed how she stood, slumped and terrified. God, she looked pathetic. She didn't look like she was heading to her first day on a job but more like she was on her way to a funeral. She stood up straight and pushed a smile onto her face before she walked out of the lift and knocked on the door.

"Come in, it's open," she heard a deep voice say. So she turned the handle and pushed the door open.

Remember to be professional and always provide good customer service, Nikita thought remembering the agency mantra. She walked in and the first thing she thought was 'wow'. The apartment was beautiful. Floor to ceiling glass panelling ran along the whole side of the living area, allowing so much light into the room. The morning sun was gleaming through the windows. In the centre of the lounge was a brick built fire place, with a solid dark oak shelf. The theme was minimalistic but it worked. With a few paintings thrown in, Nikita could only dream of having a place like this one day.

She introduced herself. She held her hand bag under her arm and she switched it from one arm to the other nervously and pushed her hair behind one of her ears.

Jai watched her as she extended her hand but she didn't look directly at him.

"Hello Mr. Singh, I'm Nikita Heer. The agency has sent me to fill the vacancy you advertised."

An Indian girl, Jai thought. He'd never have guessed from the name. Other than his modelling contract years ago, he hadn't worked with Indians; you didn't really get many in his field of work.

Oh God, I hope she knows what she's doing, Tabitha better not be wasting my time he thought. Jai put his hand out and took Nikita's extended hand. He was sure he could feel her trembling.

She was very simple looking, nothing like Semee, more the opposite, except for the crimson shoes and lipstick. There was definitely a wild side hidden in there somewhere. She was small, petite, but rounded in all the right places. He appraised her but he could see it made her feel uncomfortable. She was a pretty little thing; he had to give her that.

Let's see what she can do.

Nikita tried hard not to stare but this man was incredibly handsome. Standing at about six foot tall with tanned skin, broad shoulders and brown hair, he was more magnificent than any man she had ever laid eyes on. His eyes were a dark amber shade, with so much depth. Nikita stood, stunned. His features were striking, with a sharp jaw line and a perfectly crafted nose. Nikita's breath came in sharp. No wonder he was an actor she thought. He wore his crisp white t-shirt with the sleeves rolled up over his biceps. He smelled of shower gel and soap. Reacting purely on instinct, Nikita took a step back and looked up at him.

Focus, she thought to herself. This was one of very few men she had spoken to in the last year and her legs were turning into jelly already. She had to be smarter than this, she'd made a promise to Tabitha and she couldn't let her down. Shit, he made her feel so nervous.

Nikita prayed he wouldn't be able to feel her hand trembling.

"Please, call me Jai, I'm so glad you're here, let me show you around." He started to walk her across the apartment. "Did you have to travel far?" he asked making polite conversation.

His deep raspy voice exuded sexiness. Nikita felt her temperature rise just a little, which felt at odds with her normal behaviour. She was completely annoyed with herself, getting all flustered while he stood there all bold and self assured.

"No, I'm Birmingham based," she answered.

"Oh, you don't seem to have a Brummie accent. Did you move here from elsewhere in the country?"

Damn, he picked that up quick, but what was she going to tell him? If she didn't answer his question, it would be rude and she didn't like lying to people, so she decided to give him part of the truth. She wasn't very good at lying anyway and he'd catch her out sooner or later. Nikita's lips went dry and she licked them before answering. "I come from the Hertfordshire area originally and I moved up here a few years ago." Please don't ask me anymore she thought.

"Oh, that explains it."

"Explains what?" Nikita asked.

"Your spoken English, it's very posh. It's very different to the way people speak here in the Midlands."

"Is that a problem?

"No, no, not at all. Here, take a seat," he said and he ushered a nod towards the dining chair.

Nikita sat down nervously; luckily he didn't sit too close to her. Distance was good.

"Would you like a tea or coffee?" he asked.

"No, I'm okay at the moment thanks." She would have loved a cup of tea, but the nerves were overriding all her emotions.

"Well I need one; I haven't had a drink this morning. I'll be back in a second." Jai ran off towards the kitchen.

Nikita looked around the apartment and it was beautiful, spacious, open and clean, except for the pile of paperwork on the desk in the corner. It was a typical man's apartment. No fancy cushions on the sofa or flowers in vases. There were a couple of small pictures on the fire place, but she was sitting too far away to make them out.

Jai popped his head from around the kitchen door and made her jump. Get a grip!

"If you feel like a drink later, the kitchen is over here, help yourself," he said.

Nikita nodded.

She placed her handbag on the table and dropped her hands onto her lap. She fidgeted and rubbed her hands nervously.

Jai came back and sat down, putting his mug onto the table. The large cup had the image of a star and had the word 'superstar' printed on it.

Not in the least bit vain are you? Nikita thought.

Jai leaned back onto the rear two legs of his chair and stared at her.

She still couldn't look at him. Come on Nik, you're going to look like an idiot; you need to get a grip she taunted in her head. She took in a deep breath and looked up and forced herself to smile.

"Did you find the address okay this morning?" Jai asked.

"Yes, it was fine. I made a dry run yesterday; I didn't want to be late this morning, first impressions and all that."

Proactive he thought, that was good point number two.

He took a swig of his hot drink.

Nikita watched him put his mug down and she knew she needed to ask some questions about the role. "So tell me Mr. Singh, what does the job entail?"

"Please call me Jai."

"Please Mr. Singh." Nikita put a hand up to stop him talking. "Right now I would prefer to call you Mr. Singh, if you don't mind. That is until I feel comfortable to address you by your first name." Remain professional she thought. She also didn't like the thought of being on a first names basis with a man she didn't know. She just felt it to be too personal.

Feisty little thing he thought and he liked it. He was going to have some fun with her.

"So, do you have a job description for the role? It would be good for me to have a copy; I like to know what I'm expected to do."

"Well, I'm afraid I don't have a job description, but you're welcome to write one once you get to know the role better."

"Oh, but if you don't have a job description then how did your previous employee know what to do?"

"Well, she just did whatever I asked her to."

Nikita stared at him; trying to control her eye brow from raising itself. The previous P.A. did whatever he asked her to? Oh please, give me a break. I wonder what that included, she thought.

"Okay. Exactly what does, 'whatever you asked her to' mean exactly?" Nikita asked emphasizing the word 'whatever'. She rolled the 'r' a little like the Americans.

Jai grinned, he'd got her. So easy to find out how to push her buttons and he continued to wind the key. "Whatever means whatever I wanted," he shrugged. "She was very efficient, never said no to anything I requested."

Nikita was startled at what he was saying. Well, just because he's some semi-superstar and his previous P.A. did whatever he wanted, didn't mean that she had to. As a matter of fact she couldn't stand to be talking to this man a minute longer. Who did he think he was? Come to think of it, he wasn't even semi-famous, she had never heard of him. Nikita stood suddenly, pushing the chair back. It almost toppled over. She decided to get out of there.

"Right, I'm sorry Mr Singh; I don't think I'm the right person for this job. I'm very sorry to have wasted your time. I think I'll be leaving now."

Jai grinned slightly as he leaned back on his chair and something in his eyes told Nikita he was winding her up.

Nikita stood pushing her chair back. "Mr. Singh, I don't appreciate you trying to make a fool out of me. Maybe it's best that I leave now and you can contact the agency and get someone more suitable to your needs. It was nice to have met you." Not, Nikita thought. She picked up her handbag and turned to walk away.

Jai ran around and stood in front of Nikita, blocking her exit from the flat. "I'm sorry, I was only teasing. Please, that's just my sense of humour, sometimes I don't know when to stop and seeing as I don't even know you, I should have refrained from exposing my wonderful personality traits to you so early on. Please come back and sit down. Let's start again."

Nikita thought twice about continuing with the placement. She was never going to last if she kept getting upset with every little thing she didn't like. She decided to give it another go. Nikita sat back down on the dining table chair and put her handbag to one side. This time she placed her hands together on top of the table.

"Okay Mr. Singh, would you like to tell me what the job really involves?"

"Okay, I will behave now," he smiled. "Semee, that's my previous employees' name, organised all my meetings, took phone calls for me, attended meetings with me, drafted letters and because I'm self employed she dealt with collecting all my receipts and invoices and preparing them for the accountant. To be honest, I'm a bit lost without her. Organisational skills are not one of my best personality traits, along with my sense of humour, but then you've probably already gathered that."

Nikita gave him a wide eyed look in agreement.

"Do you think maybe you could sort all this lot out? She arranged for me to attend all these appointments but didn't book anything into my diary so I don't know when or where I'm supposed to be," he complained. "She never told me she was leaving until the last minute but it looks like she started winding down a few weeks ago, so everything's a mess."

Looking around, Nikita decided to give it a go. "Here, let me have a look," she replied. She pushed her chair back and went over to the desk and sat down on the office chair. Switching on the PC, she started trawling through the mountain of paperwork while the computer loaded itself up.

As she worked, Jai wandered around the living room. He spent some time on his phone, then picked up a rather thick document and started reading through it.

Nikita couldn't help watching him from the corner of her eye. She felt self-conscious being alone in an apartment with a strange man. It made her nervous and she questioned whether this was something she could continue doing.

She hadn't considered that she might end up working like this. What were the chances? When she had applied for office and administrative roles, she was expecting to be given a job in an office with many employees.

She turned and looked away, back at the pile of unopened mail. She needed more space to sort the paperwork, so she took the pile back to the table. Having taken off her jacket, she started to relax and sorted through the small mound of mostly unopened mail. Everything was placed into neat piles. Appointments, events, junk mail and bills and they were all sorted in the order of dates and priorities. Bills were the bane of her life but she was glad these bills didn't belong to her. Rather him that me, she thought. Nikita took the pile of appointment letters over to the computer and booked everything into Jai's outlook diary.

Those short courses she had taken at the local community centre were now coming in handy. It was Jazz who had recommended to Nikita to take up this opportunity. A local voluntary organisation was delivering support to help people back to work, and the computer course was one of many free educational programmes available. It gave her the confidence she needed to carry out the computer related tasks. If she hadn't trained, she would have been a nervous wreck.

Jai had started to behave himself and to her surprise he was well mannered and polite. When she'd finished he thanked her for her help.

"Don't worry about it," she told him, "It's my job."

It felt good to do something right for once and to start the journey to claiming her independence back. Getting this job and keeping it was the first step.

Jai pointed to the filing cabinet at the side of the desk. There were papers scattered all over it. "Semee used to do all the filing, but all this has piled up in just a few days, can you help sort it?"

"That won't be a problem Mr. Singh. My dad had businesses and I used to deal with the accounts for him; I filled out all his account books, recorded invoices and receipts. I'm sure this will be very similar."

Nikita thought about her dad and just as quickly waved it away; she didn't have time to get emotional here.

"That's great, I was getting a bit stressed about all these invoices, and I don't need the tax man on my back."

"You won't," she smiled back.

"I wish you wouldn't call me Mr. Singh. You make me feel so old. If I ask nicely will you call me Jai?"

Nikita thought about it for a few long seconds and then agreed, smiling. "Okay Jai, seeing as you asked so nicely, I will."

Jai smiled. He was glad that they had got off to a good start, well after the initial hiccup. He needed someone he could get along with. That was important. Jai spent a lot of time with his P.A.

For a while Jai watched her as she worked while he pretended to be reading a manuscript. Petite little thing isn't she? He thought.

He lifted his head to stare at her more intently. As she turned and noticed, Jai quickly tried to cover up by asking a question. "Have the agency talked to you about the hours you will be required to work?"

"Tabitha told me that sometimes I will be expected to attend meetings and events. I'm guessing that some of these will be in the evenings?"

"Will that be a problem for you, I mean with your family?"

Nikita wished she did have a family to worry about. Someone who questioned where she had been, when she would arrive home late or was working evenings and weekends. But she had no one.

"No, I live with a girlfriend, so it won't be a problem."

"Okay, here's my phone. If you get any calls for me, take messages and I'll get back to them. If people want to meet, check my dairy before you book them in," he said.

"Okay, do you want me to hold onto the phone?"

"Yes, this one will be for your use, but I have to warn you, this is the number that goes out to agents, so it's forever ringing. But also if ever I need you while you're not at work, then I will be able to contact you as well."

"You mean contact me while I'm off work?

"That's why I pay good money honey. You're paid to be on call."

Nikita thought it through for a few short moments. The agency was paying her a higher hourly rate compared to other similar jobs. What the hell, Nikita thought. She needed this job and the money and it wasn't like she had any other commitments.

Nikita spent her first day organising, sorting and filing. She loved it. There may have been a time when she would have thought this sort of work was boring or monotonous, but today, it excited her. She felt so good to have done an honest day's work for the first time in nearly two years. Even though, at the end of the day her feet were hurting, she had paper cuts on her fingers and her eyes were aching from concentrating on the computer screen, she felt satisfied and she looked forward to the next day.

Nikita worked with Jai for more than a month. Two weeks into the placement, the agency had contacted Jai to complete a satisfaction questionnaire. He had given exceptionally good feedback.

Nikita felt proud and confident to be praised in such a way. How time had flown by, she couldn't tell but she loved every minute of it. Nikita was up every day at the crack of dawn. She couldn't wait to get into work. Sometimes she arrived much earlier than her contracted hours but she thrived on this job and she was good at it.

Jai was really easy to work with. He didn't throw tantrums and they got along well. He had a great sense of humour and she always got paid on time. Nikita decided that he seemed like a very calm person. She couldn't imagine him flying into a rage, but if he ever did, she wouldn't want to be on the receiving end of it. He was muscular and strong, and she came to the conclusion that if he ever got into a fight, chances were that he could cause a lot of damage. Nikita didn't want to think of Jai in that way, but she didn't think that Sam was capable of it either. After hearing all the stories from the women in the refuge, she realised that no matter how confident you are with your partner, you never really know them fully.

Nikita sent Tabitha a thank you card with a small bunch of flowers. She felt lucky. She had a great job, a great boss, she had the best friend in the world and she could do what she wanted. Life was starting to look up at last.

Chapter 12 - The Dinner Party

Jai's phone rang and Nikita answered. "Jai Singh's phone, you're speaking with Nikita, how can I help you?" Nikita always put on her best voice, chirpy and cheerful. The call was from the caterer.

Tonight was a very important night for Jai. He was planning a lavish dinner party for some close colleagues and their friends, and people with influence in the media and arts industry. He had planned it at home to keep it personal. It wasn't good news. The caterer said his head chef had been involved in an accident and that he was really sorry but, he wasn't going to be able to provide the catering for the dinner party that evening. He already had a very large banquet to take care of and he didn't have anyone else to send out for Jai. He was very apologetic, but Nikita knew that Jai was not going to be happy about this.

Reluctantly, Nikita went over to Jai and explained about the phone call. He was getting ready to attend a meeting this morning. His expression changed and she could tell his temper had just turned up a few notches.

"What the fuck am I supposed to do now? Who am I going to get at such short notice?" he yelled. He started pacing.

Knowing his anger wasn't aimed at her, she still felt very uncomfortable and subconsciously she took a step back. She felt that same tingling feeling, like spiders were crawling over her skin. It reminded her of how she felt when Sam was about to erupt. She knew that Jai wasn't Sam, but the feelings took over her whole body and she couldn't shake it off. Her breath caught in her throat and she knew she wasn't going to be able to hide it for long. She felt hot and flustered and her palms had started to sweat.

"That bloody Pedro, I'm never taking any business to him again," he continued, walking over to Nikita. Jai reached out to grab Nikita's shoulder and...

It must have been an impulsive move but Nikita flinched and jerked her hands up in defence to protect her face. She almost curled into herself and then for a few long moments, she heard nothing.

Jai stood startled. He stared at her timid and terrified face. He was pissed off, he had to admit that, but he would never hurt Nikita. What made her think that he would? Why did she react in that way? Jai thought for a few long seconds and he almost heard the penny drop.

Nikita looked over her hands slowly and Jai was staring at her, confused.

His anger quickly subsided inside him.

Nikita straightened up quickly, embarrassed to her bones.

"What's wrong Nik, what did I do?" he asked as he reached out to stroke her arm, but she shrank away not wanting him to feel her trembling.

"Nothing," she said quickly, her voice weak. She could feel her cheeks turning the same colour as her lipstick.

"I'm sorry, did I frighten you? I didn't mean to."

"No", she lied.

Jai stood staring.

Nikita met his gaze and she could see his eyes wide with confusion. She noticed him staring at the scar under her eye and she lowered her eyes so that he could no longer stare at her.

Jai saw it for the first time. He could have kicked himself; he'd never noticed it before. She was always very shy and never held his gaze for long, but now he saw the remains of a pink gash under her right eye. He recognised the familiarity of the scar. When he was younger he'd often got into fights at school and he wasn't a stranger to physical violence. Jai knew that it had come from someone striking her. It made sense now.

"It's nothing," she responded, but Nikita could feel that he was reading her entirely. She felt faint and took in a deep breath; she needed to get a grip. She wished she could get away from him, go into a dark room and pull herself together. However, that wasn't an option right now, it would create more questions. Questions that she wasn't ready to answer.

Nikita quickly changed the subject. "So what are we going to do about this dinner party?"

Jai's face dropped. He guessed that this was her way of telling him, that what had just happened wasn't up for discussion.

He sighed. "I'll have to go down to some shitty take away won't I and get some food. I can't cancel tonight, it's too short notice and it won't look professional."

"I could cook the food?" Nikita responded quickly without even thinking.

Jai looked at her surprised. "You? Cook?"

"Why not," she said. "I'm an Indian woman and my mum taught me all there is to know about cooking."

"Yeh, but Nik, please don't get me wrong, there will probably be about twenty people coming this evening and I really wanted to impress."

"Are you doubting me, Mr. Jai Singh?"

Jai looked at her with wary eyes.

"Look Jai, I've never let you down before, so I'm not going to start now. Let me do this for you. Cooking for twenty people is a piece of cake. I used to do it all the time when my family would..." She didn't finish what she was saying. It reminded her too much of the hole in her heart.

There was a deep sigh and he agreed. "Okay," he said and went over to his desk to get a piece of paper off his note pad. Maybe he was going to make her a list of what he wanted for the dinner party. He walked back and handed Nikita the piece of paper. It had four digits written on it, 1973.

"What's this?" Nikita asked.

"It's the pin number for my credit card. Pickup what you need to get and pay for it using this," and he handed Nikita his card.

"I'll need to purchase, pots and pans, cooking utensil, the lot," she explained. "You don't have anything in your kitchen." Jai didn't have much in the way of any cooking utensils, or anything else for that matter.

Typical man. He was used to eating readymade meals and takeaways, albeit good quality takeaways.

"Get whatever you need," Jai said. "And don't worry about the cost."

He soon left to attend his meeting leaving Nikita with his card and pin number. She slipped it into the side zipper of her handbag.

Nikita was quite surprised at the gesture. Jai must really trust her. They had quickly built up a friendship, although neither talked about their past. She knew as little about him as he knew of her.

People would be arriving from around seven o'clock onwards and the time now was ten o'clock. If Nikita got to the supermarket and did the shopping, then got back by around one o'clock, she would have plenty of time to prepare and cook. She estimated the time it would take her and worked backwards from there. Quickly grabbing her jacket she headed for her little Corsa which she had picked up for only two hundred and fifty pounds, a week or so earlier. It wasn't great, but it drove well and right now it was all she needed.

Jai felt troubled on his way to the meeting. He couldn't help but think about Nikita's reaction earlier at home. He tried hard to focus on his upcoming meeting and mentally prepare for it, but his thoughts kept drifting back to her. Jai realised he had started caring for her, as a friend, nothing more. However, if he was honest with himself, he did look forward to seeing her every morning. He put the feeling down to just having someone around to talk to. So why was her reaction troubling him so much? She was just an employee whom he got along with, and whose company he enjoyed and that was it. But the cut under her eye. He wondered why he hadn't noticed it before. Could it really be what he thought it was? Why would someone want to do that? She was so timid, shy and reserved. Granted he felt that she had a wild side but nobody deserved to be hit, so why would somebody want to strike her?

Nikita went to the local supermarket and bought everything. Some meat, vegetables, serving dishes, wine, spices and a beautiful table cloth and a silver runner to go down the centre. She grabbed some flowers, a couple of vases and while she was at it, she got some scented candles to make the apartment smell fresh as well.

She hurried back to her own flat, grabbed her hair dryer, Jazz's GHDs, make up and a little black dress that she had bought from the supermarket in the sales. After cooking, she would have to have a shower otherwise she would stink of onions and garlic. Nikita quickly ironed her dress and placed it onto a hanger. She put it flat on the back seat of her car and headed back to Jai's apartment.

His apartment was very beautiful and had a lovely view of the city. Nikita could only dream about living in a place like this, but there was no way that she would ever be able to afford it in reality. She opened the French doors to the balcony, switched on the radio and made herself a cup of tea. There were two chairs out on the balcony with a small coffee table and she sat putting her feet up for five minutes. It was lovely sitting here soaking in the sun. She could get used to this, she thought.

Nikita's expertise was in Indian food so it was safer for her to stick to that. The next few hours were spent chopping, preparing and marinating. She put all the drinks in the fridge, set the table and calculated the cooking time to ensure the food would be ready for seven o'clock.

Jai called no less than five times throughout the day, checking on how Nikita was getting on. He was so nervous.

"Will you calm down? Everything's in hand," Nikita told him firmly.

"Are you sure?" he asked.

"Don't stress. Carry on and finish up your meeting and I'll see you when you get home," and Nikita flipped the phone shut.

Jai got home at five o'clock and needed to start getting dressed for the evening. He walked towards the kitchen and

Nikita could see his nose trying to sniff out the aromas of the different dishes.

"You're not allowed in the kitchen. It's a surprise."

"It smells divine, what are you cooking?"

"Well, if I told you that, then it wouldn't be a surprise would it?"

He stared at her curiously and then said that he was going have a shower.

"You look tired, feel like a cuppa?" Nikita asked.

"Yeh, that would be nice, but hold fire until I come out."

He stared at Nikita and she could see he wanted to ask her something. She flushed. She could guess that it was probably something to do with her stupid reaction this morning, but she didn't want to talk about it, so she quickly trotted back to the kitchen and put the kettle on.

Jai went off to his bedroom to have a shower.

Nikita made his tea and walked through the lounge and towards his bedroom. The flat was an open plan apartment, so it always felt very spacious. She knocked on his bedroom door and shouted, "Are you decent?"

"Yeh Nik, come in," he shouted back.

She walked in and she almost dropped the tea on his lovely cream carpet. She steadied herself.

He was standing in front of his wardrobe mirror with only his bath towel wrapped around his waist. Water from the shower was dripping down his beautiful torso. Nikita felt awkward. She looked away feeling like a pervert for staring at him, not to mention it was highly inappropriate of her to be standing there, gazing at him in this way.

He lifted his hand and pushed his hair back away from his face. He was even more handsome than she had ever imagined. She thought about what it would feel like to be held in those arms, to be pressed up against the bare skin of his broad chest. She looked away again. Stop thinking like that, she told herself. She realised she seemed to be drifting off in her thoughts quite often these days.

She felt like a fool because she'd been here before. When she came across Sam, he seemed like the most pleasant, friendly, gorgeous man she had ever met. She had never contemplated that a man so stunning was only wearing a mask which didn't lift until it was too late for her. Ignoring the tickle in her throat, Nikita said, "I have your tea."

"Thanks Nik," he said.

She put it on the bedside cabinet and just as she turned on her heel, Jai called her back.

"What do you think Nik, which shirt shall I wear? What about this one?"

Nikita turned around reluctantly; she didn't want him to see her drooling over him.

He was holding up a white Tommy Hilfiger long sleeve cotton shirt, which was nice, but a bit dull. "You want to make an impression tonight, don't you? That's a nice shirt but it's a bit boring. No disrespect, but you need to wear something that will make you stand out. I would go with something a bit brighter," she lectured, as though she was some fashion expert. She knew she wasn't but she could tell what looked good on him and this shirt just wasn't going to do him any justice.

Nikita waved her hand, gesturing him aside and walked over to his huge wardrobe. She rummaged through his shirt section and she pulled out a white and pink striped Ralph Lauren shirt.

"Don't you think that's a bit too bright?" he asked.

"No" she said, laying it on the bed. "It's perfect."

Jai looked unsure.

"Look," she said. "It's your party and your choice, but you asked for my opinion and I like this one. Wear the white if it makes you feel more comfortable."

Jai looked at her and picked up the Ralph Lauren shirt. He slid it over his strong arms and smoothed it over his gorgeous chest. He did up a few buttons and continued to look in the mirror, moving from side to side.

The scent of Armani was wafting around her and it smelt divine. She felt a little lightheaded and something in the pit of her stomach started to stir. A sensation she'd never experienced before.

Nikita realised Jai was saying something but she hadn't heard a word.

"Sorry, say that again."

"I said that Tina would never let me wear anything like this. She thinks these colours make me look gay, not that there's anything wrong with being gay or anything," he quickly corrected himself. "She prefers simple colours," he continued.

Nikita had never met Tina, or ever seen her face to face but Jai had a picture of her in his living room on top of his fire place. She was very beautiful. She had gorgeous long black hair, beautiful big hazel coloured eyes and was stunning. Nikita could see why he was with her.

When Jai was in meetings or otherwise busy, Nikita would answer his personal phone and she could tell that Tina didn't like it. She was always very rude. Nikita wound her up by being over polite and although Nikita would never admit it, deep down she enjoyed it a little. This girl didn't even know her, so why all the cattiness?

Nikita knew very little about Tina, only that she was the director of a company that her dad had set up and that she was always very busy. Nikita didn't think Jai and Tina saw much of each other and he didn't talk about her much either. But Nikita wasn't with him twenty four-seven, so maybe they caught up with each other late at night. Either way, it was none of her business. She wasn't paid to keep a track of his personal life and nor did she want to. His professional life was complex enough.

Jai was still contemplating on his shirt.

Nikita watched him for a few more moments. "You know what Jai?"

He turned to look at her.

"You should wear whatever you want to wear, do what you want to do. Don't let people dictate to you. Live your life the way you want to live it, otherwise you'll end up regretting it. It's not nice to live with regrets in your life, trust me, I know."

Jai stared at her blankly.

Nikita noticed his eyes soften. She saw the questions in them again. Before he could say anything she made an excuse about checking on the food and headed for the door.

"Jai," she said as she turned around. "Is it okay for me to use your shower? My clothes really smell from the cooking so I want to have a quick wash and change before our visitors arrive."

"That's fine," he said. "There are fresh towels in the cupboard by the shower."

"That's okay, I've brought everything with me," and she hurried back to the kitchen.

The food was coming along really nicely and it was close to six o'clock. She'd decided on making a buffet, which included, tandoori chicken, lamb kebabs, spicy fish, Bombay potatoes, bhajis, sweet and spicy prawns in batter, roasted vegetable cous cous, and salad. For desert she had made a huge chocolate and fresh cream sponge cake and strawberry and cream muffins, topped with fresh cream and strawberries. They looked utterly scrumptious. Nikita just hoped they tasted as good as they looked. She smiled at herself, proud of what she had accomplished and she looked forward to surprising Jai.

There was only an hour to go before people would start arriving, so Nikita needed to hurry up. She grabbed her clothes and accessories and headed back to Jai's bedroom, knocking on the door again. "Is it okay for me to come in?"

"Come in Nik," he shouted back.

He was wearing the Ralph Lauren shirt with a nice pair of faded jeans and a smart Ralph Lauren jacket. She smiled at him.

"You look really good," Nikita said as she walked past him to the shower.

He smiled back; of course he already knew that.

She quickly shut the door and locked it behind her. She could feel her heart thumping and she was almost out of breath. Calm down she told herself, but she kept visualising him standing there in nothing but a towel, with his beautiful arms and smooth chest.

Stop it! Think about something else. Nikita took a deep breath which didn't help as the smell of Jai's aftershave still lingered in the bathroom. She reached over and turned on the shower which took her a few minutes to figure out. She felt stupid because she didn't know how to use it. It was a bit more technical than the one in her flat. She was almost contemplating calling out for Jai for help when she accidently hit a button and the water turned on. That was lucky; she saved herself from looking like a right idiot. She took off her clothes and jumped in. The power shower was heavenly; it was so soothing on her back. She could have stood there for the next hour letting the shower massage her back. Her shoulders and neck ached. She was tired today but there was still so much to be done and there wasn't much time.

Nikita quickly jumped out and wrapped her hair in a towel, twisted it and piled it up on her head. The hair dresser had told her not to do that, but she didn't have time to worry about that right now. Nikita wrapped the bath robe around her and tied her belt.

She was nervous going out into Jai's bedroom. She always made an effort when she came to work and for the first time he was going to see her naked face. She worried about his response. He'd never seen her without any makeup before.

She took in a deep breath. There was no time to worry about that right now, she had work to do. Nikita bit her lip and unlocked the door. Her hand clutched the collar of her robe holding them together, ensuring no flesh was on display, but completely forgetting that the thigh length Egyptian towel wrap exposed her sexy legs.

Jai was sitting on his bed putting on his shoes. He turned and looked at her as she walked out of the bathroom. The site of her hit him hard. Looking away he forced his thoughts back to focus on the task at hand and not dwell on the fact that Nikita was probably naked under that robe.

Nikita's face blushed with embarrassment. She had nothing to be nervous about because he couldn't even bear to look at her. She was stupid to have worried in the first place.

Jai stood up and did up the buckle on his belt. His shirt was tucked in around his taut waist. "You get ready and I'll go and put some music on," he said without turning around.

He quickly left the bedroom.

As he walked out, he shut the door behind him, putting a barrier between him and Nikita. He realised his heart was beating hard and he could feel the blood rushing through his veins. He was confused. There seemed to be a magnetic field between them and Nikita was slowly drawing him in. Think about Tina he told himself, but no matter how much he tried, he was drawn back to Nikita. That invisible tug seemed to affect his heart. He needed to let it go. It couldn't happen even if he wanted it to. He was with Tina. At times he felt that he had seen the signals from Nikita too, however she had an impenetrable wall built around her which he knew kept her protected.

Nikita sat down on Jai's bed and she felt a little strange. She hadn't been in a man's bedroom in this way for years and she wasn't very comfortable. Of course she had been in Jai's bedroom, but not like this, completely naked under her robe.

She'd never had much experience with men. Before she got married, she'd never been with any other man. Now and then she'd met someone she had fancied, but she had never dated anyone. Even at school, her only experience was with Scott Howard, whom she used to sit next to in Geography. Every lesson he would try and put his hand up her skirt. She didn't know why he did it, she'd never handed him an invite, but he just wouldn't take no for an answer. In the end they got asked to sit separately because there was too much noise coming from their desk. Then there was Mark, who always teased her in Maths lessons. One time he went through a whole term saying that he wanted Nikita to have his babies, and she thought he was taking the piss. After a while the joke ran dry and Nikita put him in his place, even though secretly she'd had a long term crush on him. So there it was, her life's experience with men. Then there was the marriage experience and she didn't allow her thoughts to go down that road.

Nikita didn't have much time left to get ready so she quickly opened her makeup bag and made a start. It only took twenty minutes to get ready, dry her hair and straighten it. She sprayed on a little Samsara which Jazz had bought her for her birthday and glanced in the mirror. She decided that she looked presentable. Nikita popped her silver hoop earrings in her ears, glanced one more time in the mirror and left the bedroom, her chiffon dress swaying around her.

She headed for the kitchen to check on the food and found Jai in there nibbling on the muffins, the evidence visible.

"Hey," she said to him. "You weren't meant to come in the kitchen, I wanted to surprise you."

"Nik, this food is so delicious, where did you learn to cook like this? And these muffins, they're the most delicious thing I've ever tasted." Jai took another bite. "Mmmm, mama mia," he smiled, his eyes closed. "I think I've died and gone to heaven."

Nikita gathered he was exaggerating but she smiled nevertheless.

"My mum taught me everything. She always said that an Indian girl should know how to cook to keep her..." Nikita trailed off again not finishing her sentence.

"Well it's lovely, I'll have to meet your mum one day and let her know that she taught you well," he smiled.

Nikita noticed Jai staring at her. She raised her hand to touch her face. "What is it? Do I have something on my face?"

Jai grinned. "You look lovely. I've never seen you wearing a dress before. It suits you," he said.

Smiling back, she blushed.

He took a step forward closing the distance between them and put his hands on her shoulders. Nikita's instinct was to jerk back, but she managed to control it. She felt a throb under his hand.

"You're a life saver Nik, thanks," he said and he bent down and kissed her on the cheek. It felt like an electric shock running through her body and she froze.

Jai leaned back and looked at her face, "Nik, are you okay?"

She had gone as white as a sheet.

Nikita quickly spun him around and told him to get out of the kitchen; she needed to start serving up the food on platters and laying it out on the table.

"Oh shit!" he said as he walked away. "I didn't pick up any drinks; what are we going to do?"

"Calm down," Nikita said to him. "There are lots of drinks in the fridge.

"But I didn't buy any." he said.

"Yes that's true, but I did."

Nikita saw him noticeably relax. He walked back to her again and this time he grabbed her in a tight hug. She realised at that point, she'd got the answer to the question she had posed earlier in her head. She now knew what it felt like to be wrapped in those beautiful arms.

Just then the door bell rang and Jai turned to go and open it.

Nikita quickly pulled out some bottles of wine, beer and water from the fridge and put them on the table. She returned to the kitchen to get some of the food and hurried it out.

The table was full and by seven thirty, most of the guests had arrived. They were very punctual; she had to give them that. Not like an Indian function where people always arrived two hours late and then made excuses about Indian timing, thinking it was funny. Nikita always found that very annoying. She was a very punctual person, a bit of a perfectionist. She liked routine and if she organised something, it would irritate her if it didn't go to plan. She didn't think it was obsessive; she just put it down to being a Virgo.

Nikita mostly stood in the corner of the room, answering the door when people arrived, welcoming them, showing them to the food and drinks and answering the phone when it rang. It was quite a relaxed atmosphere.

Every now and then Jai would look over to Nikita and stick his thumb up discreetly and she would smile and nod reassuring him that she was okay.

Nikita watched Jai work his magic in the small crowds of people. A forty something woman walked over to him and placed her hand on his arm. She was fighting for his attention, Nikita could see. It made her smile to see all the attention he drew. If she was completely honest, it stirred envy deep inside her; she wished she could get that close too. She watched him as he spoke in that deep masculine voice, which made her knees tremble. Nikita saw the woman whisper something in Jai's ear. He poured her another glass of wine and the woman licked her lips. Nikita could see the lust in her eyes for Jai. Nikita looked away, feeling a little envious.

With the sunlight fading quickly, she noticed the horizon turn from bright blue to a reddish purple colour with a few clouds streaking across the sun. Nikita looked out of the balcony doors and felt the cool breeze against her face. She loved the sunset; it was her favourite time of day. It couldn't have looked more perfect if it had been painted by a talented artist, she thought.

Nikita felt a little suffocated from the cigarette smoke in the flat and so she took a deep breath of the cool evening breeze filling her lungs with clean air.

Jai watched her, as he noticed the slight rise and fall of her chest, her dark hair flowing in the breeze. He noticed a golden glow on Nikita's cheeks which reflected the suns evening rays. He watched her close her eyes and take in one of nature's beauties and he smiled to himself. He looked at her as though he was seeing her for the first time. She looked stunning. That little black dress hugged her in all the right places and the belt around her waist exaggerated the fullness of her breasts. Wow, he thought.

Later, Jai watched Nikita talking to a middle aged producer, who couldn't seem to take his eyes off her face. He was standing rather close and Jai watched as she took a very discreet step back putting a little distance between them. Jai felt a trickle of contentment. For a moment he forgot he was in a room full of people until someone tapped him on the shoulder.

Nikita tried to make conversation with people when they came over to talk to her. She tried to sound professional and intelligent and she felt like she was pulling it off. She pretended to be interested when they talked about finances, or cars or investments. They didn't talk about normal things, like football, or Eastenders, or going to the pub. It was contracts, celebrities and bitching. Nikita realised that these people were from a world so different to hers and she felt completely clueless. Yet she continued smiling, nodding and responding.

Some of the visitors stuck their noses up at her, but she didn't care. She smiled all the same. This was Jai's night.

As she walked around she heard people commenting on the food and guessing with each other who had done the catering, which made her feel rather good about herself.

Nikita made sure that everyone was well looked after and it was two o'clock in the morning before the last of them stumbled out. On the face of it, it seemed like a successful evening, but Nikita was sure that Jai would fill her in later.

She was shattered by this time and Jai looked even more tired. It was Sunday morning so technically she had the day off.

Nikita started to empty the table but Jai told her to leave it.

"Nik, don't bother with the tidying up. The cleaner will be here in the morning and she'll get it done. You must be tired," he grinned, the smile not reaching his eyes.

"It's okay Jai, I just want to get the leftovers into the fridge, otherwise they'll go off and you won't be able to eat them tomorrow. You look shattered. Go and get some rest," she told him.

After she'd finished what she was doing, Nikita decided to leave. She stretched her body and bent slightly backwards, arms on the back of her hips, turning from side to side. She was exhausted. "I'm going to go now Jai," she yawned. "I'll see you on Monday."

"Stay here tonight," he said quickly.

Nikita looked at him surprised. Was he asking her what she thought he was asking? She was affronted. Just because she had become friendly with him, didn't mean she would jump into bed with him. How dare he? Nikita thought. Outrage started to build in the pit of her stomach.

Jai walked across the living area, quickly reducing the distance between them. He spoke in a low, thrumming voice.

"It's too late and you're too tired to drive. I'll feel better if you stay and rest here, you can head home in the morning."

Nikita felt relief rush over her. She was ready to whack him over the head with her handbag. She felt his gaze pass over her and she was grateful for the dimmed lighting in the apartment. Jai couldn't see her face flush with embarrassment at what she thought his comment had meant and because he was staring at her so intently now.

Jai's apartment may have been big but he only had one bedroom and one bed. His second bedroom was converted into a gym so where was she going to sleep?

"I don't think that's a very good idea," Nikita replied.

"You can have my bed and I'll crash on the sofa," he smiled.

Nikita was used to sleeping rough; her bed was cheap and as hard as a rock. Jai's expensive sofa was probably more comfortable than her bed. He was so used to his luxury memory foam mattress; there was no way that he was going to get any sleep on the sofa. But Nikita was really tired and she really didn't feel like driving thirty minutes to get home.

"I'll take the sofa," she said as she yawned again.

"Are you sure?" he asked.

"Yeh, I'll be fine here."

"I'll find you a blanket and a pillow," he said as he headed to his bedroom.

The tiredness overwhelmed Nikita, but she was still buzzing from the dinner party. A hot cup of milky chocolate would do the trick, so she went off to find the left over cocoa powder from the chocolate cake.

Nikita walked into the kitchen and even though she'd tried to tidy as she'd cooked, it was still a mess. She poured some milk in a pan and put it on the hob to heat and then added cocoa and a drop of sugar. Nikita wasn't sure if Jai liked hot chocolate, but she made him a cup anyway. As she finished making the drinks, Jai walked into the kitchen.

"I told you to leave the mess Nik; the cleaner will get it in the morning."

"I wasn't cleaning Jai, I was just making a hot drink. I thought it would help us relax."

"Yeh, it has been a stressful day," he replied.

Nikita handed him his hot chocolate and he smiled.

She walked back to the lounge and saw that he had laid out a pillow and blanket on the sofa. Jai passed Nikita a pair of pyjamas and his t-shirt and she changed in his bedroom. She came out of the bedroom and climbed into the blanket, slipping off her sandals and anklets.

She almost curled up into a ball and Jai came and sat next to her. She felt her heart thumping again. What was she doing there? This was crazy. She hadn't spent the night alone with a man since she'd left Sam and here she was, spending the night with someone she barely knew. Could she trust him not to try anything? Of course she trusted him. There was no way she would have stayed if she didn't. She could feel the closeness of Jai sitting next to her, his leg almost touching hers, the heat of his body oozing out. Why did he have this effect on her? Every time he came close, her heart would jump into overdrive like it had a mind of its own. Every sense of hers seemed to be heightened, like the sensitivity of her emotions and feelings had multiplied.

"Do you think the evening went well? Did you get what you wanted from it?" Nikita asked.

Jai smiled. "It went really well. I got some really good contacts and people want to meet with me to talk about some projects." Projects meant acting work, films and dramas.

"That's great," Nikita smiled, yawning.

"But the thing that people liked the most was your cooking. Everyone loved the food, it was so tasty. I'm so used to eating readymade meals and restaurant food that I forgot how good home cooked food tasted."

"I'm glad you liked it," she said feeling quite proud of herself. "I told you I wouldn't let you down."

"I'm so glad that I've got you around Nik. Today would have been a disaster without you. Thank you."

"Stop it Jai, you're embarrassing me, I'm not used to so many compliments."

Nikita took a sip of her drink which was still very hot.

Her mind drifted back to the time when no matter how hard she tried, she couldn't please that man. No matter how good the food tasted, he would always complain.

***

"Have you tasted this shit?" he'd say.

"What, what's wrong with it?" she'd ask.

"You're trying to give me salt poisoning aren't you?" he'd said and he threw the plate across the living room.

Nikita picked up her spoon and tasted the curry. She couldn't taste anything wrong with it.

"Sam, the curry is fine, there's not too much salt in there."

"Are you saying that I'm lying?" he screamed.

"No, I'm not saying that, but the curry is fine."

Sam grabbed her upper arms and squeezed hard until she screamed in pain. "Sam, you're hurting me."

She never saw it coming until she felt the sting on her face. Her hand shot up to cover the area that now throbbed. Nikita was in shock but she was glad that tomorrow was a Saturday, or she would've had to take the day off from work.

She could smell the alcohol from his breath as he screamed in her face.

"See, this is how fucked up everything is, you can't even cook. Is it too much to ask to come home to a decent meal?" he yelled.

"I'm sorry," Nikita screamed back. Maybe it was her fault; maybe she had lost her touch.

"Sorry? You aren't fucking sorry. You spend all your time watching that bastard television and not enough time on the things that you should be doing. That's how you fuck up all the time."

Nikita remembered the way his face had turned red with rage.

He'd made her doubt herself, doubt something that she was so proud of and something she thought she was gifted in.

It took her ages to get the turmeric stains out of the sofa.

***

She felt overwhelmed to receive such compliments from Jai, because cooking was such a passion of hers and he, that man had made her question her ability, making her feel incompetent. Nikita's eyes welled up at the pain of the memory.

Jai nudged her. "Hey, where have you drifted off to? Are you okay?"

"I'm okay," she lied, looking in the other direction and quickly wiping away her tears.

Jai could see that something had upset Nikita, but he didn't know what. He hated to see her like this. He couldn't understand it, because he hardly even knew the girl. Yes he had worked with her for a few months and they had become friends, but when he saw her like this, he felt like someone was twisting a knife in his heart and it made him catch his breath.

He remembered her face earlier in the evening, looking content, taking in the sunset on the horizon. Heat rushed over him as he watched her, she looked beautiful. There was so much difference in the Nikita of this evening and the Nikita sitting next to him right now. She looked sad and Jai couldn't help but ask the question.

"I know it's none of my business and tell me to piss off if you don't want to talk about it but what happened to you Nik? I've noticed, every now and then your face will be filled with such sadness and sometimes you say things without explaining where they are coming from."

Nikita just stared into her mug of hot chocolate.

"And then earlier today, the way you reacted, like you were frightened of me. Then there's that scar on your face." Nikita looked up at him through her wet eyelashes, then lowering them, unable to hold his gaze.

"Leave it Jai; I don't want to talk about it," she said in a low voice.

"Is that your polite way of telling me to piss off?"

Nikita smiled under her breath.

Jai didn't push the questioning. He realised there was no point in trying to find out. He was sure when the time was right she would confide in him. He knew that she had started to trust him.

Nikita wasn't used to men being so understanding and she breathed a sigh of relief when she realised Jai wasn't going to ask her any more questions.

Jai leaned into Nikita's ear and spoke in low soft voice. "Thank you for today. I would never have managed without you."

"That's okay Jai, it was a pleasure."

Nikita put her mug down on the table, leaned back onto the head rest of the sofa and closed her eyes.

Jai put his arm around her.

Nikita opened her eyes, staring at Jai, asking his intention with her expression.

"Don't worry, I won't bite, I promise."

Nikita smiled and although she knew she shouldn't, she put her head on his shoulder.

It felt so nice, to be close to someone. She hadn't felt so warm and protected in such a long time and thinking about it, she had never felt so warm and protected.

"I'm sorry I yelled in front of you earlier, I didn't mean to make you jump."

Nikita's body tensed and Jai moved to accommodate her sudden movement.

"I know that you're not ready to talk about it right now, but if you do ever feel like talking, I'm here. We're friends right?"

Something about this moment felt very right. His arm enveloped her completely and he wanted to hold her all night. It took him back a little. He shouldn't feel this way, so why was it that when he looked into her angel-like face, it took his breath away.

Nikita started to fall asleep and the most that she could manage was a, "mmmhhh."

Jai stroked Nikita's arm and it helped her relax.

The memories of her childhood came back to her and the sensation of being stroked to sleep made her eyelids become heavy.

Nikita felt a kiss on her forehead, but she was too tired to object. She was so comfortable in his arms that she couldn't help but fall asleep.

Jai moved slowly to lay Nikita onto the pillow without disturbing her. She looked so fragile, almost baby like. He pulled the blanket up and tucked it in around her, pushing a strand of hair away from her face, exposing the scar under her eye. He lightly ran his finger along it, so as to not awake her. His stomach twisted thinking about how hard the blow to her face would have been. He couldn't imagine why anyone would want to strike her.

He felt protective over her but again he didn't know why. Confusion ran through his mind because for the first time in the last year, he hadn't thought about Tina all evening.

Jai went to turn the light off in the living room. He noticed the moon shining through the gap in the curtains. It was a beautifully clear night, stars bright in the sky. He stared up and imagined that Nikita would have liked the sight if she had been awake. The moonlight shone through the living room scattering a silver shimmer. Jai grabbed the curtains to shut them. He'd never bothered to draw them before, but on second thoughts he left the curtains slightly open. He didn't want Nikita to get frightened in the dark.

Chapter 13 - Confused

Jai was woken by murmuring coming from the living room. What the hell was that? He shot up looking around for something to grab. What if someone had broken in? What if he was being burgled? Then he listened again and he realised that he recognised the whispering voice. It was Nikita. She sounded like she was crying.

Jai pushed his duvet aside and jumped out of bed. Not wanting to startle her, he put on his tracksuit bottoms which lay on the little chair by his bed. He felt like he had only just fallen asleep. He picked up his watch that was on his bedside cabinet which told him it was only six thirty. Shit, he'd only been asleep a couple of hours. Jai tiptoed out of his bedroom and through to the living room stopping when the floor boards squeaked under his bare feet. Nikita lay sleeping. She still had her eyes closed but she looked uncomfortable, her forehead creased in anguish. She moaned and shifted restlessly. Jai pushed his hands through his hair not sure what to do. She sounded as though she was in pain.

"No, no, no," she moaned. "Please get off me, for God sake stop it. You're hurting me."

Jai couldn't listen any longer. He knelt down beside her and spoke gently. "Hey Nikita, you're alright." Jai wasn't sure if he should touch her. He didn't want to startle her.

She stirred a little. "Nikita, it's okay. You're just dreaming," he said as he placed a hand on her forehead which felt clammy with sweat.

Run, run she was telling herself. She tried to send a signal from her brain to her legs, but they wouldn't move. As she looked back, it came closer. The thing she was running from was now gaining on her. She closed her eyes, she started praying. Move your legs, her mind screamed...

As Jai touched her face, she awoke startled, flicking his hand off her. "No," she screamed. "Get off."

"Hey, it's only me. You're okay."

Nikita looked up at him, her eyes wide, embarrassment written across her face.

"Bad dream?" he said lightly.

She was breathing heavily and it took all Jai's will power not to look down at her t-shirt which revealed the tops of large round breasts rising up and down.

Nikita pushed her damp hair off her face. "Yes, something like that," she said in a low voice, while straightening her top. Nikita pulled the blanket up to her neck.

He wanted to lean over and hold her, help her to feel better, feel safe. He felt the need to lift her up and lay her onto his laps, putting his arms around her, protecting her. But he knew that wasn't a good idea. The poor girl looked like she was trembling and even in the dark he could see that she was as white as a sheet.

He wanted to ask her what the nightmare was about, but given her reaction from the day before, he knew it wouldn't be a good idea.

Jai wondered if she had many sleepless nights. Did she have nightmares often? He knew if he wanted answers to these questions, he would have to wait until she trusted him enough to be able to tell him. Jai left her to go back to sleep.

The rattling of dishes in the kitchen woke Nikita in the morning. She sat up dazzled. For a short moment she had to compose herself and think about where she. Then it all came flooding back to her. Last night's dinner party, the hot cup of cocoa, the conversation. The nightmare she'd had and Jai standing over her. She cringed with embarrassment; she thought she was hiding everything so well. She thought she was getting over her past and her nightmares had become fewer, so why did this have to happen to her here, of all places? Nikita felt ashamed.

She looked at her mobile phone and there were ten missed calls from Jazz. Oh shit, Nikita hadn't called her last night to let her know that she wasn't coming home. She dialled the number back and it rang a few times, before Jazz answered.

"Where have you been? I've been trying to call you all night. Are you okay? Is everything alright? I was just about to call the police and report you missing. Why didn't you call me?"

"If you let me get a word in edge-ways then I would tell you that it's okay, stop panicking, I'm at Jai's."

"Oohhhhh," Jazz said, her tone of voice excited.

"It's not like that," Nikita told her. "The dinner party ran on until after two this morning. Jai didn't want me driving back so late and I was so tired."

"Yeh right," Jazz said incredulously.

Nikita lowered her voice to a whisper. She didn't want Jai overhearing her. "Jazz, I slept on the sofa, so don't go getting any ideas. Anyway I'll be home soon."

"When you get back, I want every single detail, blow by blow," she laughed. Nikita rolled her eyes.

"Shut up Jazz. There's nothing to tell, I told you. Anyway I'm putting the phone down now, I'll see you in a little while," and Nikita shut her phone.

She loved Jazz to bits, but sometimes she really got on her nerves.

Nikita rubbed her eyes a little, disappointed that she didn't have a mirror to hand. I must look like a mess, she thought. She combed her fingers through her hair even though she knew it wasn't going to help much. Her eyelashes were probably clogged together like lumps of coal and she hadn't even got a toothbrush. She scrubbed her teeth with her finger and used a tissue to take the sleep out of her eyes. She breathed out into her cupped hands and tried to smell to see if she had bad breath, but she couldn't smell anything. Unsure of her hygiene, Nikita decided she wasn't going to sit too close to Jai and she would try to talk without opening her mouth too much. God, I hope he doesn't notice.

Jai walked in with a tray in his hand and put it on the table in front of her.

"Morning," she said.

"Morning," Jai responded. "I made you some tea to say thank you for yesterday."

Nikita looked at him, uncomfortable.

Jai sat down next to her like he hadn't noticed.

"How are you feeling this morning?" he asked.

"I'm fine," she replied.

"I wanted to ask you for a favour if that's okay?"

Nikita looked at him suspiciously.

"I was sent this manuscript," he said pointing at a thick document, "It's for a drama that I have a role in and I wanted to spend some time practising the lines today. I wondered if you could assist me. Do you think that you could work today?"

"How can I do that Jai? I don't have a problem with working today but I have no experience of acting or role playing."

"Don't worry. All you have to do is read off the page. I'm not asking you to dramatise it or anything. I just need someone to bounce my lines off. The director is a sucker for perfection and he expects his actors to memorise their lines."

"Ummm, I don't know Jai, I need to go home and have a wash, I haven't got a change of clothes and I've got a few things I need to do."

"That's fine," he said. "Go home, do what you need to do and come back later this afternoon. I'll see you back here about three o'clock?" More a statement rather than a question.

"Why don't you ask Tina? Can't she come over?" It flew out of Nikita's mouth before she could stop herself.

"I don't want to ask her. She won't have time, so it's not even worth trying," he grimaced.

Nikita's heart begged her to agree, but her mind was saying no, it wasn't a good idea. In the end she let her heart rule her mind.

"Okay," she said. "I'll come back later."

"Great," he said and then rushed off to have a shower.

Nikita's mind wandered back to yesterday's experience of seeing him standing there in his towel. That broad taut chest and his strong muscled arms. Nikita imagined tracing every peak, every dip of his body with her hands and her stomach clenched.

She was caught up in her thoughts when the door bell rang. Just as her imagination got creative, she was interrupted. Maybe that was a good thing.

It was Marcia the cleaner. Nikita opened the door and she could see the shocked expression on Marcia's face. She looked at Nikita from top to bottom. Nikita's dishevelled hair, her creased T-shirt which didn't belong to her and the flush in her cheek. Nikita could just imagine the assumptions that Marcia was making, but she didn't mind. Marcia walked in and noticed the blanket on the sofa and her expression turned to relief.

Nikita went back to the sofa and finished off her tea. It felt so nice to have someone fuss over her, even if it was only tea and toast; it was the thought that counted.

Marcia worked around Nikita, hovering, dusting and after a while, Nikita could hear her in the kitchen clunking around with the dishes.

Nikita stretched on the sofa before getting up and folding the blanket, piling it to one side. She turned around and noticed the curtains were still drawn, although not fully. She walked over and pulled them back and pushed them behind the curtain holders. Nikita opened the patio door and smelt the cool breeze wash over her. It was cold but crisp, Nikita loved October mornings.

Jai's apartment was in a busy part of the city, but as it was early Sunday morning, there weren't many cars on the road so the air still felt fresh. No car fumes or noise to disturb the morning freshness. She breathed in a big lung full of fresh air and breathed out.

Nikita felt content this morning. She had a job, she was standing on her own two feet and she had a great boss, not to mention handsome and stunning.

Jai was still in the shower and Nikita needed to get her belongings from his bedroom. She waited for him to come out, but he was taking his time and she needed to leave. She knocked on the bedroom door but there was no answer so she decided it would be safe to go in. She walked over to the far side of the room where her bag was lying and kneeled down to pick it up. Her shoes were tucked under the bed so she reached underneath to grab them and put them in her bag.

She could hear the shower running and she felt a rush of heat run over her again. She could imagine the water dripping down the contours of his back, over his naked flesh. Just as Nikita got up, the door unlocked and Jai walked out of the shower, this time minus the towel.

"Oh my god," she shrieked and quickly turned around, her eyes shut tight. She stood there frozen.

"Oh shit," Jai said quickly grabbing a towel. "Sorry, I didn't know that you were in here."

"No, Jai, it's my fault, I was just getting my things, and I should have waited for you to come out." Her voice was almost a shrill.

"Don't worry about it," he said, "No harm done."

No harm done? But harm was done, to her heart. Her heart was beating so fast, she wouldn't be surprised if it caused her to have a heart attack. The heart palpitations couldn't be good for her. She bit her lip to stop herself from grinning. Nikita stood frozen to the ground, unable to move or turn around. Even though her eyes were shut, images of his naked body were flashing in front of her and she felt the heat rise to her face.

Slowly Nikita walked sideways trying not to look at him and spoke with her back to him as she walked out the door. "I'll see you a bit later, but it might be later than three o'clock. I'll get here as soon as I can, okay?"

"Okay," Jai said, grinning. "See you later."

"Bye," Nikita shouted as she rushed out the front door.

When she got to her car, she threw everything on the back seat, quickly jumping in and started the engine. Nikita couldn't get out of there quick enough.

There really was a God. She couldn't believe what had just happened. Wow! Those thick thighs, that firm chest and his chiselled jaw line. The thought of it made her body tingle. Nikita had flash backs of Jai standing there, stark naked. She couldn't help but visualise his flat toned stomach and the dark glistening of hair leading down to his.... well that area of his body. When she was a safe distance away from the apartment, she burst out laughing. It had been so long since she'd laughed in this way, probably since before she'd got married.

Her face dropped again. What was she doing? Did she really think she had a chance with Jai? It was the most insane thing she had ever thought. Why would he be interested in her? Or, in all honesty, the question she needed to ask herself was, is she really interested in him? Look at me and look at him she thought. Look at who he is and what he is. What could she ever offer him? To top it all off, he already had a girlfriend, who was beautiful, rich and sexy, so why would he be interested in her?

She knew he liked her as a person, even cared for her; she wasn't that stupid, but that didn't mean anything. He probably felt sorry for her. He'd seen her behave like a lunatic yesterday and then like a freak with her nightmares. How embarrassing. No wonder he felt pity for her.

Nikita tried not to think about it too much and because it was Sunday and the roads were clear, she was home in no time.

Grabbing her belongings from the back seat of her car, she ran into the building and up the stairs to the door of her flat. She rummaged around in her bag for her keys, found them and then tried to open her front door. Her hands were shaking and she couldn't understand why. She managed to get the door open and quickly walked in, shutting the door behind her. She took a deep breath to help her calm down. She didn't know what was happening to her, she'd never felt anything like it before.

Nikita walked through the living room door and found Jazz slouched on the sofa watching television. Jazz sat up as soon as she saw Nikita with a bright look on her face, her eyes wide open. She had that curious look in her eyes and Nikita knew what she was about to ask her.

Nikita put her hands up, palms facing forward. "Don't say anything. Nothing happened, he's just my boss, I was too tired to drive, I slept on the sofa and now I've come home for a wash before I go back."

"Aaaahhhh, so you're going back are you? It's meant to be your day off," she said cheekily.

"Yes but he needs some help with a script."

"A script hey? Well that's what he told you," she said with a smirk on her face.

"Jazz," Nikita sighed.

"Okay, okay, I won't say anything, but I can tell that you like him," she said in her high pitched voice excited and clapping her hands.

Nikita rolled her eyes at Jazz and went into her bedroom. She dropped all her stuff on the bed, then went and sat on the bench by her window and stared out.

Nikita started thinking about the last twenty-four hours and the crazy events. It made her smile again. Reminiscing about those arms, those legs, his chest and his face, made heat pulse through her entire body. He was so beautiful. She felt warm inside and her stomach felt hot. She felt a little embarrassed. It wasn't an emotion she was used to feeling. It was a very weird sensation to have this tingling feeling in the lower part of her belly.

Nikita didn't really have anything much to do, she was just making excuses but it obviously hadn't worked.

She had a wash, put her pyjamas on and went and joined Jazz on the sofa. Eastenders omnibus was going to be on in a little while so she would watch that to take her mind off things. She didn't get much time to watch TV during the week; she spent most of her time at work.

As she relaxed on the sofa, her phone started to ring. She looked at the caller ID and it said 'Mum'. At first she didn't answer, but then she knew that if she didn't, her mum would keep ringing her until she did. The last time Nikita's mum called, the phone rang day and night until Nikita answered it. Right now, the last thing Nikita needed was for her mum to ring her while she was at work because it would almost certainly upset her and she couldn't work like that. In the end Nikita answered the phone.

"Hello," Nikita said.

"How are you?" her mum asked.

"I'm okay. How are you mum? How's dad?"

"I'm worried about you Nikita. You never call."

Nikita noticed how her mum had deflected from the question. Her mum was good at changing the subject when she didn't want to tell Nikita the truth, but Nikita recognised that trait in her, so she asked the question again.

"I know you do mum. What about dad, does he worry about me?"

"Well, you know your father, he doesn't say it but, I know he misses you."

"Does he ever mention me?" Nikita asked.

"Nikita, you know how he is. He's still angry about what happened, but I know that he misses you. Why don't you come home?"

Nikita knew her dad was angry with her. He didn't understand why she'd left Sam. When Nikita moved into her new flat, she'd plucked up the courage to call her mum. She'd tried to explain what had happened, hoping her mum would talk to her dad about it, but they all thought she was exaggerating. Their view was that arguments happen in all relationships, there was no need to walk out. Nikita gave up trying to explain it and resorted to not discussing it at all. She had always done what her parents had asked of her, but she drew the line when she walked out of Sam's life and she'd made the decision to do what was best for her.

"I'll visit soon; I'm busy with work right now," she said.

"No Nikita, I want to know when you will be returning home for good. People are wondering where you are. Sam called as well and....."

Nikita didn't let her finish. "Mum, I don't want to hear his name. If you mention him again I'll put the phone down. I don't want anything to do with him. I don't want to think about him, I wish he was never a part of my life," Nikita said firmly.

Jazz sat upright quickly and put her arm around Nikita, her face grimacing.

Mum went quiet for a short while and then in a low voice she said, "Please stay in touch. I need to know that my daughter is okay. Take your time to think things over and call if you need to talk to me."

Nikita felt so deflated, she didn't have the energy to argue with her mum anymore so she just said, "I'll talk to you another time mum," and put the phone down.

"Don't let her talk you into anything, do you hear me?" Jazz screamed. "That man is a scum bag; you can't have anything to do with that bastard."

"Don't worry Jazz, I'm not about to let that arse-hole back into my life, not for anything or anyone."

They shared everything, their pain, their sorrow and any bit of happiness they had. Jazz was furious; Nikita could feel the anger radiating from her. Nikita didn't want to ruin the day for Jazz. Even though she felt angry herself, Nikita decided she wanted to put that aside and cheer Jazz up. She decided to tell Jazz about what had happened this morning. Nikita took a deep breath and pasted a smile to her face.

"Shall I tell you something really funny?" Nikita murmured.

"I knew it," Jazz said as her face lit up immediately. "I knew something had happened between you and Jai."

"It's nothing like that," Nikita confessed and Jazz's face dropped.

"Well, I went into his bedroom to get my bag and I was about to leave when...."

Jazz interrupted. "And what was your bag doing in his bedroom, hey?" She wiggled her eyebrows in mischievous delight.

"Will you let me finish, do you want to hear the story or not?"

"Go on then," Jazz sighed.

"I picked up my stuff and as I turned around, Jai walked out of the shower absolutely stark naked."

Jazz's eyes widened. "No way. Oh my God. What did he look like?" She asked in a deep voice. "Was he sexy? Oh my God, I can't breathe. I bet he's well hung. A man that looks as good as he does, has to be."

"Jazz!"

"Sorry, sorry, continue," Jazz said, breathing a little heavier now.

"Well, he was in as much shock as I was."

"Yes but what was he like? Did he look good?" She asked again, pointing to that particular area of her anatomy.

The truth was that she was in so much shock that she didn't really remember much but the look on his face. But Nikita told Jazz that he was beautiful and that was no lie.

"Oh my god, how did you control yourself, I would have jumped on him and made out like rabbits."

"Is that all you think about?" Nikita asked incredulously.

"Well if I had someone like that standing naked in front of me, then yeh, I would definitely have had a good feel."

They couldn't stop giggling.

They lazed on the sofa and Nikita told Jazz about the dinner party and described to her in detail what Jai looked like and how she felt so mesmerized by him.

They had a great laugh and before long Nikita had pushed the conversation with her mum to the back of her mind.

"I'll be back in just a second hun." Jazz went to her bedroom and came back to the sofa with a small Waterstones carrier bag.

"What have you got there Jazz?"

"I've got something for you babe."

"What is it?"

"Well, remember how you've always told me, how much you loved watching the Hammer horrors when you were younger and you mentioned your love of vampire movies. Well I saw this and I thought that you might enjoy it."

She passed Nikita the bag. Nikita put her hand in and pulled out a book. It was Twilight by Stephanie Meyers.

"Why have you bought this for me? You know that I don't read books."

"Babe, you do read books, but you stopped because of that arsehole. Don't let him win. You loved reading, you told me yourself."

Nikita stared at Jazz. She felt a sting in her eyes but she fought to hold back her tears.

"Jazz I used to love reading, there's a difference. These books are full of rubbish. They make you dream. They make you think there is something better for you out there, but that's not reality."

Experience had taught her that reality was about having your heart ripped out, being made to feel so small, that you wanted to crawl under a rock and die. Since leaving Sam, she hadn't read anything. She left behind all her favourite novels by Catherine Anderson and Sophie Kinsella. She stopped watching romantic movies as well, something she used to do all the time.

Jazz nudged her.

"What are you thinking babe?"

"I'm thinking about your book. Thank you for the gift. I can't promise but I will think about reading it. It's a lovely gesture. I really do appreciate it," Nikita said and she stood and gave Jazz a hug. Nikita knew that Jazz was right but it still didn't make it any easier.

"Okay babe," Jazz said. "But remember, you gave up so much for him. It's time you moved on with your life and enjoy the things you love most."

Nikita reflected on the conversation and she knew that Jazz was right, but she had to get her head around it. She couldn't just switch her feelings on and off when she felt like it. It was going to take time.

Chapter 14 - The Script

Shit, its three o'clock Nikita thought as she glanced at her watch. She needed to get moving.

She took the book and put it on her dressing table. Nikita walked over to her wardrobe and started to rummage through to see what she could wear. As it wasn't an official work day and there weren't any meetings to attend, Nikita figured she could go casual. She pulled out a full length skirt, a cotton blouse and laid them on her bed. Nikita wanted to look nice, but she didn't want to over dress. She didn't want Jai to think that she'd dressed up for him. Rummaging through her draw, she searched for a white strappy vest because the blouse was made of thin cotton which you could see through when worn. It was also getting quite chilly outside and without a vest; anyone could tell she was cold.

Jazz walked into her bedroom without knocking.

"Do you mind?" Nikita sighed, "I am getting dressed you know."

"Don't worry about it, you haven't got anything I haven't got," she said. "Now show me what you're wearing."

"Well, I was thinking, as it's not officially a work day, I should just wear something casual. This blouse is a bit low cut and you can see through it, so I'll wear this white vest underneath. What do you think?"

"No you won't," Jazz replied.

"Excuse me?" Nikita didn't understand.

"What I mean is, ditch the vest. There's no harm in showing a little flesh, is there?"

"A little flesh? Jazz, my boobs will totally be on display."

"Just the way I like it," said Jazz.

Nikita raised one eye brow at her.

"You're not living with that beast anymore, so you don't need to wear round necked baggy tops anymore, dress like you."

"This is me."

"No it's not. That's what you've been programmed to think. Honey you got some beautiful breasts, flaunt them a little."

Nikita smiled at Jazz. She could always count on her to make her feel better.

Nikita turned around and appraised herself in the mirror. She liked what she saw. It felt kind of sexy.

Jazz put the straighteners on to heat and loosely curled Nikita's hair.

Using the eyelash curler, Nikita curled her lashes and applied a little mascara. She brushed her lips with a hint of pink lip gloss and nothing else. That was all she needed today. Nikita popped in her large silver hoop earrings, slipped her feet into her flat sandals and headed out to the car. She looked good, fresh, but without trying too hard.

Nikita was at the apartment in no time.

She felt her heart beat quicken and her nerves were doing somersaults in her stomach as she arrived outside the apartment door.

She had keys for the front door but she still rang the door bell, she knew he was in. She didn't want to make the same mistake twice in one day and walk in on an awkward situation, but having said that, some mistakes were worth making twice. The door opened and Jai stepped forward to greet her.

He stared at her standing in the doorway and he felt his heart skip a beat. She looked stunning, dressed simply, and she looked as fresh as a summer breeze. She smelled of honey and lavender and for some reason it made goose bumps run over his skin. What was happening?

Nikita smiled at him.

He had started to understand the fear behind that innocent face, what it could be that kept her from relaxing. He'd noticed that often. As much as she showed him that she was confident and her willingness to carry out any task, her body often betrayed her. He'd seen it in her eyes and yesterday, he almost heard the penny drop. It all made sense to him now. He didn't want to believe it, but he knew that his instincts weren't often wrong. He wanted to embrace her, to welcome her with his arms, but he quickly decided against it and settled for a smile.

"You made it Nik, I was about to give up on you."

"Yeh, sorry about that, I got a bit held up, but I'm here now."

He held the door open for her to come in. "Would you like a drink, I was just about to get myself a beer?

"Actually I think I will. Don't worry I'll get it myself."

Nikita made herself a cup of tea and she walked into the lounge. Jai was holding a very thick document. This must have been the transcript.

He'd been signed up to a short contemporary drama that was being aired on one of the sky channels and they'd started filming for it already. Jai was being filmed the following day so he wanted to get a head start by practicing his lines. Nikita and Jai went through the scenes one by one.

It was such a laugh and for the first time Nikita felt herself relax. Jai watched her giggle and he found himself smiling just watching her. It was infectious. He stared at her as she stumbled on her lines.

Even though Nikita hadn't gone onto study at college, English was one of her strong points. She was good at it; her teachers had always told her. Lucky for her it meant she didn't find it awkward to read the transcript out loud.

What made her feel awkward was the way Jai's gaze washed over her, but she reminded herself that he was probably thinking about her reaction yesterday. Face flushed she continued reading because she didn't want him to realise that she'd notice.

Nikita was playing the part of the female character Salina. Salina was of mixed heritage, white English and Persian. The transcript described that the role had to be played in a passionate, aggressive manner. She could do this, Nikita thought to herself but she was trying without much success. Nikita was trying to imitate an accent but it kept slipping into an Indian accent, then Irish and even French.

Jai found it very amusing.

She tried a deep husky voice, like the ones you got on the chat lines, not that she had ever used any of them. She tried flicking her hair and giving him the eye and it made it even more difficult to be serious, in fact it was hilarious.

Jai got himself another bottle of beer and brought out another tea for Nikita.

She watched him as he drank and worried about how long it would be before the alcohol started to influence him to a point where he would start to behave in an aggressive manner. Experience had taught her that this was the way that things happened.

Jai noticed Nikita staring at his bottle and he decided to put it down.

"You know what? I'm going to get a cup of coffee. This beer is giving me a headache."

Nikita was surprised. Did she make it that obvious?

Jai watched her smile awkwardly and he knew he'd done the right thing.

"Let me know when you get hungry, I'll order us some pizza," he said.

"What happened to the leftover food from yesterday?"

"I had that for lunch," he smiled.

Once again Nikita felt proud she was able to help out yesterday. It had felt so good to be of use, to be able to make a difference. Her face lit up ever so slightly, her chest filled with satisfaction and pride.

"I'm okay for now, we'll order some later. Which reminds me, I've still got your credit card and pin number from yesterday. Let me grab it from my hand bag. I've got all the receipts for everything I bought as well. I'll give you them, so that you can check them against your statement."

"Don't worry about the receipts, I trust you," he replied. And he did. He trusted her implicitly.

174

"You shouldn't be so trusting Jai, I could have gone out and bought new clothes or make up or anything."

"But you didn't, did you?" he said.

"I was debating it though. Imagine, someone else's credit card and shopping at the Selfridges, with me thrown in. It would have been Dior lipsticks, Chanel eye shadows, Gucci handbags and Louis Vuitton shoes," Nikita laughed. She knew she sounded like a bimbo to him sometimes but she didn't care and Jai just laughed.

"Well, you would have deserved it," he smiled.

He helped her to feel good about herself and it felt nice to be trusted. Nikita gave Jai back his card and the piece of paper with the pin number, leaving the receipts on his desk. She'd be the one filing them away the following day anyway.

She came back and sat on the sofa. Nikita slid her sandals off and put her feet up sitting cross legged. She was glad she had painted her toe nails a couple of days before, they still looked quite pretty.

"Shall we continue?" Nikita asked. She was having too much fun.

One of her childhood dreams was to become a Bollywood actress but that was never going to happen, so this was the closest she was ever going to get to realising that dream.

They turned the page to the next scene.

"Ah," he said.

Nikita looked at her script. The scene was set in a bedroom and ended with a passionate kiss. The female character tries to seduce the male character trying to stop him from leaving.

Jai looked at her and mumbled something that sounded like, "I think we'll give that one a miss," and flicked on a couple of pages to the next scene.

"It's okay Jai, I don't mind running through the scene with you."

He looked at her, a question in his eyes.

"Really, it's okay. If I get uncomfortable I'll say."

The truth was that secretly she wanted to do it. She'd imagined it so many times, what it would feel like to kiss a man properly, to kiss him properly.

She didn't remember much about that night in the bar with that sweet guy. She'd had too much to drink and before that she'd never had a boyfriend either. Even while she was married, he never kissed her. In a way though, she was glad. When she watched people kiss on TV or in the movies, or when her friends talked about it, she felt it was such an intimate act. It was going to feel nice to kiss someone that she actually liked. Nikita had always heard people say they will never forget their first kiss and she hoped that she would remember this kiss forever.

"If you're sure," he said.

She looked at him and nodded and they started on their lines.

Dev: I'm leaving tomorrow, I won't be back.

Salina: Do you have to go?

Dev: I have to; it's all been set up.

Salina: Is it more important than us? What about what we have together? What about last week? Didn't that mean anything to you?

Dev: You've got a nerve. You're playing games with me, with my heart. If last week meant anything to you, you'd be with me, not sneaking around.

Salina: But I love you.

Dev: You're just saying it, you don't mean it.

Salina: Do you want me to prove it to you? Tell me how and I'll show you.

Dev: You don't need to prove anything to me.

Salina: Then why do you have to leave Dev? I can't live without you.

Dev: Don't make this any harder than it already is Salina, stop playing games with me.

The script then said that Salina tries to seduce Dev. Salina unbuttons the top of her blouse.

Salina: Dev I'm begging you please don't leave me, I won't be able to live without you.

Nikita started laughing.

"What's wrong?" asked Jai.

"This script is a little unrealistic. Nobody really feels that way about anyone."

"But it does happen in real life, when two people really love each other, being apart can drive them crazy. Don't you believe in true love?" he asked.

"Shall we continue?" Nikita said, diverting from the question.

Nikita opened the top two buttons of her blouse trying to get into character. She was already showing enough cleavage and now her bra could also be seen. It was a good job she was wearing a crisp white new bra. It would have been embarrassing if it was one of her greying ones. She stared at Jai, deep into his eyes. Nikita pulled herself up onto her knees so that her face was level with his, only inches away. She grabbed his shirt by the chest and said the next line on the script fighting back a giggle.

Salina: I love you.

As soon as she'd said it, something immeasurable washed over her and she immediately regretted what she was doing, but she couldn't stop herself.

Jai put his hands on her neck, stroking her cheek with his thumb. He stared into her eyes.

She felt the same electrical current run through her body again and his soft eyes made her stomach go all funny. All the humour was drained from her face.

Jai's hands ran from her face, down her neck and across her shoulders, pushing the neck line of her blouse over her shoulder as he did.

Nikita had never felt such sensuous, erotic pleasure before. Never been touched like this, even if it was only pretend. She felt her body respond automatically to his touch, no longer an act. She wanted him. But what was that feeling? She'd never experienced it before. This sensation, it was almost overwhelming and it took everything in her not to groan.

Jai leaned in towards her face and she moved in ever so slightly. His lips brushed across hers just for a second, and then he kissed her eyes, her cheeks, her neck. He broke away but leaned his forehead against hers, eyes shut. He was breathing heavy.

God, he was a good actor.

He opened his eyes and kissed her across the lips for a second. Before she had a chance to move, to pull away, to say anything, his mouth was on hers, sweet and tender, soft and wet and before she could stop, it became almost aggressive. Not to a point where it hurt her, but with pressure and wanting and before Nikita could stop herself, she moved her whole body up against his. She pushed against her knees and her breasts were pulled up against the cotton of his shirt.

His hands were tangled in her hair, pulling her in harder.

It was like a bolt of lightning that set something alight inside her, brought it to life. She felt so alive. Emotions and sensations she had never experienced before were now running through the very core of her.

When Jai kissed her, his breath came short and it confused Nikita. It was as though he was experiencing exactly the same.

He wanted to devour her, she tasted so sweet. He told himself to stop but he couldn't. Then when her lips parted, it felt like a dam had opened up and a million emotions washed over him. His tongue pushed between her lips and he tasted the sweetness of her slick mouth. Oh God, so sweet.

His hands were not under his control and they started to move over her shoulders. His fingers slipped under the strap of her bra and he pushed the horrible piece of elastic down the shoulder, revealing gorgeous, lightly freckled upper arms. Her breasts were soft and pink. They seemed to beckon to him, rising up and down at a fast pace. He wanted to put his mouth there. It was so beautiful, so passionate, so hot.

Nikita wanted to rip Jai's shirt off. This expensive designer top, felt like her worst enemy right now. It was the barrier to feeling her skin against his. She wanted it gone. She wanted to trail her hands on his chest, run her fingers over his abdomen and feel the taut muscles she remembered seeing bare this morning. She opened her mouth, allowing him to invade it, letting her tongue intertwine with his. He tasted of coffee and a sweetness that could only be him.

All of a sudden Nikita's senses came back. Her blouse was half way down her shoulders, her neck, her shoulders were bare and you could almost see her nipples poking out.

She broke off. She could feel the heat rise up in her face and she could imagine what it looked like. She couldn't look at him as she grabbed her blouse and pulled it shut with her hands. She quickly got up and made an excuse. "I, I, just need to pop to the loo, I'll be back in a minute." She hurried to the toilet and shut door. She needed to breathe. She couldn't believe what had just happened. She traced her finger across her lips then across her chest and she could smell him on her. She quickly paced over to the wash basin and stared at her dishevelled reflection in the mirror. She looked a mess.

It felt so real, even though she knew it was only part of the script. A stupid, stupid script. Why did she let herself get talked into doing these stupid things?

Nikita leaned onto the wash basin, her knees were trembling. She splashed some cold water on her face, trying to snap out of the trance she felt she was in. She felt a slick wetness between her legs and shame rushed through her. She'd only known Jai a few months and already she was drooling over him.

Nikita used the toilet and cleaned herself up. She couldn't stay in the bathroom forever, she had to face him. She decided to conduct herself as normal as possible and behave like it was all part of an act. Nothing but what the script expected and she delivered.

After about ten minutes she went back out trying to make it look like it hadn't bothered her.

"I'm sorry," Jai said. "I shouldn't have asked you to practice that scene with me. We should have just skipped it."

"It's okay Jai, no need to apologise. Was it okay? I know I'm not a very good actress, but I hope I was able to help," Nikita said as calmly as possible.

"It was great, I really appreciate your help Nik," he smiled.

Help? Yes help, that's all it was, just an employee helping out her boss, nothing more, nothing less.

"Shall we order that pizza I promised you?"

"I don't know, I really should be getting back."

"Stay for a bit, I hate eating on my own."

Nikita was glutton for punishment. He asked and she agreed.

Jai ordered pizza, some pop and some fries for the dinner.

Nikita lectured him on how bad take away food was for him. "You need some good home cooked food to keep you going, otherwise you'll burn out."

"Well I suppose that's what happens when you live by yourself," he grimaced.

"Haven't you seen Tina?" Nikita asked curiously.

He looked at her face with a blank expression.

She didn't know if he was annoyed by her nosiness. "Sorry," Nikita said. "It's none of my business."

"It's okay Nik, you're my friend, you can ask. I haven't seen her for some time. She rings every week, but she's really busy with her businesses. It's more of a long distance relationship even though she only lives a few miles away. Sometimes I don't see her for weeks. It's very difficult."

"But you love her, don't you?" Nikita asked the question more for her benefit than his.

"I suppose so," he replied. "It's just that when we first met, things were great. We spent so much time together, but now, between her businesses and my career, there just doesn't seem to be anytime for love or a relationship. Don't get me wrong, I'm really happy that she's doing well for herself, but I just feel like she's changed or maybe I never knew her before."

"What do you mean?" Nikita asked.

Jai took a deep breath. He looked like he was thinking way back in to the distant past. Nikita watched him silently, waiting for him to continue.

"Tina comes from a very privileged back ground. She's always had everything she wanted and her parents made sure of that," he continued. "Tina will click her fingers and its there. No matter how expensive, her parents always fulfil her wishes."

"But that's good isn't it? She must have a very loving family," Nikita said.

"Yes, she is lucky, but sometimes I feel that she doesn't understand where I'm coming from or my upbringing."

"I don't get it. You're both confident and comfortable people and have great careers."

"Yes, but I took a totally different journey to get here. I didn't have the privileged life that she had. My parents weren't like hers and my family was very poor. Everything you see here is everything I have worked for. That's why I don't go on spending sprees and you won't see me splashing out. I know how hard I've had to work for it and it's not because I'm stingy, or tight, but I just like to be careful," he explained.

"You should be proud Jai, you're a self-made man and your parents must be very proud of you as well."

Jai's face dropped. He looked almost angry and Nikita realised, that maybe she should learn to keep her mouth shut.

"You see, that's the difference, I don't have any parents that are proud of me, our lives are actually miles apart."

Chapter 15 - Please God, please, make it stop

"I must have been about three when I first realised something was wrong at home. I was about five when I learnt that my dad was hitting my mum. My dad hated us. Mum thought I didn't know, but I could hear what was going on every day. I would lie awake in my bedroom at night, with my hands over my ears trying to block out the quarrelling voices. I could hear the slaps and things being thrown around. I hated it. I would bury my head under the pillow and pull the duvet over the top to drown out the sound."

"Dad would come home drunk every night and it frightened me to think about what he might do to me if he came into my bedroom. So when I'd hear his footsteps coming up the stairs, I would pretend I was asleep."

Nikita didn't say anything, she just listened. She was stunned at the disclosure.

When she came here today, she wasn't expecting any of this. Or what had happened less than half an hour ago. Today was one hell of an unpredictable day Nikita thought, focusing back on what Jai was saying.

Jai took a deep breath and his shoulders shook a little.

"My mum used to talk to me about God and she would take me to the Gurdwara every week. She used to say that God listens to everyone and that I should pray. Sometimes when the arguing would get out of control, I would curl up on my bed and pray. Please God, please, make it stop; make him stop, please make him stop and I would be crying my eyes out. But you know what?"

Nikita shook her head. She couldn't say anything. A lump had caught in her throat and she knew if she tried to speak, the words would come out broken. She imagined a timid little boy, kneeling on his bed with his hands clasped together, eyes closed in fear.

"It never did stop," he continued. "God never listened to me and I hated him for it. If there was a God, why would he let my mum suffer the way that she did, why didn't he do anything about it? She was a good person. She prayed everyday and went to the Gurdwara, sometimes several times a week. Yet, she got nothing for it. Slowly as time went by, I stopped believing."

Nikita moved over to Jai and rested her hand in his hand. Jai didn't know why he was telling her all this. He'd never felt comfortable enough to talk to anyone about it. Even Tina only knew the basics, but Nikita was really easy to talk to and once he'd opened up, he couldn't stop. There was something about her which urged him to open up. Something in his heart told him she was the right person to share this with and that she would understand.

"She couldn't speak to the milk man or the post man without my dad making accusations. He would call her all the names under the sun for just smiling at someone. Slowly she cut off ties with all her friends and family to make that man happy, but nothing worked. That's why I don't have anything to do with any of my relatives. Many of my uncles and aunties knew what was going on, but nobody ever did anything to stop it. No one intervened. They just shut their eyes and let it continue. I couldn't do anything to stop it. If I tried to stick up for my mum, he would beat me as well. I remember once he beat me with a belt. After that day my mum would not let me argue with him, she always stood in the way.

"That man would only refer to me as 'bastard'. Whenever I heard him talking about me, I could hear him saying, that bastard this, that bastard that. He never loved me and I hated him as well. He even made me question my mum's fidelity for a while. Maybe he hated me because I really was a bastard. Maybe I was the product of an illicit affair my mum had had and my dad hadn't ever got over it. Maybe that was why he treated her the way he did."

How could Nikita explain to him that it probably had nothing to do with his mum? That violent people were sick in the head. But she couldn't say anything without encouraging Jai to ask more questions about her and she didn't want that.

"When I was about ten years old, I really started to hate my mum. I hated the fact that she never left him and kept me there to listen to his shit. I felt she could have left him but chose not to."

Nikita felt like she needed to say something. "It's not that easy, Jai," she interrupted, her expression dark. "People who go through this don't leave because they're always thinking about other people around them, their family and their community. It's difficult enough for people to walk away from a relationship like that in this day and age. Can you imagine what it was like for your mum? In those days nobody walked away from a marriage, especially not women from our community."

"I know that now," Jai replied. "But at the time I hated her as much as I hated him. I gave her a really hard time you know. By the time I was fourteen, I was bunking off school and I got involved with guys much older than me. They introduced me to drinking and smoking. My mum didn't know what to do with me, but I didn't care, even though I could see how much it hurt for her to see me like that." Jai cast his mind back to how badly behaved he was. "But she never gave up on me, never stopped loving me and now I wish I hadn't behaved like that. I only added to her problems."

"In the end, mum came to realise that I knew what was going on, but when I'd confront her about a black eye, or a cut lip, she would lie to me. She fell down the stairs, or she walked into a door. She could never admit the truth about what was going on." Jai took a deep breath fighting back the lump in his throat. A tear rolled down his face.

"Where is mum now? Do you see much of her?" Nikita asked.

Jai realised that Nikita had noticed he didn't mention her much.

184

"She died nearly fifteen years ago," he told her as another tear rolled down his face.

Nikita reached up and stroked his face across his wet cheek and wiped the tears away in doing so. She grabbed his hand again and moved in front of him on the sofa, kneeling on the floor. Jai wasn't looking up. Nikita dipped her face to bring it level with his and draw his attention. He looked almost broken. This beautiful, confident man seemed beaten and relinquished. Nikita had never seen him like this before and it broke her heart.

"I'm really sorry Jai, I didn't realise." Nikita held onto his hand really tight.

Then Nikita asked Jai about his dad.

"He's not my dad," Jai said, his expression indignant.

Nikita's face dropped, the tone made her jump, although she tried not to show it.

"That man has never been my dad and never will be. He could drop dead tomorrow for all I care and I wouldn't give a shit," Jai grimaced. "He's still drinking a lot and he only ever contacts me when he needs money, but as far as I'm concerned, that man killed my mum. Maybe not by holding a gun to her head, but he may as well have done, it probably would have been less painful than enduring twenty odd years of violence."

There was silence for a while and Nikita stared into his face.

"Just before she died I went to see her," Jai continued. "She looked like she was broken, both emotionally and mentally and given up on life. In a sense, death was a relief for her; she didn't have to suffer anymore. He couldn't hurt her anymore. She spent her last few days in hospital because she had became too ill to be cared for at home. I went to visit her on the day she died. I sat down next to her and stroked her face, but she was just skin and bones. It felt like an old lady's skin, somebody twenty or thirty years older than she was. She laid her hand on top of mine and asked me not to be sad. She told me that she felt so blessed to have me as her son and that I was her pride and joy. She said I was the one thing in her life she had never regretted.

She said she would always watch over me and that she believed in me and my passion to become something. After that, all I remember is, she took a strained breath and then there was nothing. She'd gone."

Nikita took a big gulp trying to fight back the tears. She couldn't start crying, no matter how much she wanted to. This was about Jai, not her.

"I dropped my head on her chest and started crying, but the nurses arrived and pulled me away. I called out to her, 'mum, mum,' but she didn't respond. They started compressions and placed an oxygen mask over her face to try and revive her. I could do nothing."

"Was your dad there?" Nikita asked.

"That bastard was in the pub, too busy drinking. Even at the end, he couldn't be bothered to be there for her. The doctor arrived and checked mum over. They told me she was gone. That was it, I fell to the ground, unable to hold myself up and I cried as I sat in the corner of the room. After a while some family members arrived and they tried to console me, but I didn't want anyone to touch me. As far as I was concerned, they'd all played a part in my mum's death. Nobody did anything to help her. They stood there crying and howling but I couldn't take it. I just exploded. 'Shut the fuck up,' I screamed at them. 'Why are you crying now? When she needed you, none of you did anything to help her and now she's dead you all come running? What the fuck good are you to her now?' I yelled. They all dropped their heads in shame. The nurses tried to calm me down but I ran out of the hospital."

Oh my God. Nikita wanted to hold him. She wanted to pull him close and place his head on her chest, to comfort him, but she dare not. It must have been so hard to lose a parent at such a young age. Devastating. Yet look at how much he had achieved. He was a strong driven man and she felt pride just knowing him.

"I saw mum a couple of times after that at the morgue and then at the funeral," he told her. His face sullen and full of anguish.

"I went out and bought her a yellow sari, because when we went to weddings and parties, she always wore yellow and she looked so beautiful in it. Not many women could carry off a colour like that, but it suited my mum so well. When the coffin was brought home, I opened the sari up and draped it around her. I told her that I had bought it for her with my savings, money that she had given me over the years. I had always planned to buy her something with my first salary, but now that wasn't going to happen."

Nikita lost the battle in fighting her tears. Her nose started to run and as she blinked, her emotions betrayed her. The droplets of pure clear water ran down her face.

"Why are you crying?" Jai asked.

Nikita shook her head, unable to speak. She held onto Jai's hand.

Maybe her reaction to his anger yesterday was because of something similar. He had often seen sadness in her eyes and he recognised it, because he'd seen the same sadness in someone else's eyes. His mum's eyes. Could it be that she had been through the same things as his mum? Nikita refused to talk about it. He knew she had been married before, but she never talked about him or why the marriage had broken down. Maybe this was why. Experience had taught him that it was the most difficult subject to talk about. His mum had never discussed it with anyone either. Even he hadn't been able to talk about it openly until today.

Jai looked at Nikita, deep into her eyes and he could see he had upset her. Her eyes were overflowing with tears and it would only take one blink and those tears would be pouring down her face again. He hated seeing her upset. He didn't know why, but it did something to him, inside. He wanted to hug her, hold her, but he didn't know how she would react. "Have I upset you? I didn't mean to, I'm sorry."

"No Jai, why are you apologising? It's just such a sad story and I'm really sorry about what happened to your mum, but you have to remember that she only ever tried to protect you. She must have truly believed that by not talking to you about it, it would ensure you were kept away from it all, that you were protected. The thing is that family members do turn a blind eye, it happens in our community all the time. They like to brush things under the carpet but they don't realise that the problem never goes away."

Jai understood Nikita was talking from experience and when she was ready to tell him, he would be there for her, just the way she was there for him today. His gut told him she had been through something similar. It was all very obvious now, but every time she confirmed it by alluding to a personal experience, it was like a thump into his solar plexus. He found it hard to swallow.

"I know. I realised that after she died. I felt guilty for a long time because I felt partially responsible for driving her to her death. If I hadn't stressed her out and added to her problems, maybe she would have still been around. I just don't know."

Nikita placed her hands on Jai's cheeks and pulled his face up to meet her gaze. "You must never think that way Jai," Nikita responded. "If anyone is to blame, it's your dad. He was the grown up and he could have controlled his actions, but he chose not to. You just reacted to what was going on around you, you were a child. Don't ever hold it against yourself. Your mum loved you and I'm sure she will rest better knowing that you are free from any guilt. You were the one thing in her life that kept her going, you must remember that."

Jai smiled at Nikita. He felt like she was an angel that had fallen from heaven to come and look after him. He'd never felt so glad and grateful that his previous P.A. had left him, because had she not; he would never have met Nikita. She was a God send.

Chapter 16 - He's Dead

Nikita was so glad when Sunday came around. She was looking forward to cleaning her flat, relaxing and getting some time to herself.

Jazz was visiting friends so Nikita was home alone. These days were bliss. It meant she was able to get things done around the flat really quickly without anyone getting under her feet and she could sit and watch Eastenders omnibus without anyone complaining or disturbing her. Or better still, she could read her book in peace.

Nikita was always an early riser, even on her days off work. If she got up late she would feel like she hadn't had much of a day and before the day had started it would be over.

Nikita cleaned the kitchen, dusted the living room, scrubbed the bath, cleaned the toilet, washed her clothes and then when everything was done, she jumped in the shower. When she'd finished, she spent a few moments rubbing lavender and camomile oil on her skin, pampering herself. Her skin felt lush and moist. She chucked on a clean t-shirt and some old track-suit bottoms. It didn't matter what she wore, because she wasn't expecting anyone and she just loved her lazy days when she could put her feet up. With no underwear to restrict her, she felt relaxed and comfortable. She didn't often get a chance to do this.

Nikita settled onto the sofa and opened her book. She had made the decision she would read Twilight. The film was coming out soon so she wanted to see what all the hype was about.

She adored stories about forbidden love. It's why she enjoyed Bollywood films so much. They were mostly about the hero falling for the heroine, but trouble always got in the way of their relationship. Differences in caste, class or religion. They had to fight for what they wanted. Well, things weren't all that different in reality.

At around three o'clock there was a knock at the door. Nikita was just getting into the book and it broke her train of reading. She cursed under her breath, unhappy about being disturbed. This better be important, she thought. She got up to open the door. It couldn't have been Jazz because she wasn't due back home yet. Maybe it was one of those companies trying to sell her gas or electricity, or one of those religious groups. They often had Jehovah's Witness people knocking on the door. Nikita and Jazz would normally look through the peep hole and if it was, they wouldn't open the door.

Nikita pushed herself up on her tipped toes and looked through the security hole. Shit, Jai was standing there. Nikita froze for a few seconds. What was he doing here? Worse still, she looked like shit.

He knocked again.

After deliberating for a few moments, Nikita unlocked the door and opened it. She was about to give him the third degree for disturbing her on her day off, but something in his expression changed her mind. He looked upset, and she rarely saw him like this.

"Jai, is everything okay?" Nikita could hear that her voice sounded almost frantic, because she was dressed so inappropriately. So much for her lazy, relaxing day.

"I got your details from the agency," he replied in a very low voice.

"You could have called Jai. What was so urgent?" Nikita asked coldly.

"I had to see you; I needed to talk to you."

She didn't like the sound of that. Was he here to tell her that he no longer had a job for her? What else could it be? Nikita felt her body tremble a little as she moved to one side.

"Ummm okay, come in, but you'll have to excuse the mess," she said, even though she'd just cleaned up. It didn't matter what she did to her flat. It would never compare to his beautiful big apartment. It was so embarrassing.

Jai walked in very quietly and her heart sank. The only other time she had seen him so upset was the other day when he talked about his mum. Something had happened and seeing him like this made her feel sad.

"Sit down Jai. Can I get you a tea or coffee or a soft drink?"

"Not yet Nik, maybe later."

Later? Later? How long was he planning on hanging around?

Nikita observed Jai standing in the middle of her living room. His shoulders were a little slumped. His face lowered, not looking up to meet her gaze. She had an appalling sickly feeling in the pit of her stomach and she knew something was wrong.

Frightened at what she might hear, she plucked up the courage and asked him, "Jai, what's wrong? You look upset. Has something happened?"

Jai didn't say anything. He sat down on the sofa and put his face in his hands.

"You're really frightening me, tell me. What has happened," Nikita urged him.

Jai looked up at her, his eyes red.

She couldn't understand what was going on, what could have upset him so much.

He took a deep breath and sighed. "I had a phone call this morning from my uncle, my dad's brother. He told me that... that my dad died in hospital last night. He said it was liver failure." His voice broke as he said it.

Nikita didn't know what to say. She could see that Jai was upset but after what he'd told her about his dad, she didn't know how she should feel.

"I can't believe it, he's dead."

"I'm so sorry Jai," Nikita said as she put her arm around him. "I'm so sorry." Then she let a few moments of silence pass before she asked, "Did he say anything else?"

"Only that they would arrange the funeral and let me know. When he told me I was so stunned, I couldn't think, I didn't know what to say."

Jai's eyes welled up and the tears rolled down his face.

Nikita wanted to reach up and collect them; they were too precious to be allowed to just fall all over the floor. She wanted to hold him, make this unbearable pain a little less if it was possible, but she didn't know if that would be the right thing to do. She put her hand on his back and stroked it gently.

"Are you going to go?" she asked him.

"I don't know. I always thought that I never wanted to see his face again, even when he died. I used to wish that he rot in hell for what he did to my mum, but now that the time has come, I'm not so sure."

He rubbed his face in his hands again, creases in his forehead and he looked very confused.

"Jai, you don't have to decide here and now. I'm sure that it will take a few days for them to make the arrangements so you've got time to think it through."

Jai didn't respond. He looked like he was in shock; he just stared at the wall ahead, not looking at anything in particular.

"I'll make you a cup of tea, I'll be back in just a minute," she said as she walked over to the kitchen.

When she was out of sight she took a deep breath. Pull yourself together she told herself. This wasn't about her, but why did her stomach feel so tight? Snap out of it, she shouted in her head.

Nikita quickly made two cups of tea and went back to the living room. She put the tea on the coffee table in front of Jai.

She sat down on the sofa, turning to face him. "Can I give you some advice?" she asked.

Jai looked at her. He didn't answer.

"If you decide to go Jai, to the funeral that is, I think it would be good for you to take someone with you," she said in a low voice.

192

"I haven't decided if I'm going yet," he replied. "I really hate myself Nik. He treated me like an animal all my life. In fact he treated me worse than an animal. Even animals look after their young. I hate him for what he put me and my mum through." His voice seeped with anger.

"Hey, it's okay," Nikita said, her voice soft and calming. "Your feelings are completely justified, don't feel bad. You didn't ask to be treated that way, you were a child and he was the grown up, he was the one in control."

"But if I hate him so much then why do I feel so sad now that he's gone? Why do I feel so lonely all of a sudden? Why am I getting so emotional? I didn't want to do this."

Jai's fists were clenched and he started to push them against his forehead. Nikita could tell he was feeling very angry with himself. He was trying to control his emotions without success.

She knelt down in front of him and pulled his hands away from his forehead and lowered them. "It's okay Jai, don't punish yourself." She placed her hands on his face. Jai kept his eyes low. "Look at me," she said in an authoritative tone.

Slowly he raised his eyes.

"He was your dad and regardless of everything he did, there will always be a tie that you can never break. Nothing you can do will change that and it's okay to feel emotional and sad, that's normal. You've just lost your dad Jai; you're allowed to get emotional, you're allowed to grieve. If you feel like you want to cry, then cry. Nothing is worse than suppressing your emotions. It will cause more damage than good."

Jai dropped his head and it fell to Nikita's shoulder. She put her arms around him and held him tight. She was careful not to pull her body up against him, it was too painful. Nikita pulled away and wiped his tears and then sat back on the sofa next to him.

Jai noticed his cup of tea on the coffee table. He picked it up and he gulped it back.

They both sat in silence for a few minutes. Nikita could tell that he was deep in thought, but she didn't mind silences. She wasn't one of those people who thought that every minute of the day had to be filled with meaningless words and conversations. It was good to reflect.

"You know, when I was young, one of my earliest memories is of him shouting," Jai sighed. "I remember he used to make my mum take a small empty bucket upstairs because he couldn't be bothered to go downstairs to use the toilet for a piss and she would have to empty it every morning. He would fill it up during the night because he'd have too much to drink. Once I heard her scream and then I heard him going downstairs, I must have been about eight years old. I went to investigate and I walked into my mum's bedroom. She was sitting on the floor, the piss bucket was tipped over beside her and she was soaked. The smell was so strong. It was wet on the floor, on the bed and all over her clothes. She looked up at me and you know what she said?"

Nikita shook her head.

"She said it was an accident, he didn't mean to do it. I couldn't believe it, she was still defending him. I ran back to my bedroom and I could hear her calling, but I didn't stop. I locked the door behind me and buried my head in my pillow. I was so angry, I started punching it. I cried and I cried. I just couldn't see an end to it. But I suppose now, it has ended."

Nikita let that hang for a moment and then she spoke. "What your dad did was unforgivable. He made your life miserable and nobody can blame you for hating him, but he was still your dad and no matter what he did, you loved him. I see that now. But that doesn't mean you had to like him. Sometimes our loved ones behave in a way that we don't understand and they hurt us the most. We hate them for it, but for some reason, we still love them."

Jai didn't say much after that, he sat in silence.

After a while Jai asked if it was okay for him to lie down on the sofa. Having not slept all night, he felt drained and it probably wasn't good for him to be alone right now anyway.

194

Nikita contemplated offering him her bed, but then decided against it. Instead, she grabbed him a pillow and a blanket and put them on the sofa. He took his shoes off and lay down.

"Get some rest," she whispered.

"Thanks Nik, you've been a good friend."

"Don't mention it, that's what mates are for, right?"

Jai raised his mouth from one side, struggling to smile. Nikita stared at him with empathy. It brought back so many memories for her; his dad was just as bad as the bastard in her life.

Jai closed his eyes. She stared at him for a short while. When she heard the low rhythmic murmur of his breathing, she got up and walked over to the armchair picking up her book. She didn't want to do anything that might disturb him so she sat in silence and continued to read.

After an hour or so, Jai started stirring; he looked uncomfortable in his sleep. Nightmares weren't uncommon under these circumstances. Anyone would suffer with them if they had just been through what he had. Nikita got up and took a few steps towards him. He looked hot, his face red and clammy. Nikita stroked his forehead and it seemed to calm him down. But as her hand left his face, Jai turned to his side and grabbed it. She tried to shake it off lightly but couldn't. She twisted and turned her hand but he had such a strong grip. So she sat down next to him on the floor still holding his hand and carried on reading her book.

After a while Nikita had developed pins and needles in her legs but she still didn't get off the floor. She tried to move her toes in her slippers making an effort to fight off the prickly feeling.

She stared at his hands and they were beautiful. His fingers were thick and strong and they looked like you could find heaven in them. How would it feel to have those hands running over her body? Nikita stared at his beautiful and perfect face. There was the shadow of stubble on his chin which she'd never seen before. He was always clean shaven, but there was something very sexy about this look.

Nikita gave herself a mental slap. What was she thinking? She felt ashamed of herself. He had just lost his dad and here she was, yearning for him.

Nikita's only experience of men was a nightmare, which still continued to haunt her, even after all this time, so why was she thinking about Jai like this? Being touched by Sam caused bile to rise from the pit of her stomach, just thinking about it made her body shiver.

Like Jai, Sam was also very beautiful, but underneath all that beauty, lived an evil monster. Surely Jai wasn't like that. But then what did she know? She was no relationship expert and she obviously wasn't very good at reading people either.

Nikita leant in closer, unable to help herself. She looked at every contour of Jai's face. She felt his warm breath on her skin and it smelt intoxicating. Today he wasn't wearing aftershave, but there was a sweet scent coming from him, a natural clean smell. She never thought she would ever feel this way about anyone, but there was something very enticing about him.

Nikita looked at her watch and it was almost seven o'clock and getting dark outside when suddenly, someone came crashing though the front door. It was Jazz. She made so much noise, it woke Jai up.

"SShhhhh," Nikita whispered loudly, as Jazz walked in but it was too late and she was completely drunk.

"It's okay Nik," Jai replied from behind her.

"Oh shit, sorry, sorry, sorry," Jazz mumbled as she banged into the coffee table and headed straight to her bedroom.

Nikita turned around and Jai was already sitting up. He looked a little startled. "I'm really sorry Jai, it's just Jazz, I think she's had a few too many."

"Don't worry about it; it's time I was getting off anyway. I've taken up too much of your time already," he replied.

"It's no problem, Jai. Why don't you stay and have something to eat," Nikita asked. "It's getting late and you probably don't feel up to cooking."

"I don't think I can stomach anything right now, but thanks for the offer."

"Umm, okay, but if you need to talk, or anything else, then call me. I'll be in tomorrow anyway," she said trying to keep her voice level.

"Okay, I'll see you tomorrow. I'm sorry I disturbed your Sunday."

"It's okay Jai, no problem at all," she replied back.

Jai put his shoes on, folded the blanket and placed it neatly on the sofa. Nikita followed him to the front door and he turned to face her.

"I wish you would stay a little while longer and have something to eat. It's not a good time to be alone Jai."

"I'll be okay Nik. I think I need some time to myself anyway. Got some thinking to do."

He looked at Nikita as though he wanted to say something more and she looked back at him in anticipation. He opened his mouth, hesitant, maybe looking for the right words, "Bye," he said and lowered his gaze.

"Bye," Nikita replied with her heart in her stomach. She watched him walk down the corridor. She wanted him to turn around and look at her and if he did, she would have run to him and thrown her arms around him. He didn't turn around and she would never have really followed through on her thoughts.

Chapter 17 - Bitch

The dreaded phone call came on Monday. Jai's uncle informed him that arrangements for the funeral had been made for Thursday that week.

Jai asked Nikita to cancel all his meetings for that day. She guessed that meant he was going.

Nikita heard him make a call to Tina. Nikita wasn't being nosey, but Jai wasn't being discreet either.

"Hi Tina," Nikita heard him say. "How are you?" he asked and then there was a moment's silence. "I was wondering, would you come to the funeral with me on Thursday? I could really do with having someone with me." There was another silence as he listened to Tina's response.

Nikita would have given anything to be a fly on Tina's wall right now. As she discreetly watched, she saw Jai tense, his posture stiffened.

"But he was still my father and it's the only way I'll gain closure on that part of my life, I need to do this," he grimaced. Then silence followed.

Nikita didn't understand why he had to explain his decision to her. Tina should just support him, whatever choice he made.

"Well, okay fine, you carry on with your work and I'll do this on my own, thanks a lot," he said sarcastically. Then he slammed the phone shut. Jai sat with his face in his hands.

There was so much frustration in his voice. From what Nikita could make out from the snippets of conversation she'd heard, Tina was telling him not to go. She doesn't understand him at all. Nikita would have offered to go herself, God knew she wanted to. She would have helped him get through the day, but it wouldn't have been right for her to attend, it wasn't her place. Who was she? What was she to him? People would have asked questions. She knew what the community was like. However, Tina could have gone, she was his girlfriend. Some girlfriend, Nikita thought to herself. If Jai was hers, she would have gone with him. She would have held his hand and stood by him. She would have hugged him and kissed him until he felt better. But he wasn't hers, so thinking in this way was a waste of time.

***

Jai was getting ready in the morning when Nikita arrived.

"I don't know what to wear," he said as she walked in. He was nervous and uncomfortable.

Nikita had never seen him like this before. Her heart broke just a little for him.

"Hey, hey, hey, it's okay. Take five minutes, here, sit down," Nikita said, ushering him to his bed. She sat next to him placing her hand on top of his. She could feel him shaking.

Jai closed his eyes for a moment, taking in a deep breath urging himself to calm down. He was so agitated and restless. He hadn't slept all night worrying about the faces he would see. His mum had also crept into his thoughts, which gave him some comfort.

As Nikita felt Jai calm, she stood up. "You should wear all black," she said. "Traditionally that's the colour that men wear at Indian funerals," she commented, rummaging through his wardrobe.

Jai had a black Prada suit and a black shirt so she pulled out both.

"How long has it been since you've seen any of them?" Nikita asked reading his concern.

"I haven't laid eyes on most of them since my mum's funeral and I wasn't the nicest person to be around at the time either. I blamed them all for her death and I didn't even look at my father while I was there."

"I'm sure they all understood your reasons for feeling the way that you did and forgiveness won't even have come into the equation," she said, reaching up and straightening his tie.

Jai stared down at her. He grabbed both her hands from around his neck. She met his gaze.

"What?" she asked.

Nikita could feel a blush creeping up her face and her heart started pacing faster.

"You always know what to say to make me feel better. Thank you; you've been a good friend. I couldn't have got through this without you," he said with a soft smile.

She could have melted in those dark amber eyes but she bit her lip to mask her smile. Her knees went weak but she held herself stern, not allowing her body to reveal the way he made her feel.

"Mention not," she said trying to be casual, impersonating one of the famous Bollywood movie lines and he smiled again.

"Here," Nikita said passing him a bandana. She'd bought one a few weeks earlier, a plain black one. She liked to wear it on one of those frenzied cleaning days. It kept her hair out of her face.

"What's this for?"

"It's for the Gurdwara. If you decide to go, you'll need to cover your head while you're there. Don't worry, it's clean, I washed it last night. I thought you may need it."

Jai folded the bandana up and put it in his pocket.

"Thanks again."

Nikita wanted to wish him well but what did you say under these circumstances. 'Good luck?' 'Hope everything goes well?' In the end Nikita gave him a hug and said, "I'll be thinking of you." It was the most appropriate thing she could think to say. But having said those words, Nikita knew the truth. She knew that she would have been thinking of him anyway, no matter what the reason.

Jai took a deep breath and picked up his car keys from his desk. He set off at ten o'clock. His dad's coffin was arriving at his uncle's house at twelve o'clock before going to the crematorium.

Jai had given Nikita the rest of the day off so she went shopping. She bought the next book in the Twilight saga, 'New Moon' because she really needed to know what was going to happen next.

She bought a sandwich from a bakery and took it home for lunch. Chicken, bacon and sweet corn, her favourite. Along with that she bought a small iced bun, which always reminded her of her school days. It was the one cake that she always bought. School days were happy times for the most part. Nikita carried with her memories of her friends, her teachers and the smiles that blessed her during those years.

Slipping off her shoes and pulling her feet up onto the sofa, she opened her book.

She was absolutely in love with Edward Cullen. He was like the ideal man for any woman regardless of the fact that he was a blood sucking vampire. He was also only seventeen so Nikita felt like a bit of a pervert thinking about him in that way, but that wasn't enough to stop her from falling for him. She knew he was only a fictional character but it felt good to get so engrossed into the story and for a short while, she could forget about all her worries.

After a while, Nikita found it difficult to concentrate. She was worried about Jai. She kept glancing at her watch, thinking to herself, the coffin will have arrived at home now and they would have gone to the crematorium now, they'll probably be at the Gurdwara now. She wasn't sure if he would attend the religious ceremony at the Gurdwara after the cremation, especially after what he had told her about his childhood. She kept looking at her phone in case he called and needed to speak to her, but there was nothing, no missed calls, or texts.

She struggled on, reading until five o'clock that evening but she couldn't take it any longer.

If he wasn't home yet, then she would wait for him. He was most likely going to be distressed and she wanted to be there for him, even though she knew she shouldn't let herself get so involved, but she couldn't help it.

Nikita put a book mark between the pages she had read up to and then put the book on her dressing table. She grabbed her keys and drove over to his apartment. She had the front door key but wasn't sure if he'd be home. So even though she hadn't seen his car in the underground car park, at first she knocked and waited. There was no answer, so she took the key out of her pocket and opened the apartment door. She walked in and looked around. She could still smell his aftershave lingering from the morning and it made her fingers tingle.

She sat on the sofa and waited. He didn't come.

After a while she got up and thought she'd make something for dinner, maybe he would be hungry when he arrived home. She rummaged through the cupboards and found the ingredients to make some cheese pasta. By this time, she was quite hungry so she ate a bowl full herself.

Nikita sat back on the sofa and started going through some letters and other post. A lot of it was junk mail so she put them to one side.

Just then Nikita heard someone turning the key to the apartment door. Her heart started pacing, her hands started tingling and then as she looked up, Tina walked in.

"What are you doing here?" Tina asked in an angry tone.

"Oh, err, I'm just sorting out some paperwork for Jai," Nikita said trying to stay calm.

"Yeh right, whatever," she said in her cocky voice. "Where is he anyway?" she grumbled. "I called him but he didn't answer."

"Umm, he's not back yet," Nikita replied. Obviously he wasn't going to answer; he was at his dad's funeral she thought to herself.

Tina walked around the apartment towards Nikita. Nikita pretended to carry on going through the mail, but she could feel Tina's eyes burning at the back of her head.

"How long have you been working for him now?" she asked.

Nikita wasn't sure why she was asking, or what it had to do with her, but she replied anyway. "It's been a few months now."

"Enjoy it, do you?"

"Yeh, it's okay."

"Looks to me like you're enjoying it more than just okay," she said in her sharp voice.

Nikita tried to ignore her. She didn't like confrontations and it felt to her like Tina was looking for an argument.

"I've met many girls like you before," she groaned.

Nikita became agitated. This girl really was looking for a fight. Had she been drinking? She didn't even know Nikita and she was trying to judge her. Nikita decided she wasn't going to stand there and let Tina say what she wanted.

"What's that supposed to mean?" Nikita challenged.

"You know what I mean," she snarled through gritted teeth.

"No, I'm sorry but I don't. Would you care to elaborate?" Nikita felt a pang of guilt. She did enjoy her job, she liked working for him and she liked him more than she should. But it didn't matter, because it wasn't like she was trying to steal him from Tina or anything. Those feeling were Nikita's, they were private to her. She didn't go flaunting herself at him, she didn't ever bitch about Tina and so, Tina didn't have a point.

"Do you really think that he would choose someone like you, over someone like me? Look at you and then look at me," she growled.

Tina was very beautiful; she had the perfect lean figure, long straight brown hair and beautiful skin. She looked like the type of girl that if she visited Bollywood, they would snap her up for a movie in an instant. She also had a point, Nikita was nothing compared to her. In fact she was totally the opposite.

"Look Tina, I don't know what you're going on about, but I'm just trying to do my job," Nikita said, trying to keep her voice level.

"Don't give me that," she said in an angry voice. "They have a name for women like you and its bitch."

"What did you say? How dare you speak to me like that? I don't get paid to take shit from you. You've seriously got a problem." Nikita yelled back.

"Oh really, is that why your husband beat you, because you were trying it on with his friends as well. Women like you never change."

It hit Nikita like a bolt of lightning. She felt the same pain in her stomach as she did when Sam put his fist in it. Nikita couldn't breathe. She was stunned for a moment. Where was all this coming from? She couldn't believe how all this venom was just spewing out of Tina's mouth.

"You know nothing about me," Nikita screamed back.

"I know enough. Jai told me that your husband beat you and to be frank, I don't blame him. That's what women like you deserve. You think that you can tell him these stories and you can work your way into his arms, but he's got more class than that. He's not interested in used and abused second hand products," she shouted. "Look at the state of you. You look like a trollop. What did you do when you left home? I know all about your type. Women like you do anything for money and one man isn't enough for you, is it? If you know what's good for you, you'd better quit this job and forget about Jai. He belongs to me, get it?

Nikita's head started to spin. These accusations were slicing through her like a knife. How could a woman be so cruel to another woman? Even someone like Tina who had always had the best in life, surely she would have some compassion. Nikita couldn't believe how uncaring and cold this woman was and she felt betrayed. Jai had been talking about her behind her back. How could he? She had always tried to be a good friend to him and this is how he repaid her. She thought he would have understood, he had always shown empathy towards her. However, now Nikita knew that he had been discussing her business with Tina and probably been laughing at her.

Nikita could hold it together no longer. She grabbed her bag and ran out of the front door. As she left she saw

Jai coming up the corridor. He looked tired and drained, but she couldn't stop. Tears were streaming down her face and she ran passed him.

"What's wrong Nik?" he yelled at her from behind, but she didn't turn around and left to go home.

Nikita went straight to her bedroom and fell onto her bed. She cried uncontrollably. She hadn't cried like this in a long time but at the same time she knew Tina was right. Why would he be interested in someone like her, when he liked women like that? Women with perfect bodies and perfect faces, strong minded, career driven and wealthy.

Nikita wanted to curl up and die. It made her think about that bastard and the things that he used to say to her. Maybe she did deserve it. Maybe she wasn't good enough for Jai or anyone else.

Chapter 18 - The Funeral

Jai was so tired driving back from the funeral. All he kept thinking about was how much he wanted to see Nikita. He even thought about passing by her flat, but that would have made him look desperate. He really missed talking to her. He also knew if he spoke to her, she would help him feel better. His thoughts were selfish he knew, but he couldn't help it. He should be thinking about Tina, but the first person he thought about once he'd left the Gurdwara was Nik. Why did he feel this way? He wasn't really sure. He had been with Tina for nearly a year but he'd never felt so desperate to see her in the way that he felt about Nikita. What would she have been doing all day without him? Would she be waiting at the apartment? He really hoped that she would. He wanted to call her, but he fought with himself not to. He'd pulled out his mobile phone and typed a text message to her at least twice today, but deleted them before he'd sent them.

It was a very long day. Most of his family seemed shocked to see him there. When he arrived at the house there were so many people there. He walked in and noticed that everyone had removed their shoes before entering, so he took off his shoes as well. He walked through the crowd and entered the living room. Jai didn't recognise many of the people here. The way that women were crying seemed so exaggerated. They were making howling noises which annoyed him. They didn't need to prove to everyone that they were mourning for his dad.

The coffin had been placed on a stand and the lid had been removed. He walked towards it reluctantly and stared into the wooden box. His dad lay there in peace and that made Jai angry. He had got away with everything he had done and now he was at peace. It just seemed so unfair.

Jai's uncle grabbed his arm and pulled him towards the foot of the coffin. He told Jai to touch his father's feet, the way that tradition dictated.

The lid was then replaced and Jai's uncle told him to get to the front of the coffin to help carry it out to place it in the funeral car. His uncle and others also helped carry it. After placing his dad in the car, he went back in the house to put his shoes on.

Jai got back in his car and took a deep breath. He put his hands on the steering wheel and squeezed until his knuckles had gone white. He didn't want to cry, but every part of his body was urging him to. He felt his muscles twisting in his stomach and he felt his heart break. He always thought he hated his dad, but today he realised that even after everything that had happened, and even though he was still so angry with him, he still loved him.

He followed the funeral car to the crematorium. He didn't like being there, but he sat through it anyway.

After the service, Jai's uncle informed him that everyone was heading to the Gurdwara. There was going to be a religious ceremony to bless his dad's soul. That's if he had one, Jai thought. Jai reluctantly agreed. It was the final part of his duty towards his father and then it would be over. Closure was what he was looking for.

Nik had thought of everything. If it wasn't for her Jai would have been looking for a head scarf at the last minute. It had been so long since he'd been to a Sikh temple, that he had totally forgotten that everyone had to cover their heads. She was a life saver. His angel.

It felt really weird at the temple. He could feel everyone staring at him when he walked in. He chose to sit in a quiet corner of the large community hall and listened to the readings from the Sikh holy book. Even though he didn't understand everything that was being read out loud, listening to the words helped him feel a surge of contentment. He felt calm listening to the words from these ancient scriptures.

Moments later, his peace was disturbed as he heard the insensitive gossips on fire. There were girls who were looking over at him and giggling. Even on a day like today, it didn't stop them. He chose to ignore them. Jai did what he had to do and left as soon as he could. He couldn't wait to get back home, back to his life.

Would she be there? He wondered. Maybe, just maybe she might be waiting to see him.

When he arrived at the apartment, he saw Nikita's car. After the day he'd had, it was such a relief to know that she was there. He was right; she wanted to see him as much as he wanted to see her. He quickly parked up and ran to the lift. As he walked through the corridor he saw Nik. She was crying. She ran passed him and didn't even look at him. He called after her. "Nik, what's wrong?" She didn't turn around. Jai walked into the apartment and Tina was standing in there.

"What's wrong with Nik, Tina? Why is she crying?" he asked.

"Why does it bother you so much if she's crying?"

"That doesn't answer my question."

"And you didn't answer mine," she yelled back. She crossed her arms and was staring back at Jai waiting for him to respond.

But what was he supposed to tell her, that he'd been thinking about Nikita all the way back home? That he couldn't wait to see her?

"She is my employee and I care about her. So, I'll say it again, I want to know why she is upset. Did you say something to her?"

"And what if I did? I know what she's up to and the bitch is not going to get what she wants," she moaned.

"Tina, how can you say that about her? She's a good person and I wouldn't have been able to get through the last few days without her. You couldn't be bothered."

"Oh get over it. You should be happy that man is out of your life for good. It's a weight off your shoulders. Why would you be stressed about it?"

208

"You will never understand what it's been like for me, and there's no point in trying to explain it you any longer. Tell me what you said to her."

"Well I told her straight and I put her in her place."

"What did you say?" he repeated, each word starting to seethe with anger.

"I told her that you weren't interested in her. But she got cocky with me so I told her a few home truths. I told her that I knew about her marriage and women like that sleep their way to get what they want. They never change."

"You did what? I told you about her in confidence. It wasn't your place to say anything to her."

It all made sense now. This is why Nikita was so upset.

He had Tina all wrong. He thought she was different from other people and for a while there, Tina had him fooled, but not anymore. She had shown him her true colours and he didn't like what he saw. He had to end this now. "You know what; I can't be with a person that has such cruel intentions."

"What's that supposed to mean?"

"It means that I don't want to be with you anymore. I needed you now more than ever over these last few days but you proved to me that your work comes before me. And what you put Nikita through today is unforgivable. I want you to leave," he told her.

How could she have done this? It was so cruel, knowing what someone had been through and to use it against them. It was so wrong on so many different levels.

"Whatever Jai, I can see she's obviously worked her tricks on you and you've fallen for them. She's been used and abused, so do you really want to be touching her? Who knows what she's carrying. I wouldn't touch her with a barge pole."

These comments infuriated Jai even more. How dare this woman speak about Nikita in that way? It took all of Jai's will power not to lash out at Tina and with the day that he had had, he didn't have much patience either. "Give me the apartment keys and get out Tina," Jai almost growled. He was fuming.

Tina threw the keys at Jai and stormed out of the apartment. "You'll come back crawling," she shouted over her shoulder as she left. "And I won't be interested, just remember that."

He took in a deep breath. Now he understood why Nik was so upset. He had to call her.

Crying on her pillow, Nikita had fallen asleep. It was just after seven o'clock and her phone started ringing. Waking up startled at the disturbance, she grabbed for the hand set from her bag. 'Jai' was flashing on the face it. She couldn't answer, what would she say? Maybe he was angry with her for getting into an argument with his girlfriend, the girlfriend that knew too much about her. How could he do this to her? She'd hardly told him anything about herself, yet she knew that he'd worked it out, but that didn't give him the right to go blurting it out to every Tom, Dick and Harry he knew. She'd trusted him. He'd broken her trust. You can't rely on any man she decided. How dare he discuss her past with some stranger? The phone started ringing again and Nikita pressed the reject button. She didn't want to talk to him.

Deep down Nikita was worried about what Jai might think of her for arguing with his stupid girlfriend.

The phone started ringing again and she pressed the reject button again.

The next morning having slept on it, Nikita had calmed down a little but she still wasn't in a forgiving mood.

She wasn't sure whether she wanted to go back and work for Jai, so she called in sick, to buy her some time to think and clear her head. That was the good thing about working for an agency. You didn't have to call the client; the agency took care of everything. She called Tabitha and made up an excuse about stomach cramps due to the time of the month. Tabitha was okay about it, after all, this was the first time Nikita had called in sick since they had employed her. Tabitha didn't question her. After calling Tabitha, Nikita switched off her phone.

Jazz popped into the bedroom to see Nikita wondering what had happened. It wasn't normal for Nikita to be at home, when Jazz left for work. Nikita filled Jazz in on the eventful day she'd had in the presence of Tina.

Jazz was fuming. "I would have slapped her, the stupid stuck up bitch. Who does she think she is, speaking to you in that way?"

"Jazz," Nikita said, "Calm down."

"That's your problem Nikki, you don't fight back," she screamed. "You lecture me day and night about having confidence and self belief and yet you let that bitch get away with it!"

"Jazz, why would I fight back, when there's nothing to fight for?"

"What are you talking about? Don't you get it? She feels threatened. That's why she had a go at you. And don't tell me you don't know what I'm talking about. I know how you feel about him; I've seen it in your eyes. I've also seen the way that he looks at you."

"You're deluded, it's pity, nothing more," Nikita said in a low voice.

"I think you're wrong," she continued.

"And I think you're wrong," Nikita replied.

"We'll see," she said.

Nikita ignored her.

Jazz sighed and sat down on Nikita's bed.

"Look, I have to go to work now. I have a really urgent meeting that I can't blow off. If I could have given it a miss, I would have done. But I've been working on this report for weeks now and the presentation is today. I'll be back as soon as I can."

"Don't be silly Jazz, I'm not a baby. Go to work and don't rush back."

"I'll see you later. Call me if you need me, okay?"

"Okay," Nikita replied and she slumped back onto her pillow.

She lay there for a while and when she couldn't go back to sleep, she decided to get up.

She had a quick wash but then couldn't be bothered with breakfast, she wasn't hungry. She made a cup of tea and sat down with her book, but that didn't help her at all.

211

Reading about Edward leaving Bella, depressed her further. This was all she needed, another tragic love story. She put the book to one side and switched the TV on. She sat there for the next hour staring at it, but she couldn't tell you what she was watching because nothing was sinking in.

Just then there was a knock at the door. She wondered who it could be. She wasn't expecting anyone. She switched the TV off and sat quietly hoping whoever it was, would go away. Then they knocked again and this time it was much louder. She cursed and went to open the door.

She pulled the door open in annoyance and looked straight into Jai's desolate eyes. Nikita stared at him for a moment noticing his slumped shoulders and troubled face, and for a split second she felt her anger dissipate. It was what he did to her. But she held herself firm. She wasn't going to let it waiver. She was angry and she needed it to stay that way.

"What do you want?" she asked in a bitter voice.

"The agency rang and said you were unwell," he said.

"And that concerns you how?"

"Nik, you have every right to be angry. I'm so sorry," he said genuinely. "Tina had no right to speak to you like that."

Nikita's voice softened. "You had no right talking about me to her Jai, no right at all. I trusted you and you let me down. How could you tell her? That was my pain, those were my experiences and it wasn't up to you to go sharing them with others, no right at all."

"I didn't," he justified.

"Well she seemed to know a lot for someone who hadn't been told anything," Nikita said sarcastically.

"Look, I got the feeling she wasn't happy about you working with me, so I told her to give you a break. I told her that you had been through a lot in your previous marriage, that's all. She must have put two and two together. I promise I didn't betray you, honestly."

Nikita looked at his face and she could see the sincerity in his eyes.

"Come back to work," he begged.

"I don't know Jai. She said some things that really hurt me and I don't know if I can be around someone like that. What if she turns up again? I won't be able to hold my tongue next time and it will cause problems between you and me."

Nikita was careful not to refer to them as us, there could never be an 'us'. There was a 'you' and there was a 'me', and it had to stay that way, even though her heart ached for him.

"Well, I don't think I can be around a person like that either."

Nikita looked up at him in surprise.

"She used what happened in your past, none of which was your fault, against you and that's a very cruel thing to do. I know how difficult it is to deal with something like that. You blame yourself enough without other people telling you the same thing. It was really horrible of her to say those things to you, but you don't need to worry, she won't be saying those things again. She won't be coming around anymore. I can't spend my life with a person that is so vicious. I guess I never really knew her."

Guilt laced Nikita's emotions. "Maybe she was right Jai. She had her reasons for saying those things."

"I don't care, no matter what the reason; you don't stoop to that level and anyway, I know why she said those things."

"You do?" Nikita said, her eyes widening.

"Yes. We get along and we're good friends, we look out for each other and she was jealous," he said explaining his theory. "You know what, I let her choose my clothes, my work, where I went, but I'm not going to let her choose my friends as well. I'm not going to let her control my life anymore," he moaned.

Those words were the same words Nikita told herself when she left that bastard. She vowed he was not going to control her anymore.

"Friends?" he asked holding out his hand.

Nikita stared at his hand for a few moments. Oh, how she wanted to take it. Jai had started to penetrate every pore of her being and it frightened her. But would she be able to survive without him? She already thought about him every minute of every day. She knew she may end up regretting her actions, but she'd made her mind up. "Friends," Nikita replied, taking his hand.

This was followed by an awkward silence and Nikita reached for the one thing that had saved her so many times before. "Tea?"

"I'd love a cup," he replied.

Nikita went into the kitchen and Jai followed her in. She could feel her heart racing again and she wished it wouldn't.

He stood in the doorway of the kitchen leaning against the frame.

"Would you like spiced Indian tea or English?"

Jai thought about it. When was the last time he had drank Indian tea? "I haven't had any spiced tea since mum died."

"Sorry," Nikita said. "I didn't mean to bring back the memory."

"That's okay; it's good to remember her. I've spent so much time trying to forget the past that I haven't been thinking about mum either. I'll have spiced tea," he said with a smile.

He watched Nikita as she pulled out the spices, whole cloves and cardamoms and started to crush them with the handle of a knife.

She could see him staring at her through the corner of her eye.

"How was the funeral?" she asked. As soon as she'd said it, she knew it was a dumb question. How would a funeral be?

"It was difficult," he replied. "I didn't recognise half the people there, everyone's changed so much. They're all so grown up."

"Did you see dad?"

"Yeh, the coffin was there when I arrived. They had taken the lid off and I saw him for the first and last time in years. He looked so old. I know they wanted me to get there early so that I could help wash and dress him, but I couldn't. I couldn't bring myself to do it. Not because I had an evasion to bathing him, but we just never had a personal relationship. I felt as though I would be invading his privacy and I know he wouldn't have wanted that. Then the women were wailing so much as well. I felt like telling them to shut up."

"I know," Nikita said. "What's that all about? They always over do it." Typical.

"The family had dressed my dad in a new suit, the type he used to wear all the time, because no matter where he was going, he always dressed smart. Maybe that's why people never believed he could do the things he did. They saw him as a model citizen, smart, good looking and he was always the life of the party. A party wasn't a party unless he was there but my mum hated them. She dreaded it when people came round with invites. These functions always had free booze and mum knew what would follow once they got back home."

Jai's expression was sad and Nikita wanted to put her arms around him and tell him it was going to be okay, but she didn't have the courage to.

She poured the tea into two cups and carried them into the living room.

Jai followed again and they sat down on the sofa.

"When we were at the crematorium, my uncle told me I had to go down and put my hands on the coffin as it moved into the cremation chamber."

"Oh, that couldn't have been easy for you," Nikita said.

"I wasn't sure I wanted to do that. If I agreed, would I be pushing him in to fulfil my duty as a son? Or would I be pushing him in so that he couldn't come back? I was scared that I would feel good about doing it."

After a few moments, Nikita urged him to continue. "Go on."

"It was so confused. I didn't know what I was feeling. Then I realised, I didn't want to push him in, I wanted him back. As much as I hated him and no matter how many times I had wished him dead, for once I wished he was still here. I wanted to say so much to him, I wanted to scream at him and yell at him, and tell him how he had made me feel, but I guess I'll never get the chance now."

Nikita remained quiet for a moment, looking for the right words to say. She could see that Jai was in pain. He was struggling with himself. His forehead creased with lines that she'd only ever seen when he was anxious. When she could think of nothing else, she settled on saying, "You have to let it go."

"I know, I know. They wanted me to go to the Gurdwara and I was about to leave to come back home, but then uncle said that they were going to say a prayer for both my mum and dad. So I decided to go, for mum's sake."

"She would have been proud of you," Nikita said, placing a hand on top of his.

Jai turned to face Nikita and smiled, but it didn't reach his eyes.

"It's been years since I've been inside a temple. It felt a little odd. I got this de ja vu feeling. There were so many people there. I can't believe my dad knew so many people. We hardly ever had visitors when I was younger. Anyway, I did my bit and people came over to me and passed on their condolences. I didn't even know who many of them were. This one person came over and commented on how unlucky I was having lost both my parents at this age. I stared at him in shock. He said that I had bad fate. It was like he was blaming my fate for my parent's death. I almost leaped up and punched him. My uncle placed a hand on my shoulder to keep me calm. He must have seen the change in my expression. Some people are such arseholes."

Nikita really didn't have anything to respond with this time. She knew how old fashioned and backward thinking people could be from experience and she loathed people like that.

"My uncle wanted to tie a turban on me. He told me it was an old custom, but I didn't want it, so they just handed it to me. I know they wanted to give me my dad's status. They told me I had to because I was next in line, but I didn't want it. I wasn't going to live my life like him.

So I had some food while I was there. That was my favourite part when I was younger. When mum would make me go to the Gurdwara, I always looked forward to the food and the rice pudding was my favourite."

Nikita felt warmth travel over her body. It felt good listening to Jai opening up and talking about himself. She guessed he probably didn't have much opportunity to do that. Even though he looked sad, there was a sense of relief in his face.

Suddenly, Nikita felt very small and selfish. After the day Jai had had, she had made it even more stressful for him. She felt ashamed.

"I'm really sorry Jai. You had such a tough day yesterday. You needed support and a listening ear when you retuned. Instead you came home to what happened between Tina and me. It was so selfish of me."

"Don't you dare take the blame for what happened yesterday," he said with no hesitation. "I know it wasn't your fault. In fact, I was hoping you would be there, because I needed someone to talk to when I got back. Then I saw you running down the corridor in tears, you really worried me. When I got in, I saw Tina standing there. She looked so angry. She just stood there, glaring at me and all of a sudden all these accusations were flying in my direction. She didn't even care about where I had been. I asked her what she had said to upset you and she told me. I know how upset you were, so I didn't want to trouble you. I thought I'd wait for you to come in to work this morning, so that I could talk to you, but when you didn't turn up, I had to come and see you. I couldn't leave things the way they were." Jai took in a deep breath, before saying the next few words. "I'm really sorry she said those things to you, but she wasn't right you know."

"Right about what?" Nikita asked in low voice.

"That used and abused thing, because you're not," he replied. "I hope you realise that."

Nikita looked away ashamed and embarrassed. She developed a lump in her throat and her eyes pained and filled with tears. She didn't want Jai to see her like this.

217

Nikita thought back to the argument and all the things that Tina had said to her. Nikita was guilt ridden. Sam had made her feel like dirt and Tina had reaffirmed it to her. It made her feel like she wanted to rip the skin off her bones. She wanted to claw her eyes out, so that she couldn't see herself in the mirror anymore and feel ashamed.

She was nothing compared to Tina. Maybe that was why Sam treated her that way. Would he have behaved in the same way, if Nikita looked like Tina? No way. She was way too beautiful for any man to treat her badly. Maybe this was the fate of any girl that was ordinary like her.

As if Jai read her silence, he lightly placed his hands on her face, like she was made of glass and if he put any more pressure on, she might break. He pulled it round towards him, resting his forehead against hers. She could feel his warm breath against her skin. His sweet breath with the slight scent of cloves and cardamom spices from the tea.

"You're a beautiful, intelligent and a loving woman and never let anyone tell you otherwise."

Nikita smiled fighting back the uncontrollable urge to throw her arms around him. A man like this was a dream. Was she dreaming? How could someone like him, say what he just said, to someone like her? She took in a deep breath and filled her lungs with his scent.

"Have you ever seen that film, 'Shallow Hal'? The one where a man hypnotizes Jack Black into thinking that those big women are beautiful," Nikita asked.

Jai looked at her confused, "Yeh, I saw it years ago."

"Well are you sure no one has hypnotized you? No one has ever called me beautiful before. I think you need to get yourself checked out."

Jai let out a low chuckle. "You're absolutely mad, but that's what I like about you."

Another awkward silence followed.

He was all business like again. "Anyway, I want you back at work tomorrow, bright and early, otherwise I'll report you to the agency and tell them you've been bunking off," he smiled.

"Okay, okay, I'll be back in the morning," she laughed.

Nikita spent most of the evening with a beaming smile on her face.

Jazz returned from work and she knew something was up as soon as she saw Nikita. She looked hard at Nikita's face. "I knew it; he's been in touch hasn't he?"

"So what if he has," Nikita shrugged, as though it didn't mean anything.

"I told you he liked you, didn't I," she grinned.

"Jazz it's not like that, we're just good friends."

"For now," she replied cheekily.

Nikita rolled her eyes, but deep down inside she smiled.

Chapter 19 - The Trip

The next morning Nikita was up at the crack of dawn. To be fair she hadn't slept, she was too excited. She knew she had to remain calm, otherwise she was building herself up to be let down, but she couldn't help herself. She got ready and arrived at work very early. To her surprise Jai was already wandering around.

"Morning," she said as she walked in. "You're up bright and early."

"I could say the same for you," he said taking a sip of his steaming hot cup of coffee. "Anyway now that you're here, we have a trip to plan."

"A trip? Where to?" Nikita asked.

"I've been invited to a film event in Bradford. They want me to present an award and then they've invited us to the VIP party. They've sent me an invite, me plus one, so you're coming too," he said.

"Mmmm, I don't know if that's a good idea," she mumbled.

"Is there a problem?"

"No it's not that. It's just..."

Jai didn't let her finish. "What's wrong? Do you know someone there that you don't want to see?"

"No, no, it's nothing like that."

"Well, that's settled then. I need my P.A. with me; it's a great opportunity to network with people."

"But, where are we going to stay," Nikita asked.

"Well that's up to you. You're the P.A., book us into a hotel," he replied.

Nikita picked up the invite and sat down by the computer. She punched in the keys and typed in Google to search for hotels near the venue. There wasn't much available, nothing at a reasonable price anyway, but that didn't matter because Jai could afford something a little more up-market. Nikita booked them into the five star Bradford Country Park Hotel which had a restaurant situated by a lake. It looked stunning.

From a very young age, Nikita had been a huge fan of Bollywood movies and music. She had watched hundreds of Indian films and craved to see some of her favourite actors in the flesh. But the opportunity had rarely arisen and when it had, she didn't have a choice. Every so often, the Bollywood stars would head to the U.K. in concert. When she asked if she could go, her parents would always put her off, saying she could attend after she got married. After she got married, it was so out of the question that she didn't even dare to dream about going.

However, today there was a silver lining. Nikita imagined what it would feel like to spend two whole days with Jai. This beautiful, eloquent and gifted man. She had begun to recognise every curve of his face, the solid firmness of his chest and those piercing amber eyes. A shudder ran up her spine, just as heat started to stir in the lower part of her stomach and she blushed self consciously. To quash the feeling she directed her thoughts back to the possibility of meeting her teenage crushes and she became quite excited. Imagine if she got the chance to meet Hritik Roshan or Shah Rukh Khan? Two of the hottest Bollywood stars in the industry today. Oh my God, she would just faint! She'd probably start babbling if she tried to talk to them.

Focus, she told herself. She was letting her mind wander off again. There probably wasn't going to be any big names there anyway, except for Jai of course, so she had to keep a lid on it. She wouldn't embarrass him.

Jai went off into his bedroom.

"Jai," Nikita called from the living room.

"Yeh," he called back.

"You know you said there was going to be a party? What's the dress code going to be? It doesn't really say on the invitation."

"Umm, I don't know, I suppose it will be a black tie and cocktail dress event. The normal stuff, you know?"

Oh shit, Nikita thought to herself. She didn't really have anything to wear. Not a cocktail dress anyway. She'd have to go shopping and get something quick.

"Why do you ask?" he said as he walked back into the living room.

"Well, because I don't have anything to wear and I've never been to a place like this before, it's quite nerve racking."

"Don't stress over it too much. Hopefully it will be quite informal, but grab something nice just in case. We'll get a better idea when we get there, from the people that attend."

There were still a few days to go so Nikita had time to get used to the idea and build up some resistance to the nerves.

"Look, here's my credit card, get something for yourself, my treat," he said politely.

"No thanks," she replied, the words coming out a little sharper than she meant them to.

"Sorry, I didn't mean to offend you. I just thought that I could get you a gift for being..... such a good friend."

"It's okay, you didn't offend me, it's just that I don't want you to go wasting your money on me like that. Anyway, I do have a job you know, I can afford to buy my own clothes thank you very much," Nikita replied with a grin. "My boss pays me very well," she smiled.

"It wouldn't be a waste," he said as he smiled back.

The next few days flew by so quickly. Nikita went shopping and bought a beautiful outfit. She was looking forward to spending a couple of days with Jai away from work. She knew this whole trip was work but it felt like a mini holiday. She was so happy all week, she couldn't stop smiling.

Nikita couldn't believe how her life had turned around. For once she felt like she was in control. There was no one telling her what to do, where to go, or who to see. It was her decision and her decision alone. She had a great job, a boss that she adored and the freedom of choice. It didn't come much better than this.

With her packing done well in advance, she didn't have to rush on the morning of the journey. Jai was also packed and ready to go.

The plan was to leave early, giving them enough time to make it to the press conference at eleven o'clock.

Nikita was looking forward to the drive to Bradford. When she was younger, she loved the long distance drives, listening to music in her car, when her dad wasn't there of course.

She found it very relaxing.

If she was honest, she was looking forward to the conversation with Jai, three hours of uninterrupted chit chat. Jai had a great sense of humour and she found that she had laughed more with him in the last few months than she had in a long time.

They talked about their childhood memories, her dad's businesses, her love for Bollywood films and everything else except for the time after she'd got married.

Jai talked about his school crushes, his first kiss with a girl he had met at a day time disco, which he skived off school to attend.

She found it so easy to talk to him, he was a good listener.

Jai put the radio on and searched through the different frequencies. When he stumbled across a music channel he left it on. Nikita didn't recognise the song that was playing, but that was because she only ever listened to Indian music. She rarely watched MTV or Top of the Pops.

"You'll like this song," he smiled.

"Mmmm, I don't recognise it," she said.

"It's that guy, from the book you're reading."

Nikita was a bit confused. "Which guy from which book?"

"The book you were reading, the vampire story, you know the one," he explained.

"Oh, you mean Twilight?"

"Yes, that's the one. Well their making the movie and the guy who plays the main character, Robert Pattinson, this is him singing one of his tracks."

"Oh, okay, what's the song?"

"It's called 'Broken', you'll love it."

Nikita listened to the lyrics and at first they were difficult to make out. There was so much emotion in them and she was already in love with Edward Cullen anyway, but Jai didn't need to know that. Now he was singing this song with so much passion. Well not Edward exactly, but that was what she was picturing in her head. She listened carefully.

I was broken for a long time
But it's over, but it's over now

Nikita felt touched. It was such a beautiful song and to hear it coming from an equally beautiful person, made it sound even better.

Jai thought about Nikita and the path that she had been on. He didn't know for sure, didn't know the detail, but he knew in his heart what she had been through. When he looked at her, something he couldn't comprehend pulled at his heart strings. Seeing her face made him smile and nobody had done that to him before. She intrigued him. When she spoke, he found her captivating. She was so smart, yet child like at the same time. She balanced both so well. He genuinely hoped that things were turning around for her.

Jai tried to bite his tongue but he had to ask. "Well? Is it over?" he said in low sombre voice.

Nikita looked over to him thinking about how to respond to the question. "I don't know," she said. "Maybe not just yet, but I'm working on it."

"That's my girl," he winked, before turning his head and concentrating on the road again.

Nikita grinned. It felt so nice to hear those words and she silently smiled to herself again quickly looking out of the window hoping he wouldn't notice. She wanted it to be over. She wanted so badly to put that part of her life behind her, but would it ever? Only time would tell.

Nikita realised they were nearly at their destination when they passed by the big iron statue, the Angel of the North. She had only ever seen pictures of it before, so it was nice to see it with her own eyes.

When they arrived at the rear entrance of the awards venue, they pulled up to the electronic gates which had heavy security. Jai showed his invite and the guard smiled and ordered for the gates to be opened. As they entered the large hall, Jai was offered drinks and was pointed in the direction of the finger buffet. Nikita was feeling parched as well and Jai pulled her along towards the food.

After they had refreshed, a young man with a clip board came over to ask Jai if he was ready for interviews. The press were interviewing different artists. Some were musicians and others were actors. Nikita looked around and she could see people being interviewed with huge video cameras, recording equipment and microphones. Jai was interviewed a few times as well.

Before long, two young radio presenters approached Jai wanting to speak to him, but they said their interview was a little different and wanted to know if Jai would be up for it. They explained that it was like a fast buzzer round and he had one minute to answer as many questions as possible, except he had to choose one of two options they were giving him.

This should be fun, Nikita thought to herself.

The girls were from a local radio station and were quite amusing. Nikita could see that each of them kept glancing at the other and giggling. It made Nikita feel a little uncomfortable and although she didn't want to admit it, she also felt a little jealous. But she didn't have anything to be jealous about. It wasn't like Jai was her boyfriend or anything, and neither was he was flirting with them. Then one of them said she was about to start and asked Jai if he was ready.

"Yes," he replied looking a little nervous.

"Okay, here we go then," the girl said and she switched the microphone on and her mini disc player onto record.

"Hi, this is Ambhi and you're listening to Radio Vibe. We're in the Bradford stadium at the Film Fare Awards and we're here today interviewing one of the newest and hottest actors on the scene, Jai Singh. Hi Jai, tell us what you think of the atmosphere here today?"

"I think it's great and I'm looking forward to the awards ceremony tomorrow," he replied nervously.

"That's great, are you ready for our teaser questions," she asked in an overly bubbly voice.

"Umm, yes?"

"Okay, here we go then, your minute starts.........now".

"Bath or shower?"

"Shower."

"Leather or lace?"

"Lace."

"Romantic or action?"

"Romantic."

"Angelina Jolie or Shilpa Shetty?"

"Hmmm Angelina Jolie."

"Arnold Schwarzenegger or Sylvester Stallone?"

"Oh that's easy, Sylvester Stallone."

"Beer or spirits?"

"Beer."

"Fish and Chips or Curry and Rice?"

"Curry and Rice for definite."

"India or England?"

"England of course."

"G-string or Y front?"

"What? Neither."

"Love or lust?"

"Love."

"Ahhh," Ambi said, as she found herself drifting in to those dreamy eyes.

"Bhangra or Pop?"

"Mmm Rock."

"Front or back?"

"What?" Jai asked.

"Front or back?"

"Front or Back of what?" He asked confused.

"Of whatever you want it to be," crooned Ambi.

"Oh my God, you're trying to get me into trouble aren't you?" Jai smiled.

"I'm going to have to push you for an answer."

"Okay, okay," Jai said, rubbing his chin. "Front."

"Right, this last question is a little cheeky, but I'm sure all your fans want to know," Ambhi babbled.

Jai swallowed.

"Boobs or bottom?"

"What? Oh, I don't think I can answer that one," he smiled.

"Boobs or bottom?" she asked in a higher pitched voice.

"Okay, okay....... heart," he smiled.

"That's cheating," Ambhi laughed.

"Well, you didn't tell me that in the rules," he said cheekily and then he winked at Nikita. She was in stitches listening to this. It was a great interview.

"Thank you Jai for taking part in our teaser questions and for being so brutally honest," she finished.

"My pleasure," he said and he smiled.

The rest of the day drifted by with more interviews and questions and by the time it hit six o'clock, Nikita was really tired. Jai continued answering questions and smiling for a while longer, even though Nikita could see the tiredness in his eyes.

There wasn't much else to do for the rest of the evening. The award ceremony was taking place the following day and the party after that was going to be a late one as well. The plan for tonight was to have dinner and then to get an early night. Tomorrow was going to be a very long day.

Nikita's hotel room was a couple of doors down the corridor from Jai's. She wasn't able to get two rooms next to each other because the hotel was mostly booked up due to the event. It didn't matter anyway. She was more comfortable with the distance.

Chapter 20 - The Truth

Jai invited Nikita to have dinner with him and she was happy to oblige. It was better than eating alone and it felt nice to have some time alone with him, which wasn't work related.

Nikita opened her small suitcase and pulled out her makeup and red dress. She spent a long while back at home, contemplating if she should bring this dress or not. Was it too much of a bold statement? Was it too loud? Jazz persuaded her otherwise and now she had no choice but to wear it. She hadn't brought anything else with her to wear to dinner.

Nikita sat in front of the mirror, staring at herself. Placing her fingers on her face, she pulled at the skin under her eyes. Were those wrinkles she could see? She took a deep breath and let it out. Who was she kidding? Nobody would be interested in her, let alone a man as beautiful and handsome as Jai.

Nikita pulled out her concealer and spread some under her eyes. The dark patches were a reminder of the sleepless nights that she had been having of late. Nikita sighed and carried on applying the foundation. She applied just the right amount of makeup, kept a fresh looking face, with her lips plumped up using dark red lip gloss. Nikita stood and appraised her reflection in the mirror. This was the best that she had ever looked. Her hair was glossy and her skin glowed with the bronzer brushed across her cheeks. She looked good in the red dress, even if she did say so herself. She slipped on her little flat sandals, popped in the red crystal earrings and headed out the door. At least, he won't be embarrassed to be seen with her. She actually looked okay.

As Nikita arrived in the restaurant of this five star hotel, she looked around for Jai but couldn't see him, so she walked over to the restaurant reception desk. "Good evening. Could you tell me if Jai Singh has arrived please?" she smiled.

"Certainly madam. He is seated in our VIP area. Please follow me."

Nikita followed nervously.

"Here we are madam," he said, pulling out the chair.

Nikita walked around from behind the concierge and what she saw, almost took her breath away. She paused to take in the looks of this stunning man before she smiled and sat down.

"Your waiter will be with you very shortly. I hope you enjoy your evening sir, madam," he said as he nodded at each of them.

Jai couldn't help staring at Nikita. She looked stunning. He had always been attracted to her, but tonight she looked exquisite. The red dress looked magnificent on her and it fit her like a second skin. It showed off her voluptuous breasts, her small waist and her curvy butt. How was he going to take his eyes off her? Nikita sat with grace and elegance. He could tell she was nervous, as it was clearly written on her face.

Where have you been all my life? Jai was so drawn to this lovely woman, he felt like she had some sort of invisible magic magnet. I'm a dead man, he thought. He had fallen hard this time. When he looked at her kind face, he felt like he had to know everything about her. See everything of her. He had to have her, all of her and he knew what a dangerous thought that was.

What was he thinking? Shit. He was getting in way over his head. This girl trusted him and he was mentally undressing her? He felt ashamed. He pulled his thoughts out of the gutter and back in the room.

"Can I get you a drink?" he asked managing to keep his voice calm.

"I'll just have a soft drink. A diet coke if that's okay?"

"Are you sure, you wouldn't like anything stronger? They serve some really good quality French white wine, won't you have some?"

Nikita pushed her hair behind her ears, feeling the stare from Jai's eyes, piercing her. "No, I'm fine thank you. I don't drink at all," she said nervously.

The waiter came over and Jai placed the drinks order.

"Have you ever had lobster?"

Nikita shook her head.

"They have it on the menu; would you like to try some? It's magnificent."

Nikita smiled, "I don't mind trying it."

Jai placed the food order as well.

While they waited for the food to arrive and after a few moments of awkward silence, Nikita decided she'd had enough of the awkwardness. The whole evening would be ruined otherwise and she had learnt too many lessons in life to allow the nervous tension to ruin it. Life is too short not to take every opportunity to be happy.

Nikita started to talk about the interview that was held earlier on in the day and she tried getting the real answers out of Jai, but he wasn't having it.

"So which one would you have chosen, boobs or bottoms?"

"I can't tell you that."

"Oh come on, we're mates remember, you can tell me."

"No way Nik, I'm not going there."

"Go on, please," she smiled.

"That's not fair. You can't say that with those big brown eyes and not expect me to give in. Okay, I tell you what, if you answer the question, then so will I."

"You want to know whether I prefer boobs or bottoms?"

"Yes. Well you can have an opinion on it."

"Okay, if I tell you, then you have to tell me your answer. Agreed?"

"Okay, agreed."

"Okay, I think that my boobs are my best asset." Nikita watched him, almost challenging him with her eyes. "Don't you dare drop your gaze."

"I wasn't going to, not without your permission anyway," he laughed.

Nikita smacked his shoulder and then crossed her arms across her chest, covering up her assets.

Jai struggled trying not to let his eyes drop, but what he didn't tell Nikita was that when she crossed her arms, it just plumped her breasts up even more and it was all he could do, not to look at the cleavage between the beautiful plunging neck line of her dress.

"Come on then, I gave you my answer, now it's your turn."

"I can't believe we're having this conversation. Anyway if I was forced to make a choice, I would choose boobs as well, quickly followed by bottoms. I like both," he grinned.

"Jai, you're such a cheat. I'll let you have that one."

The food arrived and Nikita had to watch Jai to see how to eat it. The lobster was delicious. It was a messy dish but that was okay, Nikita still ate comfortably, napkin tucked down the front of her dress, pulling it down and revealing even more of her breasts, not that Jai minded. As she ate, a piece of lobster fell down the front of her top and landed between her breasts. Nikita had to reach down to pull it out.

Jai's eyes widened. "Would you like me to get that for you?" he asked cheekily.

Nikita's face turned as red as the sweet chilli sauce on her plate. "I'm sure I can manage." She smiled feeling like an idiot.

Jai peeled his eyes off her cleavage and looked back at his plate, starting to feel heat rise in his entire body. Under the table, parts of his anatomy started to harden. Shit, he had to get a grip.

Nikita's breathing became deep, and she hoped that Jai wouldn't be able to tell. She had to change the subject and quick.

"Let me ask you another question and you have to tell me the truth."

"Okay, but only if you answer my question now. I'll be totally honest with you, never lie to you, I promise, but answer me this."

Nikita knew what he was going to ask. She straightened up having cleaned her mouth with her napkin. She couldn't look at him. She'd been waiting for this question but wasn't expecting it here. She guessed he'd held off from asking for so long and she never really told him. Not what really happened to her.

"Ask me," she said in a low voice.

Jai moved his chair round the table, next to hers and he put his hand on top of her hand. "What did he do to you Nik? What happened?"

She looked up at him, sadness written all over her face. She knew that she could tell him anything, she trusted him. She also knew he would understand what she had been through, but it still didn't make it any easier to speak the words.

"Can we go somewhere quieter?"

Even though they were in the VIP lounge, there were still many prying eyes. Nikita didn't want to do this in front of anyone. Jai's reputation could be affected.

Jai held onto her hand and stood up. He led her outside, to a quiet seating area which was sheltered at the back of the restaurant. Heaters warmed the canopy so it didn't feel cold. They sat down on the conservatory furniture which was placed stylishly in this beautiful country style room. The sofas were very comfortable.

Jai stared at Nikita and waited for her to answer.

She took a deep breath. She met his gaze and then looked away before she began.

"My parents introduced me to him and I didn't have a choice. Everyone thought he was wonderful and that I had struck gold to have someone like him interested in me. They said we were the perfect match. The problem was that he wasn't really interested and he only went through with it because his parents wanted him to. I suppose that meant neither of us were happy."

"I tried really hard to make it work, I really did. But, I couldn't. He didn't love me. In fact, he hated my guts. No matter how hard I tried, or what I did for him, he was never satisfied." God, she couldn't believe she was telling him this. How was she ever going to live this down? Telling Jai that she was married to a man who never loved her. How embarrassing.

"Did you tell your parents?" Jai asked.

"I couldn't. I felt so ashamed. I just couldn't admit to them the truth about what was going on in my life. I felt like I had failed them."

"But it's not your fault Nik. It was him."

"I know that now, but at the time, I felt like I was doing something wrong. I thought it was me. I changed everything about myself to please him." Nikita sighed again, taking a deep breath before continuing. "Then he started beating me, which became a regular occurrence. If the bruising was on my back or my legs, where others couldn't see, I would still go into work. I hated being at home. But if they were visible, I'd have to call in sick."

Nikita felt Jai stiffen and his grip on her hand got tighter.

"He would argue with me and say that I was miserable all the time. He hated that I was never happy. He would ask what was wrong with me. Can you believe that? After everything he did to me, the way that he was treating me, he blamed me for being withdrawn and introverted. Once he said to me, 'I know your mum phones you while I'm not around and tells you about her problems and she stresses you out. You take it out on me. It's not my fault that those bastards are having problems.' I hardly spoke to my mum, he would always get angry when I was on the phone to her and so I tried not to phone her too often. Then when she called and he was around, I would lie to her and make excuses to get her off the phone quickly."

"If anyone ever told you there was no hell on Earth, they were lying because I was living in it. I cried myself to sleep every night. I burned every day. I felt humiliated, hurt and miserable every day of my life with him. I couldn't see a way out. I thought about the different ways I could end my life, but I never had the guts to go through with it. I'd go to work and I would smile and laugh and joke with my colleagues but as soon as no one was watching, my face would become expressionless again, the way it was most of the time. Lying next to him made me cringe and when he touched me, I felt like dying."

Her voice was so pained, Jai felt as though his heart was breaking. He just stared at her face, thinking about what to say but the words just wouldn't come to him.

"Then one day, we had a really bad argument. He said some really horrible things about my mum and I couldn't bare it anymore. He was shouting at me and he called my mum a bitch and something snapped inside me. I yelled back at him and I told him I hated him. It was the first time I had vented how I really felt about him. He beat me really badly that night and almost killed me."

Jai raised his hand and run his finger across the scar on Nikita's face.

"He did that too," Nikita said, fighting back the lump in her throat. "When he had his hands locked around my throat, I actually felt grateful because I thought that it would be over, I wouldn't have to suffer anymore." Nikita closed her eyes, as if to push away at her nightmares, but she had opened the flood gates and she couldn't close them anymore.

"Then I woke up in my bed and I realised I was still alive. That's when I decided I had to escape. That night after he had raped me and fallen asleep, I ran out of the house. I just ran and I ran and I ran."

Jai put his arm around Nikita and the tears came streaming down her face. "I called the police for help and they took me to a refuge and that's where I met Jazz and the rest you know."

"Hey, its okay, you're safe now." Jai tried hard to console her.

"He made me question everything about myself. He made me believe that I was useless and I started to question my ability in everything that I did. Even though my parents were strict, I was still happy, but after I got married I was so miserable. I felt like my life was nothing. I dedicated it to getting through day by day and just surviving it, not living it."

Jai didn't know what to say. He was so quiet. He wiped away Nikita's tears and he pulled her towards him. She laid her head on his shoulder, his body exuded warmth and affection.

"I'm sorry Nikita. Not knowing was driving me crazy but now that I know, I don't know which is worse," he said. "I've brought it all back for you haven't I? I know I've been selfish." Jai pulled his hand up to Nikita's face and he stroked it.

"It's okay, Jai. Other than Jazz, you're the only one that I've ever told about what happened. It feels good to be listened to."

Nikita felt like a weight had been lifted off her shoulders. Calmness settled over her.

They sat outside for a while longer, neither of them saying anything, but Jai didn't let her go. With Jai, even the silence felt right.

A cool breeze brushed over Nikita's face but she didn't shiver. She felt warm and content where she lay. That strong hand brushing over her face in a soft caress. She was sad, but she felt exhilarated. She had just shared her darkest secret with this man and he didn't loath her. He was still holding her and it felt wonderful.

Nikita thought about their conversation earlier, about the song they had heard on the drive over. She was surprised at how perceptive Jai was, even noticing the books she was reading.

It felt nice to have someone notice you; it was the little things like this that made her....... She stopped in her train of thought. She was doing it again, letting her mind wander and start dreaming about things that were impossible in her life and she annoyed herself.

Jai noticed the change in her expression.

"What's wrong?" he asked.

"Nothing, I was just thinking about the song that was on the radio earlier, the one you pointed out."

"Yeh, he's a great singer, isn't he?"

"Yes he is. But I was thinking about how long it's taken me to get to where I am today."

"Well, I can tell you that. It took just over three hours to get you here today," he laughed.

"Shut up, you know what I mean," she moaned.

"I'm sorry, I'll be serious, I promise," he said as he grinned.

"It's been two years now since I left him and I haven't even had the guts to send out the divorce papers. I've been more worried about what my parents will think and I haven't visited them in ages either, because I know the pressure it place on them. How am I going to tell them I'm filing for divorce?"

"Well, I could come with you if you want," he said trying to be helpful.

"Sure, that would be a great help," she said sarcastically.

"I know that it won't be over until I break all ties with him. I know that physically and emotionally there's nothing there, but that piece of paper still ties me to him and I can't stand it."

"A friend of mine practices in family law. You can speak to him and he will start the proceedings, if that's what you want. You won't have to worry about the cost, he owes me a few favours anyway," he said.

"Thanks," Nikita replied, "I might take you up on that offer."

Nikita didn't want to talk about it anymore so she changed the subject.

"So Jai, tell me about your first assignment as an actor."

"Oh my god, that was such an embarrassment."

"Sounds like there's a story in that, tell me more, I like stories."

"It's just a boring story."

"Jai, nothing you say could ever be boring. Humour me."

Jai smiled as he watched Nikita wipe the last of the tears from her face.

"Well, it was a small budget film and I only had a five minute role in it, but I was so excited because it was my first break into mainstream films. I told all my friends about it. I even went to the premiere of the film. They'd informed me of the date for the screening and I got all smartly dressed up and turned up to walk down the red carpet. But when I got there and I watched the movie, I realised they'd edited my role out of the film completely. It was so embarrassing because nobody even knew who I was. I'll never forget that day. The director never told me and I turned up like an idiot."

Jai was laughing about it now but Nikita could imagine it probably didn't feel that way at the time.

She liked to listen to his stories; some of them were so different to the world she lived in.

After more conversation and coffee, they walked back to their hotel rooms. Nikita's room came first as they came out of the lift. She pulled the keys out of her bag. There it was again, another awkward moment and she could tell he had a similar look on his face. "Good night," she whispered, looking up at him.

Jai leaned down and kissed Nikita on the cheek. He lingered for a second.

Her eyes closed as she became engrossed in his scent. She could have grabbed him and pulled him into the bedroom and she wanted to, but she couldn't. Jai pulled back and stared into her face. She watched him as his eyes followed down her arm and wrapped his hand around hers.

"Everything's going to be okay you know, I have a good feeling about it," he said quietly.

Nikita could have melted there and then. Her heart was in her stomach again, her knees were shaking. Her chest was pounding. She couldn't understand it; it was like he wasn't of this world. She'd never met anyone like him before. Not that she'd had much experience with men, but after hearing all those stories from the other women in the refuge, men like this just didn't exist.

"Good night," he said and Nikita pushed her door open.

"See you in the morning," she mumbled and she closed the door behind her.

Jai walked into his room. He was tired but he felt so agitated. He'd given up smoking long ago, but he felt like he needed a cigarette right now. He needed something and he was trembling without it.

How could she have such an effect on him? It was so easy to love her. His relationship with Tina seemed like such hard work, but this just seemed so easy. There were no complications. It was just her, as she was, a ray of sunshine. She brightened his day just like a sunflower.

He knew Nikita had been through a lot but he also knew he could help her deal with it. He could make her happy and protect her. He wanted to protect her. He felt possessive over her and no woman had ever made him feel that way. Just the thought of someone else looking at her, made his blood boil. She had to be his.

Why was he feeling like this? Was it because of his mum? Was it because he was trying to make things right, where he had not been able to when he was younger? He thought about it for a while. Was it guilt? After some thought, he came to the decision that he could not imagine his future without her. She had become such an integral part of his life. He didn't have to think about it, it was just there.

When she told him this evening, what that fucking bastard had done to her, it made him so angry. It took all his inner strength to keep from yelling out. What kind of a sick sadistic bastard did this sort of thing? How could he do this to her? She was so gentle, compassionate and kind, always looking to help in any way that she could and this is how he treated her.

Jai could feel the rage building up inside him again, thinking about that bastard's hands all over her.

This beautiful, generous woman aroused him. Just looking at her made him want her. He wanted her so badly, but he knew he would have to wait. After what Nikita had been through, he did not know if she would ever let a man near her again. But he was sure she liked him too. She trusted him. Why else would she be so honest and share everything with him?

He could not stand it. He was pacing across the hotel room. He thought about going to her bedroom. He imagined Nikita lying there on the bed, with the covers kicked off. He could visualise the shape of her curvaceous body, her beautiful breasts, and her cute little feet. He wanted to touch her face, to run his fingers across her stomach, make her feel so much passion that she would experience euphoria. But he wanted her to want him too. Did she? He walked over to the door, he needed to see her. He turned the handle and stood there for a moment but then decided against it. It might upset her. He was out of control and he needed to calm down. He needed to rest.

In the end Jai decided on a cold shower and tried to get some sleep.

Chapter 21 - Dreams

Nikita struggled over to the bed having slipped her sandals off and collapsed onto it. She could see her chest rising and falling quickly. What was wrong with her? No matter how hard she tried, she kept making a state of herself.

She lay there a little while longer and cast her mind back to the dinner with Jai. She thought about some of the conversations they'd had and she laughed to herself. She turned onto the front of her body and buried her face into her hands. She felt embarrassed even though there was no one there. She felt excited, even exhilarated and her heart was pumping hard in her chest.

After a while, once she had calmed down, she changed into her pyjamas, brushed her teeth and removed her makeup before getting back into bed. She tried to get some sleep, but it was very difficult. The bed was not the most comfortable but her body was tingling as well. It felt strange and it was agitating her. She was trembling; she'd never experienced anything like this in her life. She guessed that if she was on drugs, this is what it would feel like to have an addiction. To want more and not be able to get any. Except a drug addict knew what they wanted. What did she want? If she was honest with herself, she knew the answer to that. Jai.

There was a knock at her bedroom. Worried about who it could be at this hour, Nikita hurried over and opened the door.

Jai stood in the doorway, his eyes frightening. She could see deep into his soul and she could tell he was fighting hard to keep control. He stepped into Nikita's room, and shut the door behind him, never taking his eyes off her.

"What are you doing?" Nikita asked quietly. Her heart was pounding and her breathing came ragged.

"Something I should have done a long time ago."

Before Nikita could blink, his mouth was on hers, licking and stroking her, tasting her. There was a hunger to this kiss, which was almost primal. His hands were tangled in her hair, pulling her in deeper, wanting to feel the full softness of her mouth. He wanted to devour her.

Nikita kissed him back with just as much intensity. The kiss sent a sharp sensation straight to her stomach which intensified her emotions. More, she wanted more was all she could think. She grabbed at his clothes and started to tug at them. There was nothing she hated more right now than these horrible pieces of material, which created a barrier between her and him. She wanted the clothes gone. Nikita pushed her hands underneath Jai's t-shirt, touching him, feeling him, stroking his skin. Her hands were warm from the heat building like an inferno deep down in her core.

They fell back onto the bed and there was an unbelievable sensation running though her body. She didn't want to let go. His teeth scraped across her neck and she started to move with him. The sensation was so extreme that she begged him to take her. "Please, please Jai, please........."

Then she woke up, her whole body sweating. She had been dreaming. She was almost panting and out of breath. It had felt so real.

Nikita picked up her mobile phone from the bedside cabinet and checked the time. It was still too early to get up. She fell back down onto her pillow and stared up at the ceiling. It was such a vivid dream. How was she going to look at him later? It was awkward enough as it was and now she was going to keep having flash backs of this dream. But it was a lovely dream, she let herself reminisce.

***

There was no need to rush in the morning. The award ceremony was not due to start until later in the afternoon and the VIP party was taking place straight after, so the plan was to chill out for a while.

Nikita knew she wasn't going to be comfortable in one of those cocktail dresses so she had gone shopping and bought herself a sari to wear. She knew that she wouldn't be alone. After all, this was an Asian event, so she assumed others would be wearing saris as well, but she didn't know how Jai would feel about it. She hoped he wouldn't feel awkward walking with someone dressed in traditional Indian wear.

Some people felt uncomfortable in their own traditional clothes.

Nikita thought back to her early teenage days, when she would get changed out of her school uniform as soon as she got home from school. She had to wear traditional Indian clothes and then she would go to the park to play. Some of the other Indian girls would pick on her. They said her clothes were embarrassing and they wouldn't ever be seen dead in them. Still it never bothered her and her white English friends were fascinated by the way she dressed. Her bangles, her big hoop earrings and her anklets that jingled. Every time her parents travelled to India, they brought back bags full of goodies.

It was funny really. You often thought that it was people from different communities that showed prejudices but in Nikita's experience, it had always been the Indian girls that made life difficult for her and they made her feel like an outcast. Yet here she was today, about to dress in an Indian sari through choice, because it felt comfortable.

She got washed and dressed into casual clothes, pushed her hair back with a head band and sent Jai a text message on his mobile.

Mornin, im up, let me knw whn ur redy 2 go 4 breky, Send.

Five minutes later, there was a knock at the door and the memory of the dream came rushing back to her. Nikita took a deep breath as she reached for the door handle. She squeezed her eyes shut, prayed for her heart beat to calm down, bit back the hysterics she could feel rising and opened the door.

"Hey," he smiled. "You should have just come and knocked on the door."

He looked beautiful. His hair was still wet from the shower he had just taken and his dark amber eyes reflected a fire like glaze. Nikita wanted to melt into those eyes.

"I didn't want to wake you," she explained.

"I've been up for ages; I was waiting for you to get up."

"Okay, shall we go?" She asked staring at his face grinning from ear to ear. She couldn't help herself.

"Yeh, I'm feeling quite parched, need to get some coffee down me. Come on, let us grab some food."

The morning flew by so quickly. Jai and Nikita talked about their childhood memories, old school friends and movies. Nikita felt so comfortable around him, like she'd never felt before with him or anyone else. She didn't feel as though she had to have makeup on all the time, or her hair had to be perfect, it was just nice being around him.

After a while they went back up to their hotel rooms to get ready. Nikita knew that it would take her a couple of hours because she was going to have difficulty tying the sari by herself.

Jai walked straight passed Nikita's hotel room. "I'll see you at three o'clock, okay? That should give us enough time to get there," he said as he rushed by.

"Okay, I'll be ready," Nikita shouted back while waving.

This wasn't good for her. All she could think about was Jai. At work or at home, in his presence or not and now even in her dreams. Her life had been completely swarmed by this gorgeous, talented man. Nikita realised this would probably drive her crazy.

Oh well, right now she needed to get ready and she would have to worry about Jai at a later stage. That was what she told herself anyway.

She pulled out the sari from her suitcase, the makeup and the jewellery she had borrowed from Jazz. The sari was black in a chiffon material with silver beading and sequin work. It had a plunging neck line at the front and back and was kept from falling off her shoulders by a beautiful little draw string at the back, across her neck line.

Even though she'd invested in a number of saris in her new wardrobe for after the wedding, she'd never worn them because Sam didn't like the way she looked in them. He had told her straight, she couldn't carry them off.

"You don't have the figure for it," he would say.

Well, balls to him, Nikita thought. Today she was going to wear a sari and although she knew that Sam couldn't hear or see her, it still made her feel good.

Nikita was ready in time. She had struggled with the pleats at the front of the sari for a short while but she had managed to get them straight and to sit right in the end. The end of the sari was delicately placed on her shoulder and pinned to the blouse leaving just the correct length draping at her back. At first Nikita decided to pull the draping end of the sari over to the other side, covering her bare upper back, but then she decided to let it drop. She determined that she liked the way the neck was cut low on the back of her blouse. It looked elegant and sexy.

With one last glance in the mirror, Nikita grabbed her clutch bag and her keys and walked out to the corridor. She was heading towards Jai's room, when she saw him come out of his room. She watched him shut the door and put the key in his pocket. He started rummaging around looking in his inside jacket pocket. He didn't notice her standing there at first. Then he looked up. He looked so handsome, smart and beautiful. As his eyes locked with hers, a big smile grew on his face. He walked over to Nikita without taking his eyes off her face.

"You look amazing," he smiled.

"Umm, Shallow Hal, remember?" she grinned.

"No, I mean it, you look stunning. That sari looks gorgeous on you."

"You don't think it's too much?" she asked, looking down at her outfit.

"It's perfect," he replied.

"Thank you," she said, feeling a little warm.

Nikita looked into his eyes and the sincerity was obvious. She felt like her life couldn't be more perfect right now, as she smiled in silence.

Jai was stunned when he saw Nikita. His breath caught in his chest and he almost drooled looking down at her. God, she was gorgeous, he thought.

Jai put his arm out for her and he smiled. Nikita thread her arm through his and they walked towards the lift, to make their way down to the car which was parked in the secure underground hotel car park.

Jai let go of Nikita has he ushered her into the cart of the lift. He placed his hand on the arch of her lower back as he gently pushed her in. His hand stroked the bare flesh on her back just for a moment and it made his hand tingle. As he did, he took the opportunity to take a glimpse at the bump above her thighs and he had to control himself. He felt the urge to lick his lips.

Jai stood behind Nikita as the lift descended. He leaned in behind her, placing his nose close to her hair. She smelt divine. He knew that if he ever got to be with this beautiful woman, it would be the most erotic experience of his life. Then regrettably, he pulled away before Nikita noticed.

The award ceremony was very lively for most parts. There were elements that dragged where they had to change the stage sets for the different dance routines, but generally it was fun. Jai left Nikita for a short while to go and deliver an award, but he was back before long.

She noticed he kept looking at her from the corner of his eye, but she didn't mind, it felt nice.

She wasn't used to so many complements, especially not from a man. Nikita sat with her hand by her side and Jai let his hand rest on top of hers. She looked at him in confusion but he just smiled.

245

Chapter 22 - My Nightmare

After the award ceremony everyone was led into a large banqueting hall. This was where the VIP party was being held and by now Nikita's feet were starting to hurt in her new sandals. Jai introduced her to people as they walked around, as his friend and not his P.A.

They walked over to the bar and Jai ordered a beer. Nikita stuck with her usual, a diet coke with lemon, but no ice. After her experience at the club the last time, Nikita felt she was better off sticking to non-alcoholic beverages. The last thing she wanted was to make a spectacle of herself, especially in front of all these important people.

There were so many people at this party but she didn't recognise many of them. There were some celebrities, but none of the big names Nikita was hoping to see.

"Are you disappointed none of your favourite stars are here?" Jai asked.

"A little maybe, but no big deal."

"May be next time," he smiled.

"It's fine Jai. Not many people can claim to have come with a star either," she shouted in his ear, because it was true.

As people walked by, they smiled at Nikita. Wow, polite she thought as she smiled back. Nikita smiled at a young woman walking by but this woman gave Nikita a look that could kill. What was up with her? Then, another smile from the dark haired, slim man who walked by. Nikita quickly realised there seem to be a gender disparity in those that were smiling at her and those giving her daggers. Oh, Nikita thought. That wasn't something she was used to.

Photographers were out in full force taking snaps of anyone that would pose for them.

Jai pulled her close as a photographer came over. An arm curled around Nikita's waist, touching the bare skin close to her stomach. His thumb lightly stroking it, as he held her close.

Nikita's hand flew up against Jai's chest to keep some distance between them. Except his shirt was unbuttoned, revealing his cool firm chest with a light dusting of dark brown hair. Nikita's hand touched his bare flesh.

Jai turned Nikita to one side as he smiled at the camera.

The photographer too the picture and moved onto the next group of people.

"You look stunning Nikita, you know that?"

Nikita smiled back at him, her stomach starting to do that somersault thing.

Jai leaned down to Nikita's ear. "Honestly, you could give any of these girls a run for their money."

Nikita stiffened. "Jai, I appreciate the compliment but please don't exaggerate," she responded.

"I'm not. Haven't you noticed all the men staring at you? If that's not enough proof, what about all the girls that keep looking at you as though they want to murder you?"

Nikita looked around.

"They're all stunned at your beauty."

Nikita blushed, pushing a curly strand of hair behind her ear.

Jai caught her arm recognising the nervous gesture and moved in close to her ear. "You're breath taking!"

Not wanting to continue with the conversation, Nikita grabbed Jai and pulled him onto the dance floor. It was all she could think to do.

Nikita's feet hurt so she kicked off her sandals and let lose. She loved to dance.

Without her four inch heels, she was even shorter but that was okay, Nikita had come to accept her imperfections. She was having so much fun; she hadn't enjoyed herself like this in such a long time. The flashing lights from the cameras, added to the strobe lighting made her feel dizzy as she tried to focus, but other people were just going wild.

The dance floor was teeming but no one seemed to care. Nikita turned her back to Jai and leaned in against him.

Jai brought his hands up to Nikita's upper arms and pushed his whole body up against hers. He ran his hands stroking down each arm, down to her waist. His stomach clenched and it was all he could do, not to rub his groin against her backside. Everything in his body, urged him to.

Nikita's body trembled. She instinctively wanted to move against him, but she dared not rub herself against his warm, muscled torso. Stepping forward, she turned to face him, desperate to put some distance between them.

Jai wrapped his hand around hers and pulled her towards him again. He put his arm around her waist and spun her around.

Nikita laughed like a love struck teenager, she couldn't help herself. She couldn't take her eyes off Jai. She just kept staring at him and he must have noticed, but she didn't waver. Her mind started to wander.

Are you really that person baby, the one that's been
with me all along?
Are you that deep breath I take, is it you, is this your
song?
We've experienced nothing of each other, yet I feel we've
had so much
So little you know about me, yet we crave for each
other's touch
I watched you from a far there; so much drew me close
to you
I can't think exactly what it was, but I know that tonight
you feel it too
When you held me last night, it felt so good I had to
close my eyes
I felt so much peace in your arms, a place for the rest of
my life I could lie
Don't know where we are going, don't know what we
are doing
Are you the truth that I've been searching for?

A producer approached Jai and said he wanted to talk to him, but it was too noisy, so they decided to take the conversation to a quieter place.

Jai looked at Nikita and leaned in close, "Will you be okay for a few minutes, I won't be far?"

"Don't worry Jai, I'll be fine, I'll stay right here, take your time," she shouted back in his ear, smelling the beautiful scent of his aftershave, which made her feel all tingly again.

Jai grabbed her hand as he turned and squeezed it in reassurance and then he let go as he walked away.

Nikita stayed where she was, swaying to the music. It was such a fantastic atmosphere, everyone was enjoying themselves. She felt somewhat out of place at first, but then she started to relax. The music was amazing. They played music from around the world, it was brilliant.

A man approached Nikita with a drink but she politely refused. She knew not to take drinks from strangers; she'd heard too many stories. Jazz had also given her the motherly lecture the last time they had been out. "No thank you," Nikita smiled. "I'm with someone."

"That's a shame," the man whispered into her ear. "I've been watching you all evening and you know what?"

"What?" Nikita asked.

"All I kept thinking was, that girl is with the wrong guy."

Nikita smiled. "I'm sorry," she shrugged.

"Never mind, but if you change your mind, here is my number." He held out a business card for Nikita.

At first Nikita thought about refusing the card, but this man looked like a persistent sort of person so she took it. "Thank you," she smiled. He kissed her on the cheek and walked away. Nikita was quite taken aback by this gesture, stunned into silence. She had never been propositioned before. He must have been quite drunk she told herself.

She decided to go and stand by the bar, she felt safer there. She looked around to see if Jai was on his way back, but couldn't see him anywhere.

She noticed a man standing in the corner staring at her; it was quite dark so she couldn't see very clearly. She tried to ignore him but he just seemed to stand there. She looked away and when she looked back he was gone. Thank god. Nikita took a deep breath and let it out. She had to get a grip, she was being paranoid.

Nikita turned to face the bar and waved her hand to get the attention of the barman. Someone tapped her shoulder from behind and she smiled as she turned around. Thank God Jai was back. As she turned, she realised quickly that it wasn't Jai. As she looked up at him, she almost felt the earth rush from under her feet. The room started spinning and she felt off balance.

The man staring down at her wasn't a stranger. It was someone she recognised. A face she had tried so hard to forget. A man that had become her worst nightmare. Sam stood staring down at her.

What was he doing here? How did he find her? How did he get in here? The questions started running through her mind. He stared hard into her face, it frightened her so much. Nikita's heart started thumping and her stomach started to churn. She broke out into a cold sweat and she started having flash backs of what this man had put her through.

"Wow Nikita, you look.... you look really good. I almost didn't recognise you," he said as he lifted his hand up to her face to cup her cheek. "I've missed you," he continued in a fake tender voice.

Nikita quickly turned around to walk away. She couldn't stand there and listen to him, his voice made her skin crawl. She looked around for Jai but she still couldn't see him anywhere. Tears building in her eyes skewed her vision. She bumped shoulders with people as she walked through the crowd. People became annoyed with her. As she walked away, Sam followed. Her paranoia kicked in and she felt like everyone was staring at her.

250

Sam moved round in front of her. "Where have you been Nikita, I've been looking for you everywhere. I even contacted your parents and they wouldn't tell me either."

He tried to put his arms around her but she shrugged it off.

She looked around again, an opening or somewhere she could hide. She couldn't even see the ladies toilets.

She realised she had to face up to him at some point because otherwise he wouldn't leave her alone. She stopped dead in her tracks and turned around glaring back at him. "What do you want Sam?" she asked in a frightened voice.

"What sort of stupid question is that? I know I made some mistakes but I'm willing to put them right," he squealed.

Nikita looked at his face in shock.

"You call what you did to me, mistakes? You call trying to kill me a mistake? What planet are you on?"

"Okay, so I did some bad things, but we can work it out. You're still my wife. I know you still love me, otherwise why after all this time, have you not filed for divorce?"

"You're deluded," she screamed. "I don't want anything to do with you."

She could see people watching and whispering and she felt a rush of shame overcoming her.

"Come on Nikita. You know we were good together, even our parents want us to get back together."

He tried to touch her face again as she stared at him. She pushed his hand away.

"Don't you dare touch me, I'll scream," she shouted at him.

"But I miss you and I need you, please come back home, I'm nothing without you," he continued.

"Home? Home? A home is a place where you feel safe, where you feel secure, where you can relax, but I never felt any of those things. It was worse than hell for me."

"Oh come on, why are you being so melodramatic?" he said sarcastically.

"You're not getting the message are you? I hate you and I don't want anything to do with you," she screamed.

The soft subtleness in his voice completely disappeared. His expression became dark and precarious. He grabbed her arm and started to pull her along with him.

"Let go," she screamed.

He pulled her towards him and grabbed her by the face. "Look how you're making a spectacle of yourself. Look at the state of you; you look like a fucking slapper. You're lucky I'm even giving you another chance. You made me look like a fool when you left. People were laughing at me and now you're going to come back with me and make things right," he spat.

"Let go of me Sam, you're hurting me," she shouted.

Her eyes were filling up with tears. Her worst nightmare had come back to haunt her.

"This is nothing compared to what you'll get if you don't come back with me," he continued.

Anger was raging from every part of his body. He didn't care that people were watching. He dragged her through the crowd and no matter how hard she struggled she couldn't get him to loosen his grip on her.

She fell to the ground crying and she begged him, "Please let me go," but he didn't listen.

He pulled her back up and grabbed her by the hair, jerking her head back. Pain shot through her head, as she felt some of the pins fall out of her hair as others dug into her scalp. She was crying so much, she couldn't see anyone around her. No one came to help.

"You've brought shame on my family. All the women are talking about my mum. She can't even go to the Gurdwara without all the community staring at her," he screamed. His hand was still locked around her chin.

Nikita took a deep breath and filled her lungs with as much air as she could. It took all her strength but she pulled his hand off her hair.

"She knew exactly what was going on and she stood by and did nothing," Nikita yelled. "Would she have stood by if it was her own daughter going through what I went through, I don't think so?"

Sam became even more enraged.

"Sounds like you've grown a tongue in the last two years, but it won't bite for long, I'll make sure of it."

Nikita straightened her shoulders. "Yeh, well try your best," she shouted back. She stared at him the same way he was staring back at her. "You tried to ruin my life, but I'm not going to let that happen anymore. I wouldn't come back with you, even if you got on your hands and knees and begged me. I'm living my own life now, not yours and nothing you or your parents say, can change that."

"Yeh I noticed that, I saw you parading yourself on the dance floor like a whore with that bastard," he spat. "Been enjoying him have you. Enjoying him panting on top of you, like the slut that you are."

What was he talking about?

"When I was with you, you would lay there like a fucking log. There was nothing and now, I bet you scream his name like a bitch."

"Oi," someone called.

Nikita heard some people running over as she looked back.

"Stay away from her," she heard a firm voice say.

She tried to focus. Jai put his hand out and she grabbed it.

"So your boyfriend has come to rescue you," he laughed. "I always knew you were a slapper from the first day that I met you," he screamed.

"Go home Sam," Nikita said in a pitiful voice.

Jai squeezed her hand realising who this was.

"You touch her again, you'll have me to deal with, you got that," Jai said furiously.

"And exactly what are you going to do about it? You can't stop me, I'm her husband."

"You're nothing to me," Nikita said with a glare.

"We've all just witnessed you assault Nik, if you try anything like that again, I will personally report you to the police."

Sam could tell that Jai meant business.

"Fine, I didn't want anything to do with the fat bitch in the first place anyway, you can keep her."

He leaned in closer to Jai and lowered his voice. "Shall I tell you something else, man to man? She isn't worth it and she fucks like a dead fish, all cold and no life."

It was like he was spitting venom and Nikita wanted the earth to open and just swallow her up. She was never going to be able to face anyone after this.

Jai lunged forward with his fist clenched and raised, but people around him caught him and pulled him back.

"No Jai, it's not worth it," Nikita screamed.

Sam laughed as he walked away.

For a moment Nikita felt as though time had stopped. Everyone was staring at her. Embarrassment washed over every part of her body. The blood rushed to her face and her eyes filled with tears which she tried to hold back without success. For a short moment while her heart beat quickened, Nikita wished for death. Some sort of relief from this hideous nightmare.

Jai tried to go after him, but Nikita grabbed him.

"It's over Jai. He won't be troubling me again." She didn't have to be scared anymore and if he did cause her any more hassle, she knew she could handle him now. Well, sort of.

Suddenly a sick weakness consumed her and she fell to the ground. The lights of the strobe machine were flashing and it made her head spin.

"Nikita," Jai called.

She could hear him, but it sounded so distant. Her eyes fluttered open but the energy was drained from her bones and the weakness consumed her again.

Jai helped her up and put his arms around her, pulling her close to himself. He looked at her face, but she kept her eyes down, she couldn't look at him, she felt so ashamed.

This place was full of actors, producers and directors, one of which had asked to meet with Jai. Someone who could have made a huge difference to Jai's career and she had ruined everything. She was bad luck, an omen. She had to be. Wherever she went, trouble followed. Only her luck could bring Sam to a place hundreds of miles away.

Her legs felt like they were going to give way but Jai held onto her. She heard him mumbling something to the organiser but she couldn't make it out and then he told them he was taking her back to the hotel. They drove back in silence and then he walked her back to her room. While they were in the lift, Nikita didn't dare look up. She knew that there was a mirror opposite her, but if she looked, she would see the disappointment on his face. That was the last thing that she could handle right now. Neither of them said a word.

When they arrived outside her hotel room door, Nikita tried to get the keys out of her bag. Her hands were shaking. She managed to find her apartment key and tried to put it in the keyhole but struggled. Her hands felt numb.

When Jai could take it no longer, he grabbed the key from her and opened the door.

As the door swung open Nikita grabbed Jai's wrist to steady herself.

He walked her in and sat her down on the edge of the bed, then went off to use the phone. He dialled the number for room service and ordered two pots of tea.

Shame washed over Nikita. She needed to get away from Jai. She couldn't look him in the eye. Slowly, she got up and walked into the bathroom, locking the door behind her. A mirror could tell a million stories and this mirror reflected terror and devastation. It reminded her of the first day at the refuge and the state that she was in on that miserable day.

Her hair was a mess, some of it tumbled down around her face, knotted in places and her mascara was running down her cheeks leaving long black streaks. She grabbed onto the wash basin and let out a low sob. She couldn't control it. Pain erupted inside her stomach and her head felt like it was going to explode.

Jai overheard. He knocked on the door. "Nik, are you okay? Open this door, please." He sounded concerned.

"Leave me alone," she said just loud enough for him to hear.

He remained persistent. "I'm not going anywhere until you open this door."

What did he want? Did he want to see what a mess she was? To see a woman completely broken? Why didn't he just go away, couldn't he tell that she wanted to be alone?

"I'm still here, Nikita. God damn it, open this door." He banged on the door harder.

Nikita sighed and lifted the lock on the door.

Jai walked in, his dark amber eyes, almost as red as molten rock.

She sat on the bath with her face in her hands.

Jai noticed the pins poking out of her hair. He gently pulled them out one by one. Her hair fell along the sides of her face and he pushed it back behind her shoulders. He left the bathroom and returned a minute later, carrying her pyjamas in his hands and passed them to her.

"Here, put these on," he said in a gentle but stern voice.

Staring at the pyjamas and then looking up at him, Nikita asked, "Why are you being so nice me? I've probably fucked up your chances with all of those agents. I've made a mockery of you. These people are going to be talking behind your back for ages, and because of me they're going to be laughing at you. Don't you get it, I'm a liability. I destroy everything I touch. The quicker you get rid of me, the better it will be for you." Nikita looked away, no longer able to hold his gaze.

Jai's expression didn't change and he handed over her clothes. "Just put on your pyjamas and when you're comfortable we'll talk about it."

"What is there to talk about? Didn't you hear me? I'm a liability," she screamed.

Jai let out an exasperated sigh and ran his fingers through his hair. Turning he walked out of the bathroom.

He'll probably be calling the agency first thing in the morning, telling them he didn't want her working for him anymore. Nikita knew that if she was in his position, she would cancel her contract immediately. It was for the best, she told herself. She couldn't even begin to comprehend what she had cost him, in reputation and financially.

Nikita changed, washed the makeup off her face and headed into the bedroom.

The tea had arrived and Jai was pouring it in. He passed her a cup and she sat down on the bed to drink it. It tasted so good. Jai sat in the chair by the dressing table and she could feel the glare of his eyes.

Having seen a snippet of Nikita's past, he realised today, what she had been up against. The man that she had once married, wasn't a man, he was a fucking psycho. He had no respect for her, even after all this time. Jai always saw Nikita as a hard working, caring and funny woman. She was the type of person who would go out of her way to make anyone happy, but that animal never saw any of it.

In a selfish sort of way, there was a small part of Jai that couldn't be sad about what had happened in Nikita's life, because had her life not taken the direction it had, she would not have walked into his life and he was oh so happy that she had.

He stared at her for a long while. She sipped at the hot tea, slowly and Jai grinned internally at the slurping noises. She was so cute.

Nikita's heart beat fast in her chest as she waited for Jai to drop the bad news. He had to sack her after this cock up.

"How are you feeling?" Jai asked.

Nikita's head snapped up. What? No retribution? No blame? No shouting and yelling at her? She didn't know how to react.

She stared at him, surprised at his endearing tone.

He walked over to her, put his cup of tea on the dressing table and then took hers from her hand and placed it beside his.

Nikita felt the automatic urge to back away. She feared him, but she didn't know why. His eyes were set to hers and they didn't waver. She felt entrapped by him; she couldn't pull her gaze away from his. He stepped closer and her breath caught. Her instinct told her she needed to do something, but her body wouldn't do what her brain instructed.

Jai sat on her bed next to her and picked up both her hands. She watched him cautiously.

"I am so proud you," he smiled and then he leaned in and kissed her forehead. "You stood up to him today; you told him where to go. You should be proud of yourself too."

Nikita didn't know what to make of him. Had he just said he was proud of her? This man was too good to be true. Nikita realised she should say something but she couldn't find the words to respond.

She stared at him in silence, still enchanted by his eyes.

Jai stared at her lovely face for a moment longer. This woman awoke urges in him that he needed to be wary of. He couldn't help himself. Right now he wanted to touch her, to kiss her, to devour her, but he also knew he needed to leave. Her eyes were so beautiful; he wanted to drown in them. Her hands were warm and soft. He wanted her to touch his face with them and run them over his body so that he could enjoy the feel of them. His heart did a flip thing and his body started to tingle.

"I'd better go back to my room. You need to get some rest," Jai said reluctantly. He got up and turned to walk towards the door.

"Don't go," she said too quickly.

"What?" he asked in surprise.

"Don't go, not yet."

Jai came back and sat on the bed.

"I need to say something," she sighed.

He gestured for her to continue.

"If you need to call the agency to let me go, I'll understand."

Jai started laughing. "Why would I do that you silly girl? Actually I was thinking about employing you, on a more permanent basis."

Nikita looked at him surprised. "Even after today?"

"Especially after today," he smiled. "I need a strong and independent person working for me and you fit that job description very well," he said in adoration.

Nikita leaned up onto her knees and threw her arms around him. "Oh Jai," she said, with a smile beaming like the sun. She hugged him with such intensity, like she was holding on for dear life itself.

Jai's arms locked around Nikita, his hands placed at the bottom of her back, over her spine, and it took everything not to caress the sensitive arch. He felt a sense of calmness and relief while holding her, like he could breathe easily for the first time. He'd never realised before, that he was uptight or uneasy in life but this felt like release.

Nikita pulled away, which was followed by an awkward silence.

Jai felt the sudden urge to kiss her again. Memories of the kiss they had shared when going through his script came flooding back and there was a sudden rush of blood heading south. He remembered it clearly and if they hadn't been practicing his lines, he could have sworn Nikita had meant that kiss. She had responded to him so intently, he was sure she had wanted him too. That animal had said that Nikita was as dead as a fish, but Jai had never kissed anyone so alive and now he couldn't hold back. He needed to know how she felt, so he took a deep breath. He looked into her eyes and asked, "Would it be really bad, if I kissed you right now?"

Nikita was shocked. Did he just ask her what she thought he was asking? "Excuse me?"

"If I kiss you now, would you have a problem with it?" he asked again.

Nikita's eyes stung with more unshed tears. She had dreamt about this moment so many times and now that it was here, she couldn't let it go any further.

She dropped her gaze. "Didn't you hear what Sam said?" Her voice thick from her control. She closed her eyes for a moment and then looked straight at Jai. He didn't respond to her question, so she continued. "I am not good news Jai. You heard him. He used me and abused me and threw me away like a piece of rubbish. Granted I left him, but he didn't leave me any choice." Nikita took a deep breath. Her body slumped when she said the next words. "I can't give you anything Jai. Sam ruined me, completely. I'm not even sure if I will ever be comfortable with a man in that way. I hated every moment, because every night it happened, he cut away another little piece of me. I was violated every single day and I hated myself for allowing him to do this to me. You don't know what it's like to be forced upon, to be raped, to lay there and let him do whatever he wanted, without fighting back. I was a coward and my only way of dealing with it was to send my mind elsewhere. A place where there was no pain. When I looked in the mirror at my body, I wished I could rip the flesh off my bones. Every part of me felt dirty."

Jai still didn't interrupt. He knew he had to allow her to say what she needed to say. He pushed away at the lump developing in his throat. This girl had started to mean so much to him and he hated to see her in so much pain.

His heart ached for her. He hadn't realised when she had crawled inside his heart and created a little home for herself. He wanted to protect her and love her, and right now, his heart was swelling for her.

Nikita looked at Jai and waited for him to walk away, but he didn't. There was nothing. No disagreement, no unkind or hurtful comments.

Jai stood and she braced herself. When she opened her eyes, he would be gone. Why would he want to be near someone like her? Her heart ached at the thought, but her brain told her it was inevitable. She had to come to terms with her fate. Tears flowed down her face. This was the way it had to be.

Suddenly she felt a warm breath on her face and she opened her eyes startled. He was still there and sitting so close, so very close that she could feel his sweet breath on her skin. She felt a shiver run through her body and her breathing intensified.

He leaned in awkwardly. He didn't know why he felt so nervous. It wasn't like he'd never kissed a girl before, but it was the first time in ages that he had butterflies dancing around in his stomach. Firstly he was going to kiss those beautiful eyes of hers. He wanted to taste her tears, didn't want them falling on the floor and be wasted. It would mean that he would have a little piece of her inside of him and the thought felt so erotic. He leaned in and kissed one eye and then the other, the salty liquid flavouring his trembling lips. Her face was cupped in his hands stroking her cheeks. He pulled away from her eyes and leaned in to taste those luscious lips, brushing his mouth against hers. As he drew closer, he could hear her breath catching and it made him want her even more. His thumb caressed her bottom lip before he went the rest of the distance. He placed his mouth on hers so lightly, like the feathers of a bird and then pulled away. He had to be careful, ever so careful. He needed to be sure that if she wanted him to stop; he still had full control of his senses.

She froze underneath him, feeling her heart pace faster and her stomach start dancing.

He leant back in but this time he wanted to show her how much she meant to him. She wasn't someone you messed around with; she was someone to be enjoyed. Someone that deserved to experience all the pleasures in life and with that thought he took her mouth. He covered it with his and when her lips parted, he felt like the heavens had opened up. So sweet, so lush, so magnificent.

He ran his tongue along her mouth, controlling the need to run his hands all over her body. He'd experienced months of celibacy, he wasn't thinking straight. Oh how he wished he could caress those beautiful breasts, touch her thighs and make her sweat with wanting, but he knew he had to stop. He could have her right now, if he wanted to, he knew that. She had surrendered herself to him, he could feel it. But that thought became a mental slap in his conscience. How could he even think that way? He had to show her that he was nothing like that animal and she meant more to him than just getting his leg over. He realised he had some reflecting to do.

261

Nikita's head felt light. The way that Jai kissed her, was like a dream. She remembered the kiss they had shared when she helped him to practice his script, but this was on a completely different level. This was so intense, so passionate, so powerful, and she didn't want it to stop. She felt him become aroused, she could feel the hardness of him pushing against her leg and it frightened the life out of her. But if she said no, would he turn his back on her? The thought terrified her. She lay next to him waiting for the pain to follow. She braced herself, mentally prepared herself. Other people enjoyed it, why shouldn't she? Problem was that she wasn't ready, so how was she going to tell him? Should she tell him or should she stay quiet?

She waited, but it didn't come. She didn't feel any groping of her breasts, or pressure between her legs. It was gentle and sweet. He kissed her on her neck, her chin, her forehead and then her eyes. She waited for the heavy weight of his body to pin her, then for him to start forcing himself into her, but he didn't.

Jai pulled Nikita close to him and laid down next to her, embracing her in his arms.

She laid her head on his chest, feeling the strong muscles of his upper body wrapped around her. It felt so nice to have a warm body lying next to her. She could hear the low thump of his heartbeat in her ear, and she found it soothing. It sounded like a lullaby, helping her to drift off to sleep. She felt so comfortable in his arms. She snuggled in as close as she could and before long she'd fallen asleep.

Nikita woke a few hours later to a beautiful face staring down at her. "Hey," she said.

"Hey yourself," he said back. His smile was so radiant it filled Nikita's heart with joy.

"Thank you," she said.

"What for?" he asked, reaching up and moving strands of hair away from her face.

She liked the way he did that and she smiled back.

"For stopping when you did," she said.

He smiled at her again and kissed her on her forehead.

"You don't have to thank me and you don't have to worry, I'm never going to force you to do anything that you don't want to."

"Really?"

"Really."

Nikita knew that if Jai wanted to, he could have put the pressure on. They were in a strange city, in a hotel room, in the same bed, yet she felt so safe with him. She didn't feel in the slightest bit intimidated by him as she had done so earlier, she could trust him.

Nikita got up to get washed and after they had both cleaned up and packed, they were ready to leave to travel back home.

Nikita couldn't help but smile.

How much had changed in the last forty eight hours, was unbelievable. Jazz would be smug when Nikita told her.

"I told you so," she will say.

This had to be a dream. Things like this just didn't happen to people like Nikita.

The hotel room phone rang and Nikita answered it.

"Pardon the interruption madam. We are trying to locate Mr. Singh but he doesn't seem to be answering his room phone. Would you know where he is?"

"Yes, he's here, we were just packing, I'll pass the phone onto him."

"Thank you madam."

The hotel manager had been in touch with the award event organisers. Jai had asked them to investigate how Sam had managed to get in to the party. It turned out that the solicitors firm Sam was working for, had received two free passes to attend. Apparently they had sponsored one of the awards and so obviously they had decided to send Sam.

Nikita tried to push everything that had happened to the back of her mind. She had more important things to think about, like Jai.

The drive home was so lovely. She noticed things that she had never noticed before. She felt like she had suddenly woken up and everything looked so beautiful. She noticed the smell driving past freshly cut mustard leaf in the fields.

She realised people were smiling at her, no doubt because she had a grin on her face and they thought she was smiling at them.

Jai held her hand throughout most of the journey and they talked for most of the way home.

She twisted her body in the passenger seat so that she could look at him easily. He was so wonderful, perfect in every way. She felt the urge to kiss him again, to hold him, but she knew distracting him right now, wouldn't be a very good idea.

Sitting there watching him, made her think about how lucky she was.

It's all about the smile, that cheeky grin that makes my heart melt
Your beautiful face makes me dream even when I'm awake
Those eyes are so cute, sexy, deep and intriguing
Never seen anybody like you, so mesmerising like magic
God made you in his own vision, so perfect like no one else
How can anyone look like you? Enough to make anyone's heart melt
Wish I could run my lips across your face, feeling the shape of your jaw line
What I wouldn't do to be able to, touch your face and kiss your eyes and to have you love me

They drove back to his apartment as Nikita's car was parked underground. Jai pulled up and put the car into park. They got out and he took out Nikita's suitcase from the boot and walked over to her car. Jai opened her boot and he lifted her suitcase into it and then shut it.

"I'd better go," she told him, her voice almost inaudible.

"Come up to the apartment for a while," he said, his voice thick and deep.

A shiver ran through her body, hearing the intention in his voice. "I don't think that's a very good idea Jai. It's just

264

that there's probably loads to do at home and I need to check in on Jazz as well. I'll be back tomorrow."

"I don't know that I can wait that long."

"Wait for what?" she asked, swallowing dryly.

"This," Jai said and he pulled himself up against her. He grabbed both her hands gently and brought them up to his chest. He gazed into her eyes and leaned in and kissed her on the lips. She was pushed right up against the bonnet of her car. She reached back and pulled herself onto it. They continued to kiss and Jai's hands went from around her face, down her arms and he placed them on her waist. He pulled himself closer to her and Nikita opened her legs to accommodate him, her inner thighs brushing his hips. She felt his tongue stroke her lips and she didn't want it to stop.

Just as she realised what she was doing and her senses came back, she froze. She wasn't ready to take the next step, not yet anyway and Jai realised that something had changed. He quickly pulled away from her lips but he placed his head on her shoulder and gave her a long tight hug.

"You're going to be the death of me," he whispered in her ear.

They were both breathing heavy and Nikita felt like she was going to faint. Her heart was thumping so loud in her chest, she was sure that he would be able to hear it. She could feel the pulse in his neck as she placed her cheek on his shoulder and she knew he felt it too.

Jai helped Nikita off the bonnet and walked her round to the driver seat of her car. She got in, started the engine and let the window down. Jai leaned into the car and put his hand on her face, "I'll see you tomorrow," he said.

She put her hand on his hand and stroked it. "Yes, see you tomorrow."

He leaned into the car and kissed her again. Oh God, she wanted to jump out so that he could kiss her properly. She realised she didn't want to go home, but she knew she had to take things slowly, or she'd probably end up regretting it. She forced herself to break free from his hold and put her gear stick into first. If she didn't leave now, she would never leave.

She smiled all the way home.

Chapter 23 - Departing Friends

When Nikita got back home, she was so excited and happy that she wanted to tell Jazz everything.

Jazz was sitting on the sofa looking a bit troubled when Nikita got in. Nikita's heart sank. She hadn't seen Jazz like this in a long time. Her face had an unreadable expression and Nikita became worried that something was very wrong.

"Hey Jazz, you okay babe?"

Jazz looked up. Her expression was of shock. Oh God, I hope he hasn't found her, Nikita thought. If Max had, it would mean Jazz would have to move out and she'd have to start again somewhere completely new.

"Has something happened?" Nikita asked again.

She sat down next to Jazz, putting her arm around her.

They were like sisters and Nikita's stomach twisted wondering what could be wrong.

"I can't believe it," said Jazz. "My mum's been in touch; she wants me to come home."

Nikita felt a surge of relief rush over her. She felt selfish, but she couldn't help the slight pang of jealousy running through her.

"They said that they want to forget about everything that has happened and move forward." Jazz longed to be part of her family again.

As much as it broke Nikita's heart to encourage Jazz to return to her family, she couldn't allow her selfish emotions to get in the way.

"That's great Jazz. What are you waiting for?"

"I don't know. It's been so long, I don't know if I can go back to living that sort of lifestyle. I know that they were never strict on me but I don't know if I can deal with constantly answering to them. I'm so used to living my life how I want to, I'm not sure what I want."

"But they love you, that's the main thing and anyway, you're risking your health with all this binge drinking. It may do you some good to question yourself before going out and getting smashed nearly every night."

"It's not just that, if I move back in with them, you won't be able to stay here. There's no way that you can afford the rent on your own and we've always looked out for each other. I can't leave you in limbo like that," she replied.

Nikita knew that to be true and if Jazz moved out, Nikita also knew that she would have to look for another smaller apartment, quick sharp. But this was Birmingham, how hard could it be? Nikita and Jazz had a good track record with their current landlord, so she would get a good reference. Their rent was always paid on time and their landlord had never had to speak to them about any concerns. They were model tenants.

"Jazz, is that what you're worried about? Babe I'm really flattered that you're thinking about me but I think it will be good for you to go. Your parents have asked you back home, that's amazing. This is what you've been waiting for. You don't need to worry about me. I'll find another flat somewhere, so don't stress about it, honestly and I can visit you and you can come and stay with me as well. We'll still be best friends, nothing is going to change that," Nikita smiled.

Nikita gave Jazz a long hug and ordered her to make the arrangements. They only had to give four weeks' notice for ending the tenancy. Nikita asked Jazz to give the landlord notice from the following day. This also meant that Nikita would have to find another suitable apartment quickly. Four weeks wasn't very long to find a flat, but she didn't tell Jazz about her worries, Nikita didn't want to influence her decision. Jazz missed her family and Nikita knew that too well.

Nikita hardly slept that night. She kept thinking about Jai and the eventful few days that they'd had. She missed him already, having only left him this afternoon. She tried really hard to think about something else, but she failed miserably. What book shall I read next? Jai. What movie shall I watch next? Jai. What shall I wear tomorrow? Jai. Then she started counting sheep, one, two, three, Jai, four, five, six, Jai. It was no good. He was all she could think about and she wondered if he was thinking about her too.

He had quickly taken over her mind, her heart and her soul. Every part of her body pulsed for him. When she thought about him, her body tingled from head to toe. Just the thought of him made her heart beat quicken. His scent lingered in her pours and every minute that went by, felt like an excruciating hour. It was going to be a very long night.

The next morning Jazz called the landlord to let him know they wanted to end their tenancy.

Nikita put the radio on while she was getting ready for work and every song that was played, seemed to be about her. She could relate to the lyrics of most. She sang along to the songs that she recognised, she felt elated.

Nikita looked in the mirror and actually felt somewhat satisfied with herself. She felt a sense of pride, she was standing straight and she hadn't realised it. Her hair looked glossy; skin looked like it was glowing and her boobs looked perky. Well, she was wearing a good quality bra. The thought of Jai liking what he saw, made heat burn in her lower stomach and without thinking she clutched her thighs together. She had to get a grip.

Nikita went into work on time. She had to fight with herself not to turn up at five o'clock in the morning. She knew she'd look desperate, so she had to pace herself. She was letting herself get emotionally attached, way too quickly. If things didn't work out, she knew she'd pay for it heavily. But she told herself she could keep it under control, but then again who was she kidding? Nikita's heart skipped, she felt like she was a teenager again. She was floating, walking on air. Her nerve endings tingled and she came to realise that she had never felt more alive.

Jai was up and about when Nikita arrived at work; he was waiting for her to get in.

As soon as she opened the door, his arms were around her. He kissed her long and hard before she could say anything. He took her breath away.

"Mmmm, lipstick, lipstick," she managed to mumble.

"What?" He asked as he broke away.

"You're wearing my lipstick," Nikita said, running her finger across his lips and then holding it away for him to see.

"Oh," he replied. His lips were a lovely shade of pearl pink and he just smiled at Nikita, pouting his lips. It didn't suit him.

Nikita's head felt a little dizzy and she knew that as much as she didn't want to, she needed to lay down some ground rules, or they would never get any work done.

"Jai, if we're going to make this work, then we have to remain professional while we are working. We can't afford to spend all day kissing and canoodling, we have a business to run," she stated. "As much as I would love to, because there is nothing more in the world that I want than to lie in your arms all day long, we have to remain focused," she pleaded.

"You're right," he smiled, "But we'll start with the rules and regulations tomorrow."

"Jai you also need to bear in mind that I am still working for the agency. They have policies and procedures against employee and client relationships and boundaries." Nikita worried about how this was going to affect her employment.

"You don't work for the agency anymore."

Nikita's eyebrows rose. She was a little confused. Had they found out already and sacked her without telling her?

Jai responded as if he'd read Nikita's mind.

"You now work directly for me, so I make all the rules and you young lady are most welcome to kiss me or do whatever you want to me. That's written in my personal relationships policy. All you have to do is, pop into the agency office and sign off all the paperwork."

Nikita sighed, exasperated. "Jai, you should have spoken to me about it first. You paying my salary will be awkward. It doesn't feel right. Going forward, what if things between you and I work out, I can't expect you to pay me a salary. What if it doesn't work out, then what?"

"Look, people in relationships often work together in my field of work. Family members act as managers or associates all the time," he said trying hard to justify his actions.

"But I'm not your family, am I?"

Now it was Jai's turn to become exasperated. "Don't ever say that. You are my family. You're the only family that I've got."

Nikita mentally chastised herself. That flew out all wrong. What was she thinking?

Nikita looked at Jai and smiled. "I didn't mean it like that, I'm sorry." She held Jai's hand and pulled it up to her mouth and kissed each knuckle.

Jai's posture softened a little. "Nikita, don't ever say that you're not my family. It hurt to hear you say that."

"I know and I'm sorry. I didn't mean it like that." She felt bad for what she had said, but it didn't take away the feeling of awkwardness at Jai paying her salary. However, she brushed the thoughts aside wanting the atmosphere to return to the light sultry mood of when she arrived that morning.

As Nikita kissed Jai, his stiffness quickly dissipated and before long he had taken over. He kissed her back with so much intensity; he found it hard to control his inner most desires.

Nikita found it exhilarating.

Just then Nikita's phone started ringing. It made her jump. She pushed Jai away and she noticed him roll his eyes in annoyance. She knew what he was thinking, great timing.

It was Jazz just letting Nikita know that she had called the landlord to give the notice to leave the flat. This reminded Nikita that she had some urgent things to do, starting with flat hunting.

"Jai, I'm going to have to take an extended lunch, will that be okay?"

"Do you have to ask?"

"Thanks, I need to do some flat hunting. I know it's cheeky, but could I also use your computer to have a look online as well, I need to sort something out as soon as possible," Nikita explained.

"Why? Are you looking for a flat? Are you guys moving?" he asked.

"Well, Jazz's parents have asked her to return home, which is great, it's what she needs and I'm so happy for her, but it leaves me in a bit of a predicament. I can't afford to stay at this flat on my own, so I'll have to find something smaller, something I can afford."

"Well there's not much around that's at a good price unless you move further out, but that will increase your travelling time."

"Yeh, I need to way up the cost of travel everyday to the cost of rent. I know it's going to be hard, that's why I need to start looking straight away. Jazz has given the four weeks' notice and unless I find a flat soon, I'll be kind of homeless," she grimaced.

"How can you say that Nik?" Jai was annoyed with that comment. In fact he was so offended he let go of her hand.

Nikita lifted her hand to his cheek and pulled his face back round to face her.

"Did I say something wrong?"

Jai sighed. "Nik you call me your friend and recently we have become so much more. I've just said that you are family to me and then you talk about becoming homeless," he grimaced.

"Jai, I'm just exaggerating, it's never going to come to that and anyway, I've got you haven't I?" She smiled and his faced pulled up on one side.

Jai knew what he was about to say, might startle Nikita and maybe it was a bit premature, but may be this was a blessing in disguise. This was his opportunity to take the next step. Granted they had only just taken their friendship to the next level, but he had never been surer about anything else.

"Why don't you move in here?"

Nikita looked at his face in surprise; he couldn't really be asking her to move in with him could he?

Jai read her expression. "Only until you find somewhere else, I mean."

Nikita smiled at him. "If it comes to that, I might have to take you up on your offer. It's funny really, you keep making me offers and I keep taking them up."

"That's the way it should be, which reminds me, I contacted my friend, the solicitor and he said that he can draw up the divorce papers for you when you need. I told him that you'd call him when you are ready. Here's the number," and he handed Nikita his friends business card.

Nikita put it to one side.

Jai was such a wonderful guy, with so much to offer. She couldn't understand his interest in her. It wasn't like she had guys falling at her feet, so why did he pick her? She was ordinary, nothing special, yet he was exquisite through and through. He was extraordinary.

She stared at Jai wanting to ask him the question. She had begun to fall for this generous, kind and beautiful man who had eyes so gold and full of depth that she felt like drowning in them every time she looked into them.

Jai leaned in and kissed her, a long and sensuous kiss. As he pulled away, Nikita spoke placing her hands on his chest. "What do you see in me, Jai? You've got so much to offer and you can have any woman you want, so why go for someone like me?"

Nikita understood, may be more than most what Jai's mum had been through, but she had to know for sure that this was not the reason for Jai being with her. She didn't want pity or sympathy; she wouldn't be able to stand it.

They both had similar scars which were still healing. Hers were still raw in comparison to his, but commonality wouldn't be enough to hold a relationship together, long term. There had to be more.

Questioning Jai in this way would be painful for him, she realised that. However for her own sanity, she had to know. "I feel really bad for what happened to your mum and I know how much you loved her and wanted to protect her. I don't want you to take this the wrong way but I don't want you to want to be with me because you feel sorry for me."

"Is that what you think?" Jai pulled away slightly. "You think that I feel sorry for you?" His forehead creased and his mouth changed into a thin line. "I'm offended that you can even think like that about me. Don't you trust me?"

"Of course I trust you, but I have to be realistic. If anything, life has taught me that. I'm not the kind of girl that men throw themselves at because of the way I look, which brings me back to my question, why me?"

"You want proof, is that it?"

Nikita started to draw back, Jai sounded furious.

He stopped her, grabbing her hands. He couldn't let her recoil away from him; it wounded him to see her like this. He exhaled, calming himself. She wanted proof of his attraction to her and he could only think of one way. He pulled her hand closer and placed it on bulge in his jeans. "Is that proof enough for you? I'm so desperate for you it hurts."

Nikita stared at him, unable to move. Her throat went dry and her heart beat quickened.

"Everything about you makes me want you. You're intelligent, funny and sexy. You make me feel like I'm eighteen again. You give me butterflies."

Jai put both hands on Nikita's face and kissed her. As he pulled away he said, "I'm not going to lie to you, yes I do feel like I want to protect you, but that's because I care about you, not because I feel sorry for you."

Jai's hands dropped to Nikita's throat, his fingers intertwined with her hair. There was something almost possessive about this movement, the way in which he held her right there.

"Does this feel as though I feel sorry for you?" He stared at Nikita, his eyes intense. His face was inches away.

Nikita swallowed.

He brushed a kiss on her neck.

Her breath started to come shorter and shorter and her heart thumped in her chest.

"And does this feel like I feel sorry for you?" He asked again.

His mouth was on hers now and she knew there was no point in arguing with him. This felt too right.

His arms were wrapped around her body and he pulled her close. His hands reached behind her, stroking the soft arch at the lower part of her back. He pulled her in closer.

It took all his control not to grind his hips in between her legs. Right now it would have been so easy to rub his hardness into her soft sensitive flesh.

His breath was intoxicating. Nikita felt dizzy with emotion and she pulled away to compose herself. She had no idea of the internal struggle that went on in Jai's heart and mind.

She smiled at him. She put her head on his chest and she could feel his heart thumping.

"I'm sorry," she said. "It's just that I'm not used to getting lucky and I keep feeling like all this is just a dream and I'm going to wake up any minute."

"I'm the lucky one Nik," he smiled.

At lunch Nikita popped out to the local estate agents and registered interest with a number of them, leaving her contact details with them. Hopefully they would find her something soon.

Nikita thought about Jazz and how lucky she was. Her family wanted her to come home, forgetting about everything that had happened. She wished she could see her family as well, she missed them so much.

Chapter 24 - Home

"I've come to a decision," Nikita said one day out of the blue.

"You've made my day, you've decided to sleep with me," Jai said cheekily.

"You should be so lucky," Nikita said, scowling at him. "I'm going to visit my mum and dad."

She missed her parents dearly. Even though what they had done to her was wrong, she still couldn't help loving them, and above all she wanted their approval. Old habits die hard. She was so used to them being happy with her; she wanted them to understand how she was feeling. Understand why she had taken the steps she had and she wanted them to accept her decisions. It wasn't going to be easy. She wanted all these things, but she knew it was a tall order. Her dad was a stubborn man, stuck in his old ways. You could shift a tree from its roots but you couldn't change her dads mind once it was set.

She wasn't looking forward to it. It had been more than two years since she had been back there or even laid eyes on her parents. She missed them a lot, but she knew how they would be. She was too fragile to face them before and at the time, she couldn't stand anymore heartache, so she stayed away, but it was time to make amends. She was stronger now, and she had the confidence to stand her ground.

Nikita had spoken to her mum now and then on the phone, but they were always very short conversations, very awkward conversations. After getting the formalities out of the way, the subject would always revert back to the same thing, him. It shattered Nikita's heart into a thousand pieces every time she spoke to her mum. Her mum was only interested in one conversation, but Nikita made it clear that she would rather die than get back with that demon of an ex-husband of hers. Nikita would always find an excuse to get off the phone, being busy; a knock on the door, late for work, anything so that she didn't have to discuss it.

No matter what her parents had done, she still loved them dearly. Her self-esteem had grown and she wanted to see them and she decided she would take whatever they threw her way without holding a grudge. Her eyes craved, and her heart wept wanting to see them.

Jai read the worry in Nikita's eyes. "Would you like me to come with you?" he asked in a concerned voice.

"Oh yeh, that will really impress them," she said sarcastically. "They'll probably strangle me as soon as they saw you and then kill you after that, and anyway, I'm sure he's filled them in on the eventful evening in Bradford. God knows what bullshit he's fed them."

"What does it matter what he says. They're your parents and anyway, do you really give a shit?"

"Of course not. I couldn't care less what that serpent has to say," she threw back.

"Good," Jai said. He walked stepped towards Nikita.

She buried her face in his chest. He felt so warm and comforting. Jai stroked her back slowly, sending shivers up her spine.

"You know, you don't have to do this alone. I can still come with you if you want, just drop me off somewhere in the city centre. I'll have a browse around and grab a cup of coffee while you see your parents, then you can come and get me."

Nikita let out a low chuckle. "You think that Letchworth has a city centre? You don't know anything about it do you?"

"Know anything? I'd never even heard of it until I met you."

"Well, you can walk around the shopping centre in five minutes flat, so I don't know how long you'll last shopping there."

"That's okay, I'll walk very slowly."

277

"Umm, I'm not sure and that's not really fair on you as well."

"Don't worry about it. I'm sure there's a pub there somewhere. I mean, there is a pub isn't there?" he asked doubtfully."

Nikita smiled. "It's not that bad, of course there's a pub."

"Then I'll be fine. I'd like to see the little town you always speak so highly of."

Nikita's heart felt overwhelmed. Never had anyone ever made her feel so important, so valued. Jai wanted to be with her, he chose to spend time with her. He never complained about anything. Her confidence had grown so much over the last few months, she actually felt worth something.

Sam had not once complemented her or said anything remotely nice to her. He only ever put her down, made her feel incompetent and worthless. Jai had taken all that pain away and replaced it with kindness, compassion and benevolence.

He cared so deeply for Nikita but every time he tried to tell her, he couldn't find the right words. Never in his life had he felt so strongly about a woman. Every day he thanked his lucky stars for allowing him to meet such a kind and generous person. She had so much love to give and Jai wondered if she would give him some too.

"Umm, okay, you've got a deal," Nikita smiled. "Thanks," she told him, hugging him again.

***

On the morning of the trip to Letchworth, Nikita went to Jai's to pick him up. It was going to take them approximately two hours to get there and the same back, so it was good to have some company.

It was so nice talking to him, she didn't feel any anxiety.

Nikita had brought along some of her favourite CD's to play in the car. She was quite surprised because although Jai wasn't very clued up on current Bollywood music, he recognised some of the older tracks. He told her how he used to watch the films with his mum and dad when he was

278

very young. It was one of his happier childhood memories. When he recognised a song, he'd try to sing along with it. He made her feel weak at the knees and he was distracting her while she was driving.

"*Tum jo milgai ho, to yeh lag ta hai, ke jahaan milgaya.*"

Now that I have found you, it feels to me like I have got the whole world.

"*Beto na dhoor humsi, dekho kafa na ho, kismet se milgai ho, milkar joodha na ho.*"

Don't sit so far away, don't be upset, we have met by fate and may we never part.

"Will you stop it," Nikita giggled. "You're distracting me."

He lifted his hand and stroked her face with the back of his knuckles. "Does this distract you as well?" he laughed. "And what about this?" he asked as he stroked the inside of her thigh. It made her jump and she couldn't concentrate on driving. "Stop it," she laughed.

Nikita noticed a service station as she approached a junction, so she indicated left to move into lane and quickly pulled off the motorway.

She parked the car in the huge service station car park and switched off the engine. She had pulled into a parking space away from all the other cars which allowed them some privacy and as it was Jai's car, it also had slightly tinted windows. Nikita took off her seatbelt, pushed her seat back turning her body in the seat to directly face him.

"What?" He looked at her innocently.

Her stomach was doing somersaults and she felt ripples of tingling all over her body. She could feel the hair on her arms standing on end. She placed her hands on his face and pulled him in to kiss.

He responded by deepening the kiss. The passion was electric between them. He easily made her forget all her fears and feel like she could do anything. She felt the pressure of his arms around her waist and slowly he moved his hands up until they were placed just under her breasts. Her breath caught.

Jai thought about whether or not he wanted to move his hands up any further and he fought with himself not to. He wanted her so badly it hurt, but he controlled himself as much as he could. Every day it got harder. At times like this, Nikita really tested his limits.

Jai became aroused and his hands were everywhere. His breathing became ragged and he let out a low groan. Nikita pushed him away.

"Jai stop it." He looked at her and she couldn't read his expression. His eyes looked eager and desperate and it frightened her. She saw what may have been hunger and need. "I can't, I won't, and I'm not ready." She said it almost with a shrill. She wanted him too, she knew that, but as soon as things got any further than a kiss, she would clam up. She froze because it frightened the life out of her.

She didn't know how long Jai would wait. Normal people didn't behave in that way and Jai deserved more. Nikita turned her face away and looked out of the window. "I'll understand if you don't want to continue with this. You're a man. I know you have needs."

That struck Jai like a slap. He cared for this girl, a lot, but she sure as hell didn't make it easy for him. Didn't she trust him? God, she drove him crazy.

He pulled her face back to look at her.

"Is that what you think? Is that what you think of me Nik? I thought that you trusted me?"

"I do," she said. "But you're also a man and a man has needs. And it's not like you've been celibate all your life. You were with Tina for a while and I'm sure that you two..... well you know, and I'm sure she didn't keep you waiting like me. But I'm not like that, I just can't. I'm too fucked up. You should move on, for your own good."

Jai scowled at her. "Nik, I'm not going to lie to you, of course I want to, but do you think that I would force you? I got a bit carried away and I'm sorry for that, but I'm not going to be sorry for wanting you, because that's not your problem, I will deal with that. I'm not going to force you to do anything that you don't want to. I'm falling for you and I had hoped that you felt something similar for me too."

280

This statement struck Nikita like a bolt of lightning. She had no idea that Jai felt so strongly for her.

"Why do you look so surprised? Come on! You can't tell me you hadn't realised I felt this way."

Nikita couldn't find the right words to say.

Jai was so exasperated. "Why do you have to be so god damn self deprecating? Why can't you believe for once that you deserve better? Why can't you just tell me to behave myself instead of making me feel like I don't mean anything to you, because you keep telling me to move on? Why wouldn't someone want to be with you? You're beautiful and intelligent and strong." Jai let go of Nikita's hand and turned his face away from her.

He was angry with himself as well. He could try harder to control himself, but she made it so difficult. When he brought his hands up towards her breasts, they were almost screaming at him to grab them. It took all his will power not to do anything he might regret, but God she made it hard for him. He cared about this girl a lot and he never wanted to ever do anything to hurt her. She infuriated him so much. He wanted her to challenge him. If he got out of hand, he wanted her to scold him, tell him to stop and be confident. He knew she had it in her, but she always made out she wasn't good enough for him and that drove him crazy.

Nikita placed her hand on Jai's face and tried to pull it back to face her, but he wouldn't. "I'm sorry Jai, I shouldn't have said anything. I know you're not like that, I know I shouldn't judge you with my past." When he didn't make eye contact, Nikita jumped out of the driver seat and ran around to the passenger side and opened the door.

Jai still wouldn't look at her.

She knelt down next to him and pushed her face into his face. "I'm sorry." She held his hands and because he wouldn't let her lift them up, she leaned down and kissed them, while they were in his lap.

"Nik, what are you doing? People are going to think you're doing something else. Stop it. We'll get arrested for an indecent act. There are kids in this car park."

Nikita could see him trying to hold off a smile. "I won't stop, not until you forgive me and my big mouth."

"Okay, okay, I forgive you, now please get up."

Nikita smiled a big grin. Inwardly she felt so angry with herself for hurting his feelings like that, when he had only ever been good to her. Never again, she promised herself.

"I think I need to pop to the toilet," he said and he seemed to blush.

"Okay, I might as well come with you," she replied.

"I thought we just established we weren't going to take things further. Did I miss something? I mean, the men's cubicles aren't the best place to get it on, but there's always a first time for everything."

"Shut up," she said blushing. "I meant that I need to pop to the ladies."

"Oh well, I can only try."

Nikita looked at Jai with so much love and wanting. "And I want you to keep trying, because when I am ready, you will know."

Jai got out of the car and grabbed Nikita's hand as they walked towards the restaurant entrance. She couldn't take her eyes off him. She wasn't used to the public show of affection either and he made her feel so proud to be with him.

Nikita got to her parents house at around twelve o'clock after dropping Jai into town. Her mum was looking out of the window, waiting for her. Nikita worried about what they would think of her appearance when they saw her. They hadn't seen her hair so short and they'd never seen it coloured. They'd never seen her dress this way either and she was mostly concerned about how her dad would react. She thought about tying her hair back and not wearing so much make up but then she wouldn't be true to herself. She decided it was time they accepted her as she was.

Her mum opened the door before Nikita had knocked. She pulled Nikita into a motherly embrace as Nikita stepped in the front door.

"How are you my dear?" she asked.

"I'm doing good mum, how about you?" Nikita asked getting the formalities out of the way as usual. "How's dad?"

"Why don't you ask him yourself, he's inside," she replied.

Nikita felt her heart shudder. She felt like a little girl again, nervous and frightened. It would only take one look from her dad and she'd know that she was in trouble. Ever since she was little and even up until the day she left home, she never did anything against her dad's will, not unless she could hide it from him. If he ever disapproved of something she was doing or saying, he would give her the look with those piercing eyes to say 'stop it' and it frightened the life out of her. Today she felt the same fear wash over her again. She walked in and looked over to where he was sitting.

He had his own comfy chair, where no one else would dare sit and he had the television remote control resting on the arm of it. He was changing the channels, furiously.

Nikita greeted her dad putting her hands together. "Sat Shri Akal. How are you dad?" she asked in a quiet voice but he ignored her. His eyes didn't leave the television set as he continued to flick through the channels. Panjabi news, Panjabi music, religious channels, but he didn't even glance at her.

Nikita stared at her dad with nervousness rushing through her, which made her fingers tingle and her stomach do somersaults. She lowered herself onto the sofa and her mum went in the kitchen to make some tea. Nikita sat for a moment but decided she was too uncomfortable sitting there, so she followed mum into the kitchen to see if she could help her with something. She walked into the small square space, remembering all the time she had spent in this room learning about spices and starters, curries and desserts. When she lived here, it was her favourite room in the whole house.

Nikita sighed and went straight for the dishes.

"Don't worry about those love, I will do them later."

"It's okay mum, I don't mind. It will only take a couple of minutes," Nikita replied. She would do anything to keep herself busy. It helped to erase her nervousness a little and made her feel useful. She stared out of the kitchen window at the miniature apple and plum trees which she didn't recall seeing before and therefore must have been newly planted.

Returning her gaze back to the dishes, Nikita remembered the altercation with Sam and felt a shiver run up her spine. Nikita knew she was imagining it, but she could have sworn she could still smell his breath on her neck. His dirty alcoholic mouth whispering in her ear. Even now, she still remembered every word of that conversation. The memory was so vivid in her thoughts, like it had only happened yesterday. So many of these horrible memories were etched deep across her mind and Nikita wondered if they would ever become more distant.

Mum made small talk, asking Nikita about her work, her flat mate and life in Birmingham, but Nikita knew that her mum was itching to get onto a particular subject. Before long, mum brought up the conversation.

"Sam called," she said.

Even though she was expecting it, it hit Nikita like a punch in the gut. Just the name made her cringe. Then anger coursed through her heart. After everything that he had done to her, he was still calling her parents. How dare he? Nikita shot mum a cold glare. "Mum, I don't want to talk about him," she sighed.

"But he's been ringing since you left and he keeps telling us about how much he loves you and wants you back. Why don't you give him another chance? Whatever happened, he's sincerely sorry."

That was it, her mum needed to hear the truth. Nikita had hidden it from her parents for far too long and it was time they learnt about their so called, sun shining out of his arse, son in law.

"Did he also tell you that he strangled me and beat me to a pulp? Did he tell you that he would accuse me of flirting with his friends? Did he tell you how he beat me until my face was black and blue and that he broke my ribs?"

Mum's eyes widened in disbelief. "You're exaggerating, why would he do that? He is a very smart and educated man." She was mumbling the words, still in shock at the revelation.

Typical, Nikita thought, her mum didn't believe her.

"Mum, why would I lie to you about this. The police have evidence. They took photos of my injuries and they encouraged me to press charges, but I didn't."

"You involved the police?" Mum said, her voice almost a shriek.

It was as though Nikita was the one who had done something terrible, not him.

"Mum, I needed help; I had no one to turn to."

"But he told us that he saw you in Bradford with another man. His mum called me as well and she was shouting insults at me down the phone, saying that we had brought our daughter up to have no shame."

"Mum, I really don't care what that battle-axe thinks. I was in Bradford, but I was there with my boss Jai, we were on a business trip."

"You stayed overnight with your boss Nikita?" she said, her tone of voice rising a notch or two. "Is this how we brought you up?" Nikita's mum banged her hands against her forehead, not knowing what to do.

"Mum, he had his own room and I had mine, it wasn't like that, it's my job," Nikita argued. "Did Sam tell you what he did to me in Bradford, or did he forget to mention that part as well?" she asked.

Mum shook her head.

"He pulled me out of an event, in front of hundreds of people and when he got me to one side he grabbed me by my hair because I wouldn't listen to him. There is no way that, that man is ever going to step foot in my life again," she whispered in anger. "I'm filing for divorce," Nikita told her mum.

"But why? What will people say? You will be the talk of the town. We won't be able to show our face to people in the community, but above all, how are you going to get through life on your own. Life is a very long journey. A woman needs a man otherwise other men will look at you and think you are public property and who will want to marry a divorcee?" she moaned.

"Mum, that is so backwards, lots of women live on their own. I'm not the only one to have gone through this and anyway I don't care what people have to say and with regards to my life, if it is in my kismet to meet someone new, I will. I know you won't like it mum, but I am going to do things my way from now on."

Mum had never heard Nikita speak like this before, she couldn't believe it.

Nikita took a sip of her tea standing in the kitchen. She looked at her mum in frustration.

"Mum, would you have preferred to be carrying me out in my coffin, rather than me leaving that animal. It sounds like that you'd rather I'd have died than to have left him and all for what, the community? A community that has problems of their own, they haven't got time to be gossiping about others. And even if they did have time, how long could they keep it up for? Before long someone else would be the talk of the town."

"Don't say that child. Of course we don't want you dead, you are our eldest daughter, our pride and joy," she said.

Nikita sighed. "And that's why I put up with it for so long. To protect you guys. Mum, you have to trust that I would never do anything to bring shame on the family, but I had no choice. And now you have to let me live my own life. All my life, I did everything that you and dad asked of me, but now it's time for me to make choices for myself. If they are wrong choices then they are my mistakes and I will learn from them, but you have to let me live my life," she cried.

Nikita's mum sighed and didn't say anything. She was angry with her; Nikita could see that, she wouldn't look at her.

Nikita went back into the living room and walked over to where her dad was sitting. He still didn't look at her, but kept staring at the TV.

There was a knock at the door. Nikita went into panic mode and headed back to the kitchen to hide. It was probably going to be one of her aunties or another relative but she couldn't face them, not yet. Mum pushed passed her to open the door and Nikita looked through the serving hatch from the kitchen.

She heard a man's voice and then saw him walk through the door. She had been deceived. Her own parents had betrayed her. How could they do this to her?

"What is he doing here?" Nikita screamed as she came out of the kitchen.

"Don't be like that Nikita. I'm here to see you. Your parents want us to get back together, so your mum invited me over after she found out you were visiting. She knew how difficult it was for me to get in touch with you. Don't worry honey; I won't hold what happened in Bradford against you."

Nikita couldn't believe what she was hearing. He was playing them. He was such a liar and he was so good at it. She could see why he had them fooled.

"How many times have I told you, I don't want anything to do with you?"

"You see, mum, dad, this is how she speaks to me," he barked.

"Don't you dare call my parents mum and dad, they aren't anything to do with you," Nikita spat.

"Come on," he said and he tried to touch her face.

Nikita hated him with a vengeance. It made her shudder to feel his skin against hers and it gave her flash backs of what she had been through. It made her cringe and she couldn't breathe. She felt like she was having a panic attack.

"Oh it's all an act. Stop faking all this shit," he shouted. "What's wrong with you? I'm offering you everything and all you want to do is carry on living your life as a prostitute. How many more men have you had since, hey?"

"That's enough," Dad shouted and he got up out of his chair. "I'm not going to sit here and listen to you talking to my daughter in that manner."

Nikita stared at her dad, not believing that she had just heard him stand up for her. She felt a rush of pride.

"But dad, she's lying to you," Sam shouted.

He grabbed Nikita by the hand and started to pull her towards the front door.

"Let go of me," she screamed.

Mum started crying, she didn't know what to do. Nikita pulled free from Sam and he grabbed her from around the neck. "I should have finished the job the first time round," he whispered in her ear.

"Let go of her," dad said, every word emphasized, "or I'll call the police."

Sam let go and pushed Nikita away. "Keep the bitch; I never wanted to marry her in the first place. You people should be ashamed of your family," and he looked Nikita's dad over.

"Get out of my house!" dad said distinctly, anger pulsing through him.

Sam gave Nikita one last glare and walked out of the front door.

Nikita took a deep breath, as she rubbed her neck. Her mum sat on the sofa and just kept crying. Dad didn't look at her and sat back down in his armchair.

Nikita kneeled down next to her dad and put her hand on his. He pulled his hand away but didn't look at her. "Dad" she said. He didn't even twitch.

"Dad, I know you're angry with me, but I haven't done anything wrong. Do you remember the day you said to me, 'never give you a reason to ever lower your head?' Do you remember that? Since that day dad, I've never given you any reason to doubt me, so why can't you trust me on this? I don't blame you for what happened to me. You didn't know what kind of man he was, but you have to trust my decision to leave him. If I didn't then maybe I wouldn't even be sitting here right now, you would have cremated me."

He still didn't look at Nikita but she saw the frown across his forehead and she wished he would give her a hug. But he didn't.

Nikita looked over to her mum and told her she was leaving.

Mum looked at Nikita through her tear ridden eyes. "When will we see you again?" she asked.

"I don't know. I don't know if I should come back, whether you want me here. Dad's still angry with me." Nikita said it loud enough for him to hear. "I have to go, bye mum," she mumbled as she headed for the front door. "Bye dad." He still didn't look at her.

Nikita quickly headed to the car fighting back the tears and as she drove passed the house; she could see her mum looking through the curtains with tears still running down her face.

Nikita turned down a quiet road and pulled up. She put her face in her hands and cried her eyes out.

She hadn't seen her dad or spoken to him for two years and even after witnessing everything with his own eyes, he still couldn't bring himself to look at her. He hated her. He saw her as a disappointment and he was ashamed of her. She hated herself for putting him through this, but what else could she have done? The questions ran through her head again and again and again.

Pull yourself together, she told herself and she drew out her mobile phone from her handbag.

She called Jai and arranged to pick him up from the shopping centre where she had dropped him off. She met him outside the arcade and he could see how upset she was.

"I take it, it didn't go too well?" he grimaced.

"Yes, you're right," she answered. "He turned up while I was there."

"Oh my god, are you okay? Did he touch you?" His voice was laced with anger.

"It's okay, my dad threw him out."

"So he did touch you." Jai's hands were curled tight into fists.

Nikita felt sad that the animal was also affecting Jai as well. It shouldn't have to be like this.

"I'm sorry Nikita. I should have dealt with him the last time, and then he wouldn't have had the nerve to turn up today."

"It's not your fault," Nikita replied.

"It is. I should have ended this in Bradford. I feel like such a coward for not having done anything to sort him out."

"Jai please don't say that. I cost you enough that day. Imagine if the press had caught you in a fist fight. It would have been awful. I would never forgive myself and you can't jeopardise your career in that way. Ever. It's over now anyway. I don't think he'll be back. My dad threw him out. But do you know what the worst thing was?"

Jai nodded.

"My dad couldn't even bring himself to look at me. He hates me Jai, I can see it."

Jai relaxed and he put his arm around Nikita. "He doesn't hate you; you need to give them time to adjust. It's all a big shock to them as well, they'll come round in the end, you'll see," he smiled.

"I don't know Jai. I can't believe my mum; I don't know how they let him in the house," she grimaced.

"I suppose he's a bit like my dad. People thought he was a wonderful man. Nobody really knew what he was like," Jai explained.

"Look, you're not in a state to drive, let me," Jai said and Nikita moved over so he could jump into the driver's seat.

Nikita didn't say much all the way back home and Jai didn't push her to talk either, but he held her hand for most of the journey and that made her feel a little better.

"I'm going to call your solicitor friend and ask him to begin the proceedings Jai. I have to put an end to this now," Nikita said.

"Go for it babe. You deserve your freedom and you deserve the right to get that monster out of your life once and for all," he replied.

When she had Jai around her, she felt like she could do anything. He gave her so much strength and she loved him for it.

Nikita stopped in her train of thought. She loved him for it? She loved him? Did she? **She did**. She realised for the first time in her life, she was in love and it made her feel warm inside.

Chapter 25 - My Best Friend

Jazz paid her share of the rent until the end of the contract and decided she wanted to make the move sooner rather than later. She'd managed to get a transfer in her company and as the new post had been vacant for a while, they wanted her to take up the role immediately.

Nikita drove Jazz to the train station with all her belongings. The train wasn't due to arrive for another forty minutes so they decided to grab a cup of coffee while they waited.

Jazz was more than Nikita's best friend. She was her sister, her family and had been her everything for the last year. Nikita felt like she had known her all her life. Jazz had helped Nikita through the worst of times. When she'd felt like giving up, or felt like hurting herself and when she considered going back to that bastard, Jazz gave Nikita the courage to be strong and believe in herself. Jazz changed Nikita's life.

Nikita was really going to miss her and wondered how she was going to cope. Nikita promised herself that she wouldn't let on how sad it made her feel. It was hard enough for Jazz as it was, she already felt guilty and Nikita didn't want to make it any more difficult for her.

"Promise that you'll keep in touch Jazz," Nikita said, her voice shaking.

"You'll always be part of my life babe. Just because I'm further away doesn't change anything. I'll still love you. And anyway, you need to keep me up to date with what's going on with Jai," she giggled.

"Don't worry, I'll keep you posted, not that anything major is going to happen any time soon."

"Babe, you deserve to be happy and I can see that he really does care about you. You need to take the risk and go for it."

"I am trying to Jazz, but just at my own pace," Nikita grimaced.

"Yeh but, I know that you've been holding back because of what happened in the past. You need to understand that he is nothing like that bastard and Jai won't treat you like that arsehole did. I can tell by the way Jai looks at you, he's really into you. I think that this could be the real thing you know."

"I don't know. He's lovely, beautiful and intelligent. He's kind, caring and everything a girl could want, I can't fault him. It's just that sometimes I feel like it's too good to be true and I'm frightened of getting hurt again," Nikita explained. "I keep feeling like there has to be a catch somewhere."

Nikita had mastered developing an invisible shield around her emotions, which made it hard for anyone to penetrate. It also kept her strong and safe and she was never going to give anyone the chance to hurt her or break her heart. She'd learnt that from Jazz.

"Babe, you are all those things too, you two are perfect together, but you just have to give him a chance."

"Okay, okay, stop lecturing.....So, when you get to Manchester, make sure you text me to let me know you got back safe and sound. I want at least one telephone call every week to let me know how you're getting on," Nikita demanded.

"I will, I'll probably be on the phone everyday and you'll get fed up with me," she laughed.

Just then the announcement came. The train would be arriving in five minutes so Nikita helped Jazz take her bags down to the platform. She embraced Jazz in a big hug, fighting back the tears.

"I love you, don't ever forget it and make sure that you come back and visit me okay?" Nikita said feeling emotional.

"Just try and stop me," Jazz replied with tears running down her face.

"Remember to call me when you get home okay?"

"I will," she said and she climbed onto the train.

Nikita waited as the train left the platform and waved at Jazz as the distance increased. She was really going to miss the craziness around her.

She was left standing on the platform, people running around, busy, late, going to work, coming home, meeting friends, but she didn't feel like moving. She was alone again.

Nikita didn't want to go back to an empty flat. She called Jai to see if he wanted to come around for dinner. If anyone could chase away her loneliness, it was him. She also knew he would come to her if she asked. She could rely on him, something she had never been able to do with another man.

"Hey Jai, it's me."

"You okay Nik? Has Jazz gone?"

"Yes, I'm still at the station, the train's just left."

"Are you okay?" he asked.

"Yes, I'm okay, I'm just going to miss her. I feel like I've lost a piece of my heart," Nikita said pushing back the tingling in her eyes. "Anyway, I was wondering if you'd like to come to mine tonight for dinner."

"Umm, okay, I haven't got anything planned, what time do you want me there?"

"I'll be home in about twenty minutes so anytime after that will be okay," Nikita said.

"Okay, I'll see you in a bit then," he replied.

"Bye babe."

Nikita hurried home to get the dinner on. She had some left over cauliflower and potato curry in the fridge so she thought she'd make some fried chapattis stuffed with that, just the way her mum used to make them. Served hot with cold natural yogurt, was mouth watering.

Jai arrived just after she'd finished cooking and she opened the door to him. Nikita walked straight into his arms as he entered her flat. With his height, she buried her head in his chest.

He wrapped his arms around her and squeezed lightly to reassure her.

Nikita had come to find comfort in his arms and she missed them when they weren't around her. As the realisation struck her, she discovered she had become dependent on him to make her feel better, so with a tinge of regret, she pushed out of his embrace and looked up at Jai.

"My offers still open you know, you can come and stay with me for a while. You don't have to stay here on your own," he said.

"I know and I may have to take you up on that offer but it's something I'll have to think about," she replied.

Jai smiled and kissed her on the forehead. He was so tender, so warm, it was just crazy. His body heat radiated and when Nikita placed her face back on his chest, she heard the low thrumming of his heart beat. It was the most beautiful sound she had ever heard.

Nikita pulled away and Jai followed her into the kitchen.

"So what are we having for dinner? I'm starving," he complained.

"Don't get too excited, I didn't make anything special, just stuffed chapattis, I hope that's okay?"

"Are you serious?"

Nikita's heart sank. He was disappointed.

"I can make something else if you want."

"No, what I mean is, are they stuffed with cauliflower and potato curry?"

"Yes"

"Wow, I haven't had those since I was very young. My mum used to make them for breakfast on Sunday mornings. They were my favourite."

Nikita's spirits lifted. "Great, would you like yogurt?"

"Yes please and will you hurry, my mouth is watering just from the smell."

Nikita smiled and poured the yogurt into bowls and passed Jai his plate.

"Mm mm mmmhhhh!" Jai said, his eyes closed like this was the best meal he had ever had. "Wow Nikita, this tastes better than sex."

Nikita blushed.

"Well actually, I don't know if they would taste better than sex between us, but I'll let you know after."

Nikita smiled, not knowing how to respond.

They relaxed in front of the TV and ate with their plates on their laps, something Nikita enjoyed.

"This is the tastiest food I've had in ages," he smiled.

"Ahh, thank you, I'm glad you enjoyed it."

"Being with you always takes me back to my childhood," he stated, his voice a little sad.

"You really miss mum don't you?"

"Yeh, lately I've been thinking about her a lot, especially since dad passed away," he said.

Nikita switched the television off so she could listen more intently.

"I feel lonely," he said. "Since dad passed away, I feel like I have no one. I mean, I've got my friends, but I don't have that connection with anyone else."

"Not even with me?" Nikita asked.

Jai looked at her and smiled. "I've been hoping that you will fill that void in my life but I don't know that you want to."

Nikita frowned, taking a moment to respond. "I do Jai, but I'm scared," she said quietly.

"Scared, scared about what?" he asked.

"I'm scared of getting hurt. I know you're not like that, but I have a fear which is deep in my heart and no matter how hard I try, I can't seem to shake it. I want to be the one to fill that void, I really do, but it's just going to take a little time." Nikita dropped her gaze.

She looked sad and Jai felt his heart sink. Right at that moment he knew this girl was the most important person in the world to him.

Jai placed a finger under Nikita's chin and pulled her face up to level his. "Nik, I want you in my life, no matter how long I have to wait." He paused for a moment. "No that's wrong. I need you in my life. I can't stop thinking about you. When I can't see you, I feel a great big gaping hole in my heart. I think that....." and he didn't finish.

"You think what Jai?" Nikita asked.

He took a deep breath. "I think I'm in love with you Nik. I can't seem to stop thinking about you. I can't stop thinking about the way you kiss me, the way you hold me, your Bollywood one liners, your stories. My mum would really have loved you. She would have been proud of me for wanting to spend my life with someone as brave and as strong as you."

Nikita didn't know what to say. She was in shock. She had dreamt about someone saying these words to her but now that it had happened, she couldn't think what to say back. She just stared at him. It made her realise that she was scared about getting hurt because she felt the same way about him. Her feelings were a defence mechanism. She loved him too and she had done so for some time now.

"Now would be a good time to say something," he smiled.

The problem was, Nikita couldn't find the right words to respond with.

"Please, I can almost hear my heart shattering here," he joked, his eyes mischievous.

She looked into Jai's eyes and leaned in to kiss him, but this time she didn't hold back at all. She dropped her guard. The invisible shield around her heart had melted away. She kissed him on the lips, on his cheeks, his forehead and as she kissed his neck she continued down undoing the buttons on his shirt so that she could bear his chest. She didn't know what she was doing, but she knew she wanted him. She pulled his shirt open to bear his muscled chest and shoulders. Her breath caught and even though she'd seen it before, she couldn't believe how magnificent he was. His skin was beautifully tanned and with the light reflecting on his skin, it had a golden shimmer. Amazing she thought. How could a man be so exquisite? She ran her fingers over his shoulders, his taut chest and then over his dark nipples. She heard his breath catch just a little. His eyes were sparkling gold and she stared into them using her own eyes to tell him, she loved him. His scent swirled around her, touching her every nerve, making her shiver with desire for him. Nikita pushed herself up placing her legs on either side of his hips and when she lowered herself, Jai shuddered in pleasure. He let out a groan, a deep guttural sound, which made Nikita clench between her thighs.

He shuddered under her hands. Jai pulled back up to kiss her lips again. Her mouth tasted so sweet and her lips felt soft. He kissed her, caressing down her neck and down to the top of her breasts.

"Jai," Nikita said almost a whisper.

He pulled back to look at her.

"I don't have any experience in this." Even though this was not the first time for her, this was the first time that she had wanted to do anything like this. What that bastard did to her made her feel violated and he never kissed her. She was very in-experienced and she didn't know if she would please him.

Jai stopped and pulled her back down putting his arms around her. He fought every nerve in his body to do what he had to do right now. He realised if this went any further, she would probably end up regretting it and he couldn't risk that. She was too important to him. Nikita was like the earth and the air, something that was essential in life, something he couldn't live without. She was so beautiful, yet so vulnerable, so he knew he had to tread carefully. His heart broke to have to do this but it had to be done. "You're not ready yet Nik and I don't want you to feel you have to because of what I've just said to you. I don't want you to feel pressurized."

"I don't Jai, I want to," she said, her voice sounding almost desperate.

"You do? Okay, come here then," he said and she leaned forward. He kissed her again but this time with so much more passion, it was breath taking. She tasted delicious. He started to undo the buttons on her top and when it revealed two beautiful pink breasts with a slight dusting of freckles, it was almost his undoing.

He pushed his hands into her hair and it was the most erotic feeling that Nikita had ever experienced.

Jai pulled her down, his lips meeting hers, almost painfully with wanting, with need. He placed his hands on her chest and then brought them down to her breasts.

Nikita looked at him direct, unsure and she realised she couldn't go through with it.

Jai saw the hesitation in Nikita's eyes. He caught her hands in the moment when she was about to curl away from him. He couldn't allow her to distance herself. He pulled her blouse closed with one hand and put his arm around her with the other. He held her tight, her body stiff with discomfort. After a few moments he felt some of the tension dissolve and she relaxed into him.

He couldn't allow her to curl into a little ball at the end of the sofa as though she was frightened of him. He'd caused her to feel that way before and he wouldn't have been able to take that right now. He had been a fool, pushed her too far, stupid, stupid man. He had to start thinking with his brain and not with what was going on in his trousers. What an idiot.

"It's okay Nik; I know you're not ready. I'm sorry; I should never have pushed you," he finally said.

Nikita relaxed realising Jai was right. She should never have pushed him.

Nikita looked up at him, "I'm sorry," she said.

"Don't be sorry, I shouldn't have tried to prove a point."

Nikita was like the sun on a rainy day, the scent of red roses, and the smell of the ocean. She was the most wonderful thing in his life. He stroked her back, "Hey, it's okay. When you are ready, I'll be waiting."

They sat holding each other for a while longer, neither saying anything, but that was okay. There wasn't a need. They didn't have to fill their time together with words. Lying in each other's arms was more than enough.

After a while, Jai looked over to the clock and he realised it was getting quite late. "Hey honey, it's time for me to get going. Would you like to come with me?"

Nikita thought about it for a moment. "Not tonight Jai, I think I'll stay here, but I'll see you in the morning won't I?" She was worried she might have upset him.

"I'll be there first thing but then I have a meeting so you'll be home alone for a little while," he explained.

Jai got up, straightened and buttoned his clothes, covering that gorgeous muscled chest of his. Nikita felt a pang of disappointment. A man like that was not meant to cover up; he wasn't made to wear clothes. She wished that she could rip the shirt off his back.

Jai must have noticed the lustful look in Nikita's eyes because he said, "please don't look at me like that. I have little control as it is and with you staring at me with those sexy eyes, I will lose the restrain I have on myself."

Nikita blushed.

Jai walked over to the door, his stride a little awkward.

"Is something wrong Jai, are you hurt?" Nikita asked. "Why are you walking like that?"

Jai smiled, "Don't worry, it's nothing. I'll be fine."

Then as she looked down at his legs, she noticed the bulge in his trousers and she realised why he was walking awkwardly. She felt herself flush again.

Jai opened the door and turned to face her. He kissed her on the forehead.

It took everything in Nikita let him go. She wanted to ask him to stay and spend the night with her, but she just couldn't bring herself to say it. What was wrong with her?

"See you tomorrow honey," he said as he walked away.

'Honey,' she liked the sound of that and she smiled internally.

Jai walked down the corridor urging himself to leave. Today Nikita had taken him to the depths of his will power. Usually girls were throwing themselves at him and he was fighting them off. Then there was Tina and even though they hadn't slept together for a while, they hadn't remained celibate throughout their relationship.

300

Jai got into his car and looked around. There was no one around and he was parked under a lamp post that wasn't working. He undid his belt and put his hand down his trousers and straightened himself up. At least now he could sit straight.

Chapter 26 - Her First Time

A few weeks went by but Nikita hadn't found the right flat. She had no choice but to take up Jai's offer and move in with him, and she kept on searching, when she had time. All her furniture had to go into storage. She was literally living out of a suitcase.

Jai was such a gentleman. He didn't try taking advantage of her, even though secretly she wished he would. He'd purchased a new sofa bed, to replace the old sofa in the lounge, not that it looked like it needed replacing. She knew it was for her benefit. She insisted on something cheaper, but he wouldn't listen. This sofa bed was more comfortable than her old bed. It had to be, especially when it cost a small fortune.

Jai was out at a shoot and Nikita was home alone again. She'd done all the work she could do by the afternoon and then started to get bored. She hated being without him.

They spent every hour of every day together except for when he was out filming or when they slept.

She decided to put on one of her Hindi CDs and started to dance around the apartment. One of her favourite songs came on, which had a real Spanish feel to it. Opening the doors to the balcony to let in the fresh air and gorgeous sunlight, she turned the music up loud and swung her hips. She stood in the middle of the lounge area, dancing away feeling the music. Her body moved seductively. All those years of Bollywood dancing had made her body supple and agile. Her hips moved like Shakira and she danced with the confidence of Beyonce. Music always lifted her spirits. When she hears a song she loves, shivers run up her spine and make her body tingle. She loved a variety of music. It all depended on how the song appealed to her. Sometimes it was the lyrics and other times it was the harmonies. Nikita felt confident by herself, shaking her hips just that little bit more, swinging her arms around her body in bigger gestures. There were some moves that she only felt comfortable doing alone.

She felt someone come up against her. Placing his hands on her hips, he started moving with her. She turned around, startled, because she hadn't heard the door open. "Jai."

He smiled a wide, gleaming smile and Nikita was reminded how lucky she was. Her breath caught and her heartbeat quickened. His beauty was extraordinary. The way that he looked at her, made her knees go funny. He was so refined in his walk, the way he carried himself, it was astonishing.

Nikita breathed him in, which tickled her belly. Butterflies darted around her stomach making her feel giddy. She was in awe of him.

He had returned home early. Jai pulled Nikita in close and placed his hands around her waist. He moved to the music, encouraging Nikita to move with him. The song came to an end and he hugged her smiling. The next track started which was an old Kishore Kumar song and one of Nikita's favourite golden oldies. Perfect timing she thought.

This song was so beautiful, the lyrics so romantic.

Nikita reached up and put her arms around Jai's neck, threading her hands through his hair. She loved the feel of his dark brown locks. Jai and Nikita swayed from side to side as they gazed into each other's eyes. She could feel his love running through her and it made her feel warm inside.

Jai leaned down and kissed her. He slowly urged her mouth open and Nikita felt his tongue stroke hers.

He tasted so sweet and delicious. She opened her eyes to look at him and she could see the lines of frustration on his face. She knew it was hard for him to control himself, but he always did, for her. She pulled away from the kiss and he looked at her in confusion. It was the perfect moment with him and she felt as though this was the moment she was made for. She knew she didn't want to be without him. She needed him and she wanted him. He was the greatest happiness she had ever known and she knew at that moment that she couldn't be without him, ever. The feeling was immensely overpowering, stronger than anything she had ever felt in her life. Without saying a word, she started to move towards his bedroom and she pulled him by his hand. Jai walked behind her.

They sat down on the bed and he looked at her.

"I love you," he smiled. "I've never felt like this about anyone before," and he touched her face.

"I love you too," Nikita replied. "You are everything to me, but I'm scared."

"Don't be. I promise I'll look after you, I promise to share my joys and my pain with you, and I won't let you down. You are the only one that really knows me and you have given me the opportunity to open up and talk about things I have never spoken about and I love you for it," he smiled again.

He stroked her face.

Nikita moved in and whispered into his ear, "I'm ready."

He searched in her face for reassurance. He needed to be certain. "I don't want you to feel pressurised, I can wait," he promised.

Jai was desperate to make love to her, to show her what she meant to him, but he had to get it right. The consequences of getting it wrong could lead to devastation and he couldn't risk that. He had imagined it for months, what it would feel like to be one with her. He knew it would be worth the wait.

Nikita whispered in Jai's ear. "Jai, I don't want to wait any longer and I trust you." Nikita smiled and suddenly felt a little embarrassed.

She quickly moved in to kiss him, unable to bare his piercing molten eyes staring at her. It made her feel shy but he was so gentle. She was really worried that she would freeze, or become anxious, but Jai was so tender, he made her feel comfortable. Slowly they started to undress each other and when she got down to her underwear, she felt uncomfortable. They lay down next to each other and she buried her face in his chest. He placed his finger under her chin and lifted her face up to meet his.

She ran her finger around his face and followed the line of his chin. She traced his lips with her finger and moved up and kissed them, not holding back.

He pushed her back onto the bed holding her down. With the sensuous tip of his finger, he trailed it along her forehead, down her nose, over her lips and across her breasts. He reached underneath her and unhooked her bra and lifted it off.

Nikita covered her face with her hands.

He gazed at her plump round breasts and his breath caught. He felt the electricity shoot to his groin and it was all he could do, not to rip her pants off and take her right then. He touched her breasts and traced her curves down to her waist, across her hips and followed down her thigh. He pulled her hands away from her face but she kept her eyes closed.

The sensuality ignited something deep inside her, another new experience.

"You're beautiful," he whispered into her ear.

He bent down and kissed her again and before long they were lying naked next to each other, their bodies entwined. He pushed his body right up against hers and pulled hers towards his. He kissed her everywhere. Long, deep, intense kisses.

Nikita didn't realise she had forgotten to breathe and when she became aware that she needed to take a breath, she stopped moving her mouth.

He didn't let her move her lips away and he continued to breathe into her. She tasted so sweet and as he pushed the hot sugary air into her mouth, she breathed in deep into her lungs.

She felt like his love was being carried around her body with the oxygen. It pushed into every artery, every vein and every vessel of her being. His love was running through her blood stream. Warm, hot pulsating love.

His body was so beautiful, like that of a Greek God. His stomach firm, the muscles solid with a sprinkling of curly hair down below, the colour of treacle. He was so refined. He had a face which could break a million hearts, but he was hers. He had chosen her and this turned her on even more.

He made love to her so softly and passionately. Jai groaned in pleasure. He watched her, as he loved her, unable to take his eyes off her. She was the most exquisite being he had ever seen.

She was so hot for him. Her breathing became ragged. "Jai," she whimpered. Her words coming out a blur and all she knew was, she wanted him to continue doing what he was doing. "Don't stop."

Jai became even more aroused. The sound of her voice sent an electrical current through his body. He wanted to feel her shake with wanting and pleasure. He wanted to feel her sweating, digging her nails into his back, because she couldn't contain herself. He wanted to hear her scream in pleasure and he wanted her to demand more.

Her breasts were soft but her nipples turned into nubby cherries when he rubbed his finger tips over them. She writhed under him.

Nikita realised her thoughts from earlier were wrong. **This** was the most perfect moment with him and this was the moment she was made for. But then she also realised she was going to have many more perfect moments with Jai and from this point on, her life was going to change forever. It was the greatest happiness she had ever known.

Jai made sure she experienced pleasures Nikita had only ever dreamt about.

Nikita lay sprawled across his chest and for a moment she thought about her parents but not for long. She told herself she would deal with whatever they felt because she had found her true happiness, Jai.

Nikita looked up at him as he lay there as peaceful as anything, fast asleep. He looked almost vulnerable with his guard down, but still as beautiful as an Angel. Nikita watched his taut chest rise and fall as he breathed and she felt the urge to run her fingers over it, circling his dark syrupy nipples. But, she didn't want to disturb him; he seemed to be at such peace. Quietly she pushed her fingers into his hand and he moved to accommodate her, wrapping his large strong hands around hers.

This was the first time anyone had shown her so much love and she felt needed, wanted and enjoyed. Jai made her feel good about herself, feel beautiful and he made her feel like a woman.

After a while, she slowly got up so as to not disturb Jai and looked for her voice book. She felt like writing about him. Before she had always written about her pain, but today she wanted to write something about her happiness. She wrapped a bed sheet round herself and went into the living room with her book and looked for a pen. She sat down on the sofa and started to write.

Lost and broken with nothing to live for
Down and sad with no one to live for

Until the day that I met you, my angel my soul mate
You are my ray of light, it happened just like fate

You came as a dream, which became a reality
You became my friend, then everything to me

You tell me you love me, I can't believe
You are so precious and love so perfectly

You gave me strength and you made me your pride
Made me your own and in you I confide

You know how to lift me, no matter how I feel
Make me smile, I can't believe, is this for real?

I love you forever, without you I can't live
My life without you, I cannot forgive

Jai woke and the realisation dawned, there was something missing from his arms. He looked around. For a second he thought she had gone. His life flashed before him. Had he pushed her too far? Did she regret it? Why would she leave? He jumped out of bed and pulled on his jeans. Without buttoning them, he walked out of his bedroom, barefoot.

He placed his hand on his chest without thinking, feeling a sigh of relief wash over him when he laid eyes on her. He let out a breath he hadn't realised he was holding. He smiled, crossed his arms and leaned against the frame of the bedroom door. He watched her, sitting on the sofa with the crisp white cotton sheet wrapped around her beautiful body. She simply glowed. Her hair was tousled, her face still pink from the love making and her neck and bare shoulders were exposed where the sheet had slipped off. It was stupid but he envied that piece of material at that moment. He wanted to be the one wrapped around her, keeping her warm, touching her, caressing her.

He felt himself stir below; he wanted to kiss her flesh again. He felt so warm inside, when the thought crossed his mind. 'She's mine.'

He watched her, deep in thought, then writing, then the tip of the pen in her mouth, thinking again. She was so cute, there was something very child like about her. He loved everything about her.

Nikita didn't realize when Jai came and stood behind her.

"What are you writing?" he asked.

"Oh umm, nothing," she replied, hiding the book under the sheet.

"Let me see."

"No, it's embarrassing. You're going to laugh at me."

Jai hooked Nikita's chin and pulled her face up. "I would never laugh at you and if you think that, then you don't know me at all."

Nikita grimaced. She felt her stomach tighten in embarrassment. These were her most intimate thoughts.

Thoughts that she had never shared with anyone, not even Jazz.

"I'll find your book later and read what you've written anyway, so you might as well let me see. Is it about me?" he asked.

Nikita nodded.

She took a deep breath and handed the voice book over to him.

"Move over then, I want you to wrap that sheet around me as well," and Nikita opened one side up for Jai to climb into, revealing a bare thigh and stomach. Jai stared down at her, licking his lips without realising.

He shook his head and sat down next to her.

She laid her trembling head on his arm.

He sat there for quite some time, much longer than what it would have taken him to read what she had written. She looked at him confused; he looked upset, almost like he was going to cry.

"It's beautiful," he smiled with a tear in his eye. "I can't believe you wrote this about me."

"I wrote it because that's how you make me feel."

"I love you," he smiled.

"I love you too," she said and she kissed him.

Jai turned to the front of the book to read the other pages and although she knew he would see the nightmares that had haunted her for years, she didn't stop him from looking. He sat there for a while longer reading through the pages, reading about her pain and her deepest, darkest thoughts. He didn't say anything.

After a while he took a deep breath and shut the book. He embraced her in his arms without saying a word. He held her so tight. He never wanted to let her go, to never be apart from her. He wished they could be one again. Jai wanted to erase every single one of those nightmares and replace them with sweet loving memories.

They sat for a few minutes and she moved to lay her head on his chest. Neither of them said anything and although it was quiet, the silence felt right. After a while Jai spoke. "I feel like killing him. I've never hated anyone as much?"

"It doesn't matter now Jai. It's over. He can't hurt me anymore," she said, leaning her face against his heart.

This was her favourite place in the world.

"I will never put you through that, I promise," and he smiled and kissed her forehead. He tugged on her chin to release her bottom lip. When her lips parted and she took in a quick gasp of air, Jai felt like he would lose all control. Heat raced through his body and he moved in to take her mouth.

Nikita pulled away to look at Jai. "I want you to touch me everywhere," she said, lifting his hands up to her face. "I want you to replace every dark memory with a new beautiful one. When I look back, I want to remember you and how you made me feel, not him. Erase my pain with your pleasure, with your love. Wipe the slate clean with your passion."

Those words struck Jai, right at the centre of his heart. He wanted to do exactly that and now Nikita had told him that she wanted the same. He breathed in deep. She was irresistible and alluring. She had cast a spell on him because what he felt for her was crazy.

They made love throughout the night and it was very late when they both fell asleep.

Nikita could have stayed in bed with Jai forever. She didn't want anything to change, but she knew they had to get up at some point so she persuaded him to get out of bed and anyway, she needed a cup of tea.

Over breakfast, Jai decided he wasn't going to go to the film shoot so he called in and told them he wasn't very well.

He decided he wanted to invite his friends round in the evening for a drink. He wanted to introduce Nikita to them, so they put on their tracksuits and started planning. Jai made some phone calls and invited as many of his friends as he could get hold of.

Nikita planned the menu and although Jai insisted on ordering the food in, she insisted on cooking.

"Let me do something," she said. "I really want to."

"I don't want you to have to spend all day in the kitchen. You don't know my friends, they eat like pigs," he replied.

"It's fine, I don't mind, honestly. You know how much I love cooking."

"You're in the wrong line of work baby. Don't get me wrong, I think you're a fantastic P.A. but you should be in the catering business," he smiled.

Nikita knew that Jai didn't want to trouble her but she enjoyed cooking and she really wanted to do this. Besides it was a great way to impress Jai's friends.

Nikita went to the supermarket and picked up everything she needed.

Jai had given Nikita his credit card and pin number again to use to purchase all the ingredients.

Nikita was back home within a couple of hours and she made a start straight away. Home, she liked the sound of that, but she changed her train of thought, because she was getting ahead of herself again.

Jai's friends started to turn up around seven o'clock in the evening.

Nikita had all the music prepared, but it was more to her taste rather than Jai's but he didn't mind.

All his friends knew her as Jai's P.A. and friend and they were all very polite to her. Nikita felt nervous. What would they think of her? They had all heard that Jai had broken up with Tina and some of them thought he was crazy.

"How could you let her go? Did you see the legs on her?"

"Are you crazy, she was beautiful?"

Nikita had heard all the comments from his friends and she knew she would never compare to Tina. This unnerved her even more.

There was a football match on TV that evening, so it wasn't long before all of Jai's friends were settled to watch the match, after guzzling down most of the food and beer.

She started to clear the table, but Jai called her to come and join them to watch the match. Nikita told him she wasn't really interested but the truth was that it brought back too many horrible memories for her. As much as she wanted to watch the gorgeous David Bekham play for England, she couldn't bring herself to sit with the boys. It made her feel anxious and uncomfortable.

Jai kept looking over to her and smiling. As she took some of the dishes into the kitchen, he followed her in with some of the plates. As she put them in the sink, Jai grabbed her from behind and kissed her neck. He spun her around and leant down and kissed her passionately on the lips. She wished this giddy feeling would never end. Each kiss felt like it was the first and it gave her butterflies in the stomach and made her weak at the knees.

"I love you," Jai smiled.

Nikita's chest expanded with pride. "I love you too," she smiled, giggling at his pink lips. She wiped off the gloss for him, and he went back out to join his friends.

After a few moments one of Jai's friends joined her in the kitchen saying he wanted a glass of water. Kevin was one of Jai's best friends but he'd been working away for a while and so she hadn't met him before now. He had moved back into his apartment on the other side of city recently, but he hadn't been able to visit sooner due to other commitments.

"So, you're the new P.A. are you?"

She didn't like the tone of his voice. "Yes I am," she replied in a similar tone.

"And you're his cook and cleaner too are you?"

"No," she replied with an underlying tone of irritation. "I'm just helping him out. Is there anything wrong with that?"

"Did I say there was anything wrong with it? I just hope you're getting paid for the extra work you're doing." He said it emphasising the word 'extra'.

Nikita may not be highly educated, but she wasn't stupid. She knew what this guy was implying by the using the term 'extra work'. What an arsehole, she thought.

"I don't think it's any of your business what extra work I do for Jai," she told him firmly.

"Hey, I was just joking," he laughed.

"Joking? I didn't find it very funny," she said.

Nikita's confidence had grown, and it showed in the way she challenged Kevin with all his nonsense. She felt proud as she stared him down.

"Sorry, I get carried away sometimes. People tell me I'm an arsehole; I didn't mean to upset you."

"Well you didn't," Nikita exclaimed. She didn't want him to know that he got under her skin.

Jai looked around his living room, noticing that Kevin wasn't there. His eyes drifted to the kitchen and he saw Kevin standing in the doorway. Jai's heart did a little flutter. Kevin was a good friend, but Jai knew him well. Sometimes he didn't know how to control his mouth and not everyone appreciated his sharp tongue and sarcasm. Jai decided he would give it another minute and then he would check on Nikita to see if she was okay. He hadn't laid eyes on her for the last few moments and he missed her already.

"I'm Kevin by the way," he said as he put his hand out to shake hers.

"Hi Kevin, I'm Nikita," she replied with a smile keeping up the pretence. She didn't like this man one little bit, but she shook his hand never the less.

"I've heard a lot about you. I was looking forward to meeting you, until now," she said with a hint of sarcasm.

"Okay, I guess I deserved that," he smiled. "Jai and I have been friends for years. He used to bring Tina over to my place all the time. Those two made a really nice couple, you know?"

He really was a bastard, Nikita thought. She didn't know what to make of him. Why was he saying these things to her now? Hadn't Jai told him about his and Tina's relationship ending? Nikita tried to keep a straight face and managed a little smile and went back out to collect more dishes. When she returned to the kitchen, Kevin was still standing there messing around with his phone. Why didn't he just go back to watching the football match? Why was he still standing here? She didn't want to talk to him anymore.

"Take a look at this picture Nikita, it's of Jai and Tina."

She didn't want to look but she couldn't help herself. Why did he have a picture of Jai and Tina? It was over. This guy had to be bluffing. Nikita moved round to see the mobile phone screen, still not believing he could have a picture of them. Kevin held out his phone and as she looked, she felt like someone had kicked her in the stomach with full force. It was a picture of Jai and Tina kissing. A cold rock settled at the bottom of her stomach and she couldn't find any words. She spoke slowly.

"When.....when was this taken," she mumbled.

"Last week," he replied. "It was really hard to tear these two apart you know, they were kissing, even in public. I told them to get a room," he continued.

"Last week, last week," she said confused.

"Yes, last week."

Nikita looked at Kevin. He held his expression. Was he bullshitting? Why would he, he had no reason to lie. Could it be true? How could it be? Jai told Nikita he wasn't with Tina anymore. This was months ago, so why was he kissing her in this picture taken last week? Nikita felt the soul drain from her body. It was as though she could feel nothing; her whole body had gone numb. A moment later she found she couldn't breathe and she was finding it difficult to stand.

"Look, if you're ever looking for work, come and see me. I pay well, especially for the extracurricular activities, if you know what I mean?"

She felt the blood rush from her face. What did he think she was? Nikita felt dirty and what made it worse was that this time she had walked straight into it with her eyes wide open. Yet, she never saw it coming.

Nikita gave him a contemptuous look. "I have to go," she said feeling like her legs had turned to rubber.

She pushed Kevin out of the way and headed straight for the front door.

How could she have let this happen? How could she have fallen for such lies? Jai had been lying to her all along, their whole relationship had been a farce, but she couldn't understand why.

She ran down the stairs of the building, too impatient to wait for the lift and headed briskly down the street. She walked and walked and just kept walking. Why would he do this to her? What did she do to deserve this? Maybe it was her; maybe she was an easy target for these men. Maybe she was a magnet for punishment. Was he just using her? And then to listen to this man suggest profanities to her, she felt used and abused all over again.

When she was in the refuge they had often said how some men had a radar for vulnerable women. They could easily pick up on the ones that went into the same sort of relationship, time and time again. She was one of these women. She had fallen for the same old bullshit again.

She cursed Jai, cursed her life, and cursed the world. She felt like she was in a building and the walls were caving in around her. She couldn't breathe; she couldn't think clearly, she only knew that she had to get as far away from him as possible.

God, she hated him. She felt like screaming, yelling. She felt like scratching deep into her arms so she could experience a different pain, anything to take away the feeling of this unbearable pain which she felt right now.

"What did you say to her Kevin? Where has she gone?"

"I don't know. I was just joking with her. It's not my fault if she can't take a joke."

"What do you mean joking with her? What did you say?" Jai could feel the anger building.

"I just showed her a picture of you and Tina kissing which I took ages ago and I told her it was taken last week," he laughed.

"You fucking twat. Do you realise what you've done?" Jai grabbed Kevin by his collar, his other hand coming together into a fist. He felt like punching him. He knew that he was a good friend but sometimes he really hated his guts.

"Look, if she doesn't trust you, that's not my problem and you'll be back with Tina in no time. You got what you wanted. We have to do what we have to do to get what we want. Everyone plays around before they settle down, and when you've finished with this one, hand her over. She's got tits the size of melons. "

Jai lost all control. He took a swing at Kevin and in the next few seconds, Kevin was on the floor, holding a bleeding broken nose."

"Get the fuck out of my house." Every word was laced with fury. Jai felt like killing him.

He went over to where all the boys were sitting and asked them all to leave. He looked over to Kevin and told him to get out. "I never want to see you again," Jai told him. Kevin didn't seem too fussed but Jai didn't have time to waste on the low life, so he pushed him out the door.

Jai picked up his phone and dialled Nikita's number. He heard the phone ringing in the bedroom and realised she had left it behind. It was a long shot but he thought about ringing Jazz. She was the one person Nikita trusted with her life and maybe, just maybe Nikita will have tried to contact her. If she hadn't yet, there was a good chance Nikita would.

Jai dialled Jazz's number using Nikita's phone.

"Hey baby, two calls in one day, I really am privileged today," she said as she answered the phone.

"Jazz, it's Jai. Please listen. Have you heard from Nikita in the last fifteen minutes or so?" He heard his voice break.

"No, should I have done? What's happened? Is she alright?" Jazz asked suspiciously.

"There's been a mistake."

"What do you mean a mistake?" Panic quickly started to build in Jazz's stomach.

Jai sighed. "One of my so called friends told her I was with Tina last week and he insulted her. She got upset and ran out."

"You did what? You arsehole, how could you......."

Jai cut her off. "Look, it's not true. My friend lied to her, none of what he said is true. Look, if you hear from her, please encourage her to come home. I'm going out to look for her now, but please trust me; I haven't seen Tina in months."

"You better not be lying to me Jai. She's strong, she managed to handle the pain of her marriage breakdown, the continuous rape from Sam and the loss of her baby, but she will never get over you. You have to find her," Jazz said, anxiety rushing through the very core of her.

Jai felt like a bomb had detonated in his brain. His head throbbed with pain. "Nikita was pregnant?" he asked, his voice almost a whisper.

"She never told you." More a statement rather than a question.

When Jai didn't answer, Jazz took that to mean he hadn't known.

"When she arrived at the refuge she was in a really bad way. At the time she didn't know she was pregnant, until about three days after her arrival. She started bleeding and was taken into hospital. They informed her that she was around eight weeks pregnant and the doctors told her that more than likely the stress and the assault inflicted on her caused her to miscarry."

Jai couldn't find the right words to respond.

A baby.

"I have to go," was all he could say and so he grabbed his car keys and left to look for the one woman that meant everything to him in life.

Where could she have gone? Why didn't she just ask me, he thought? And that fucking prick. Jai had a pretty good idea why Kevin did it. He constantly asked questions about her and when Jai told him they had got together, he had seen the disappointment on Kevin's face, but Jai never thought that Kevin would pull a stunt like this.

It was already dark and the temperature had dropped rapidly. This December evening had a chill, which wasn't only to do with the weather. Jai was very worried about Nik. She just ran out of the flat as she was. She didn't even have her coat with her or anything else. She must be freezing, he thought. Jai started to get desperate. He thought about reporting her to the police but there was no point. They wouldn't do anything just yet; she had only been missing an hour or so. He drove around and around the streets looking for her.

Ever since he was a child, he had stopped praying to God, because he felt his prayers were never answered, but tonight he prayed, "Please God, please, help me find her."

Jazz had always said to Nikita, "Never give a man one hundred percent, always keep some back for yourself because if you don't and they let you down, you've got nothing to hold onto."

Nikita remembered Jazz's words clearly and she was right. Nikita had shrugged off the comments at the time. She had given Jai her all and she had nothing left to hold onto. He had taken everything away from her. She couldn't even hate him because she loved him so much, even though he had hurt her. As she wandered down a street, she came passed a nearby park and Nikita spotted a bench. She walked over and sat down on it.

Nikita hadn't thought to pick up her handbag as she left the apartment. It had her car keys and her bank card in it.

She had nowhere to go, because stupidly she had become complacent in looking for a flat since she had moved in with Jai.

Her heart ached painfully, even to think his name. The tears started to pour from her eyes and she put her face in her hands and let out a low sob. She wanted the earth to open and swallow her up. She didn't want to exist anymore.

Sam had put her through so much, but she'd dealt with it because she had never let herself get attached to him in anyway. Even when they slept together, her body might have been there but her mind would be elsewhere and that was her way of coping with what was happening to her.

Then she lost her baby. It broke her heart, right there and then. Even though Sam was the father and she hated him, this was her baby. She was going to loved it, nurture and cherish it and give it a life filled with joy. She never found out the sex of the baby, she'd never asked. Sam had taken that away from her as well. In a way, she was glad at the time as she hadn't known about the pregnancy. Her periods were so irregular because of the stress, that when she didn't have her period due to the pregnancy, it didn't come as a surprise. If she had known, she would have built a bond with the baby, fallen in love with it and then when she lost it, she most definitely would have died.

However with Jai, she had surrendered everything to him. Her heart, her body and her mind. She allowed herself to become attached to him in every way possible and the pain of being ripped away from him was far too excruciating to bear. She felt like someone had taken a knife and cut out her heart.

What was she going to do? She had nowhere to go. She didn't even have her mobile phone with her to call anyone for help, and anyway, even if she had, who would she call? Jazz was miles away, so there was no way she could come and get her tonight, and calling her own family was out of the question. She couldn't let them know that she had failed them and herself again.

Nikita's body felt heavy and her head started to spin. The buildings surrounding her seem to close in on her. She had no strength to lift her arms, to shake her head, or fight anymore. She wanted to leave the world behind and be truly alone. She feared life more than anything right now.

She thought about going to the police but they would put her in a refuge and she couldn't go back there again, she just couldn't. She was meant to be moving on with her life, not going back to square one. If she had the keys to the Corsa, she would have been able to crash in the car for the night, but the keys were in the apartment as well.

It was dark. She looked at her watch and it was almost midnight. She didn't know where the time had gone. She couldn't stay on the bench all night, she could hear drunken people at a distance and she couldn't risk any of them coming over to her. It was too quiet where she was sitting so she decided to start walking around again on the main road, while she thought about where she could go. At least there were cars driving around and it would be safer than a bench in a quiet park where no one could see her if anything happened.

She walked around for another hour, wrapping her arms around herself, trying to keep the feeling of ice coming through her clothes. People were horning at her as they drove passed but she ignored them. A man pulled over and wound his window down.

"Hey baby, you looking for a ride?" he smiled.

"What? No!"

"Come on, don't play games. I can make it worth your while," he said. He was driving a Mercedes Benz. It looked silver in colour and he was dressed in a smart suit and looked well groomed.

Nikita started walking quickly and he drove up beside her again.

"How much?" he said, annoyed.

"What the..." she said as she came to a halt. "Do I look like a prostitute to you?" Nikita glared at him, outraged.

"You're the one walking the streets honey. What would you call yourself?"

Nikita walked on infuriated. Men... they are all the same, the bastards.

She didn't look at him again and carried on walking. He must have got the message because he drove off.

Fucking wanker, she thought to herself. Why didn't he go home and ask his mother or daughter how much they charged, arsehole. Nikita cursed the man and hoped that he would crash his car and die a painful death.

Did she really look like a prostitute to him? She felt disgusted and she shivered violently at the thought. If she never slept with another man again it would be too soon. Then the thought crossed her mind. She was the one who was walking the streets at one o'clock in the morning.

Nikita remembered meeting a girl at the refuge. She was only eighteen years old. So young and inexperienced, she remembered thinking. Her name was Zara, and her boyfriend had introduced her to drugs. Once she was hooked on heroin, he forced her into prostitution. Initially, he gave her some sob story about how he was struggling to pay the dealer and the only way he could protect his own life was, if she agreed to sleep with one of the dealer's men.

So, she did.

Before long he started to pimp her to other men to help feed her habit. She was on the streets for a whole year before she realised he did this for a living. He had groomed many girls before, forced them to develop an addiction to drugs and then pushed them into. He made so much money from them, but the girls didn't care. If one of them refused to do as he said, he refused her drugs. When a girl didn't get the drugs, she felt like she was dying. Her body would scream in pain, and then she was ready to do anything to get rid of this feeling.

Zara said she had met many men in the year she was on the streets. These were men that had high profile jobs like solicitors and barristers and many other men who worked in trusted professions. Some of them were supposedly happily married with children and they were still out looking for sex. Their wives didn't have a clue. Zara had been through so much trauma.

While she was on the streets, she became pregnant twice because sometimes the men refused to use protection. After her second abortion, she decided she had to get away. She was originally from Scotland and she came to Birmingham to get away from her ex. She feared for her life because if he ever found her, the chances were that he would kill her.

Thinking about all these stories from the refuge made Nikita feel hatred towards men even more.

Were they all abusive bastards?

As Nikita walked, the rain started to come down in huge, heavy droplets. She didn't even have a jacket, so she wrapped her arms around her body and kept moving. It was the only chance she had of keeping her blood pumping around her body to keep her warm. But she was getting soaked and her teeth were chattering.

She was going to get sick, she could just feel it.

A car pulled up beside her again, but she didn't look back at it this time. Then she heard the door to the car open and shut.

Jai saw a soaked figure walking along the street and his heart skipped a beat. Was it her? He couldn't see clearly, the rain was coming down pretty hard. He wound the window down and he breathed a sigh of relief. He had found her. Guilt sent a shock through him; he was to blame for this.

Look at her, he thought. She was soaked through to her skin. Her hair was stuck to her face, her makeup running down her cheeks. Her arms were wrapped around her and he wanted those to be his arms. He had promised her that she could trust him. He said he would look after her, but he wasn't doing a very good job.

The last few hours had felt like days.

This feisty woman had bewitched him, cast a spell on him, he could think of nothing else. He had fallen hard for her, and right now, he would be willing to do anything for her. Life was unimaginable without her and these last few hours had just re-affirmed his inner, most deepest feelings for this beautiful person. He got out of the car and shut the door. He had to get her home before she got really sick.

"Nik, where have you been babe? I've been looking for you everywhere," he yelled over the noise of the rain and the traffic.

Nikita couldn't believe Jai was calling her babe. He had lost that right this afternoon. After everything he had done, he thought she was going forgive him, just like that. Well, she had news for him and she wasn't going to put up with any more shit. She'd had enough. She turned and stomped towards him unleashing everything she had. "Don't you dare call me babe, Jai, just don't. You bastard, how could you do this to me? I trusted you," she shouted, poking a finger into his chest.

He raised his hands to cup her face.

Nikita pushed them away. "Don't touch me."

Jai dropped his hands and sighed. "Nik, look, I know you're angry, but please just come home with me. Let me get you out of the cold and then you can scream at me all you like," he said in a lower voice.

Nikita wanted to hit him, she wanted to bang at his chest using both her fists, but she was never going to bring herself down to the same level as her bastard ex. She chose not to behave in that way, he didn't.

"That's not my home," Nikita said through gritted teeth.

"Please, come with me, it's not safe for you out here," he said. "Please."

"So now you give a shit? You can drop the act Jai, I've got your number you fucking arsehole."

Jai cringed at the use of language. It hurt him to think she thought of him that way, but he also knew she was hurting even more.

Nikita looked around and sighed. There was nowhere else for her to go. She had no choice but to go with him, but only for tonight. Tomorrow she would pack her bags and leave. She didn't know where she would go but she just knew she would have to leave. He had used her, so tonight she would use him too, use his apartment.

Nikita turned around and walked to the car. She didn't look at him. Quietly she climbed in the passenger seat.

Jai got in the car and started the engine but didn't say anything. He placed his hands on the steering wheel and took in a deep breath. In his heart he thanked God that he had found her.

Nikita looked out of the window, because she did not want him to see the tears running down her face. She quickly wiped them away with her cold hands but as soon as she did, they were replaced with more tears. She wasn't able to control them no matter how hard she tried. Was this all her life was about? Her, crying like a fucking idiot. Getting slapped in the face by life? Was there any point in anything?

It took them a lot longer to get back to the apartment than she thought it would. She must have walked much further than she had realised. He parked up in the car park and she got out and headed for the lift. She didn't wait for him.

He ran to catch up and he noticed the zombie like expression on her face. He tried to put his arm around her to comfort her, but she shrugged it off.

She only planned to spend the night there and as soon as the morning came, she would to be out of there. Maybe she could go and stay with Jazz for a few days until she could decide what to do. Yes, that's what she would do.

When they got into the apartment, Jai shut the door behind her. Nikita fell onto the sofa. She was so tired, and drained and soaked by this point that she couldn't even stand. Her legs had turned to jelly, her fingers were frozen numb and her body still shook with anger. Jai put a blanket over her and then went straight to the kitchen and made a hot cup of tea.

"I don't want it," she fought back. "I don't want anything from you." She shot him a fierce glare. Her eye liner and mascara were all running down her face.

Jai wanted to reach up and wipe the rain from her face. He wanted to sweep her up in his arms and take her into the bathroom, run her a hot bath. He knew if she didn't get out of those clothes soon, she would become very ill.

"Nik, please drink something hot. You've been out in the cold for hours, you'll get sick," he begged.

"What do you care, Jai? If you cared about me, you wouldn't have been all over Tina last week would you?" she cried.

"Nik, I wasn't."

"Don't lie to me Jai. Kevin showed me the photo. He told me he took the picture last week."

"He was lying to you, I promise."

"Why would he lie to me Jai? Why would he?" she shouted.

"Nik, he was lying to you. Did he show you the date of the picture on his phone?"

"No."

"He lied to you because he likes you and wanted to cause a rift between us."

"What? Don't treat me like a fool Jai. Do you really think I'm going to believe that? And do you know what else he said?"

A lump settled in Jai's throat.

"He told me I could come and work for him and do the same favours for him, which I have done for you."

Jai tried to put his hands on Nikita's shoulders but she didn't want any of it. She pushed them away.

"May be I will Jai. May be, I'll go and fuck him, just like I fucked you. Everyone thinks I'm a fucking prostitute anyway. Tina, Kevin, the people on the street." The tears rolled down Nikita's cheeks.

Jai saw the agony in her face and he could hold back no longer. He pulled Nikita into an embrace, pulling against her trying to push him away.

She punched at his chest but he didn't move. His chest was as hard as a rock and after a moment he grabbed her arms and held them to his heart.

"Why did you do this to me?" She whispered, her whole body trembling.

"Nik, I love you. You have to believe me, I'm not lying to you. That photo was taken more than 6 months ago when Tina and I were together. Look, I spoke to him about you a few times on the phone over the last few months and when he turned up tonight and he saw you, he asked if you were dating anyone. So I told him about us. He congratulated me but I could tell it wasn't sincere, but I didn't think anything of it. I didn't think he would try anything like this and when I found out what he had done, I threw him out. He was meant to be my best mate. I can't believe he would pull a stunt like this," Jai said exasperated.

She had to believe him. Jai didn't know how else he could convince her and he couldn't imagine life without her. Life without Nikita would be like, the ocean without water, flowers without scents, butterflies without colours. Life would have no point.

"Please don't lie to me Jai. I won't be able to handle it if you are lying to me. Just tell me straight if you are still seeing her, because if you are, I will walk out of your life and never come back."

"That is the truth Nik, I promise you. Do you really think I can survive without you? I need you."

Nikita looked into his face for a long moment and his eyes were honest. She watched him as he stared back at her with pleading eyes. Her eyes welled up and the tears started again. Jai lifted his hand up and wiped the tears from her face and as soon as he touched her, she felt the same electricity flow through her body. She burst into tears uncontrollably.

"Jai, please don't do this unless you really want to. Sam did what he did and I got through it, because I never loved him, not the way I love you. If you were ever to break my heart, I don't think I would be able to survive it. So if you're not sure, say it now, finish it now, it will be hard, but I will deal with it. But if we carry on as we are, I won't be able to live without you," she cried.

Jai threw his arms around her and this time she didn't shrug them off. She let him. It felt so warm to have him hold her again.

"I want to be a part of your life Nik, if you want me to. I've never felt like this about anyone before, I feel like I've found the other half of me," and he smiled a little.

Nikita leaned in and put her face into his neck under his chin. The painful knot that had embedded itself in her stomach, started to loosen. She could feel it unravelling.

He moved his face back and kissed her forehead. He leaned over and picked up the tea from the table and passed it to her.

She grabbed hold of the mug and quickly threw it down. It felt so warm and safe in his arms again and she was so comfortable, she started to fall asleep.

Jai lowered his face and placed his lips on hers. Kissed her lightly.

"Honey, you have to get out of these clothes, you'll catch pneumonia."

He walked Nikita to the bathroom and sat her on the toilet seat having dropped the lid. Placing the bath plug in the drainer, he turned on the hot water tap and poured in some of Nikita's favourite lavender and camomile bath salts. He dimmed the lighting, frightened he might make her feel uncomfortable and helped her undress. He held her hands has she stepped into the bath. She sat back and relaxed, the hot water warming her body from head to toe.

Jai grabbed Nikita's shampoo and washed her hair. There was something very soothing about this action. It brought back memories of her childhood and tears prickled in Nikita's eyes once again. She felt good, loved and content.

"Jai," she said, almost a whisper.

"Yes honey," he replied.

"You don't have to do that, I can get it."

"I want to do it. Am I doing it right? You're not getting shampoo in your eyes are you?"

"No. It feels wonderful." Nikita felt so relaxed that she could have fallen asleep in the bath.

What a day it had been. It had started out as the best day of her life. She was on top of the world and then it was like there had been an earth quake and everything was falling on top of her. She had felt suffocated in her own skin, having difficulty breathing. Then here she was again, in Jai's arms, back where she was this morning. It had all felt like a long dream, a nightmare she didn't care to visit again.

Nikita woke early in the morning finding herself alone in Jai's bed. She could hear him in the kitchen moving around, then appearing in the doorway with a cup of tea and some toast. He put the tray in front of her and sat down next to her.

"I need to use the bathroom," she told him.

Jai felt a tinge of disappointment. Nikita still hadn't forgiven him and that worried him. He also realised that pain like what Nikita had experienced yesterday, couldn't be forgotten overnight.

Nikita brushed her teeth and washed her face. Every time she closed her eyes, she saw a picture of Jai and Tina together, kissing. She believed Jai. She had no doubt the picture was old, but she couldn't get the image out of her mind. She felt red with jealousy. It was stupid really. She knew Jai and Tina had been together for a year, so it went without saying they had slept together, but that didn't help Nikita with her irrational thoughts.

Jai didn't say anything at first and just watched her as they had breakfast. It warmed Jai's heart to see her back here, sitting up in their bed. The events of yesterday seemed like a distant memory and he was very glad to have her back. Jai cursed Kevin in his mind, but then reminded himself that he could do that later. Right now, he was having breakfast with the woman he wanted to spend the rest of his life with and the thought made his breath catch a little.

"I'm sorry," Nikita said.

"Why are you apologising? It's that moron that should be saying sorry."

"Still, I shouldn't have doubted you and I should have come to you. What does that say about me? Look at what I've done. I've caused a rift between you and your best friend as well, I'm cursed," she grimaced.

"Don't you dare take the blame for this. None of this is your fault. Yeh okay, maybe you could have asked me but that arsehole shouldn't have lied to you. His behaviour is unforgivable and what he implied? It was downright disrespectful and I'll never forgive him for it. But I know why he did it. I can see his attraction," and he smiled a little.

Nikita looked at him sceptically.

"You don't see it do you? You don't see why someone would be interested in you?"

She looked at him and he could see the question in her eyes.

"You're beautiful, kind hearted and funny and in case you hadn't noticed, some men like women with curves," he smiled.

He leaned in and kissed her on the lips. She threw her arms around him and pulled herself up against him.

"If you're ever unsure about me or anything else, promise me that you'll ask me no matter how silly you feel the question is."

"I promise," she replied.

He leaned down and kissed her again as they sat there. He touched her face and it felt like heaven.

Nikita cuddled up to Jai, she smiled internally.

"Can I ask you something?"

"Yes, sure," she answered.

"Please don't take this the wrong way and I'm not angry or upset with you, okay?"

Nikita's heart sank. What did he want to ask her?........Jazz.

Her eyes dropped, she knew that he knew.

"You know, don't you?" She asked, her voice a low whisper.

"I'm sorry, I know this must be hard for you, but it kept bugging me. You never told me, and when I called Jazz, she said it, she thought I already knew. Why didn't you tell me? I could have helped you."

"Because the pain of losing a child is a pain like no other. I didn't even know I was pregnant, so it wasn't like I had time to build a bond with the baby. I hadn't even thought about being a mum and then what that bastard did to me, it killed my baby. When I found out, I told myself that it was for the best. What could I give a child? I didn't even have a place of my own to live, how was I supposed to bring up a baby?"

Nikita put a hand on her stomach and stroked it gently. "But it was my baby, my flesh and blood and he took that away from me as well. You don't know what it was like for me. I felt defeated by life itself. I thought that I was being punished for doing something really bad, maybe something in a past life. I saw my life as a failure and I wished I hadn't been born." Nikita looked in the other direction and laid her head on the pillow.

Jai pulled himself up, flush against her body and put his arm around her waist laying his hand on her tummy. He whispered in her ear. "One day, you will be a mum and you'll be the best mum in the world. You'll see."

Nikita kissed his hand and placed it over her heart, because that was what he had become to her, he was her heart.

Chapter 27 - We Miss You Child

The next two months were the best months of Nikita's life. Jai was doing really well in his work and she was doing well in hers. She gave up on looking for an apartment and became comfortable where she was. Nikita laughed like she had never laughed before. She grew in confidence, comfortable enough to say what she wanted without holding back and Jai loved it. She learnt to tease and flirt with him, without getting a flush in her face and often initiated the bedroom drama.

Valentine's Day came and went. Jai took her out to the best restaurant in town, showered her with roses and chocolates.

Nikita wore a beautiful red dress which hung just above her knees and had a plunging neck line, which revealed round plump breasts. Jai asked Nikita to walk in front of him; just so he could watch her back side wiggle. Nikita turned saw what he was doing and she swung her hips a little more.

"If you carry on shaking that gorgeous ass in front of me like that, I won't let us get to the restaurant. We'll go back to the apartment and celebrate in bed," he said in a low raspy voice, which reminded Nikita of sex and chocolates.

Nikita laughed, knowing what effect she had on him.

She walked past the canal, heading towards a restaurant overlooking this beautiful part of Birmingham. Nikita loved it here. Even though it was only February, daffodils were already blossoming in the window pots and displays. Yellow was one of her favourite colours, it always made her feel like the sun was out, even on a rainy day. Different music came from the different restaurants, 'I knew

I loved you' by Savage Gardens came from one and 'Could I Have this Kiss Forever' by Enrique Iglesias from another. Jai listened to mainly English music and Nikita had learnt to appreciate it. Lyrics were what interested her and some of these songs sounded as though they had been written specifically for her. They conveyed to Jai, the feelings she sometimes felt difficult to articulate.

She turned and came to a halt.

Jai took a step forward, bringing himself flush against her.

Nikita ran a red perfectly painted finger along his taut chest, teasingly. She licked her plump red lips slowly and he almost turned back, there and then.

"You keep that up young lady and you'll have to pay later," he said teasingly.

"Do you promise?" she teased. "I'll look forward to it," she continued, her voice low and seductive.

Nikita turned to walk towards the restaurant.

Jai took a deep breath. He had to get a grip, otherwise everyone would know what he was thinking. All they had to do was take a glance at his trousers.

They didn't make it to dessert. Nikita had made things very difficult for Jai, running her finger along her cleavage, sitting close to him, stroking his thigh. She licked her glass as she took slow sips of her lemon and mint cocktail. She loved it. It was like flicking on a switch, she knew exactly what to do. She spoke in a low seductive voice and it brought Jai to breaking point. He couldn't keep his hands off her any longer and when Nikita said, "let's pass on dessert," his will power dissipated. He just about held it together long enough to ask the waiter for the bill.

They hadn't even got in the door of the apartment and they were already ripping each other's clothes off. Making love to Jai was Nikita's favourite pass time. She'd never have believed that she would enjoy it so much. She enjoyed him so much; he left her insatiable, always wanting more. She had learnt new tricks and through practice, she had worked out exactly what he liked. She loved to hear him groan, it turned her on even more.

Jai felt ravenous around Nikita, which didn't help, as they spent so much time together. He loved to make her writhe underneath him. She would twist and squirm sometimes demanding what she wanted and he loved to please her. They spent most nights sweating and out of breath, only falling asleep when their passion and desire for each other had been satiated and they were both exhausted.

The next morning Nikita got up and threw on Jai's shirt. He gazed up at her and felt a stirring in his groin.

"I think you should always wear my shirts in the morning, you look so hot."

Nikita smiled, turned and lifted the back of the shirt exposing a naked bottom as she walked out of the bedroom.

"That's not fair," he yelled and Nikita laughed as she entered the lounge.

She walked through the lounge and over to the kitchen, picking up their clothes as she went, and put the kettle on.

Nikita could hear her phone ringing. She tried to remember where she threw her bag when they arrived home the night before. She listened out for where the ringing was coming from and found her bag behind the sofa. She pulled her phone out and saw that it was her mum. She hadn't heard from her mother for months, since she had visited the last time. Nikita wondered what her mum wanted. Had something happened to dad? Why was she ringing her all of a sudden? Nikita answered the phone.

"Hello."

"Hello Nikita, how are you? You haven't called for so long."

"I didn't think that you would want to talk to me after what happened the last time."

"Don't be silly, you are our daughter, of course we want to speak to you. Your dad has been asking about you."

"Has he? What did he say?" Nikita sounded almost hopeful.

"He asked when you were going to visit again."

Nikita couldn't believe it. Her dad actually wanted to see her. It was the only other thing she wanted in her life and now it felt like she was going to get it. She felt so excited, like daddy's little girl again.

"I will come down mum. I will make the arrangements and call you, okay? I've missed you."

"Please daughter, come soon."

Nikita was so ecstatic after she put the phone down; she ran into the bedroom and jumped on Jai to give him a big hug.

"Whoa, what's happened?" he asked.

"Mum's called and she wants me to visit. Dad's been asking for me as well, can you believe it?" Nikita grabbed Jai's face, "I can't believe it, he's been asking for me Jai." Nikita sat on the bed, her face full of optimism.

"That's great news babe. When shall we go down?"

"Umm Jai, I don't think it's a very good idea for you to come with me, let me check the waters first, before I break it to them. They won't like it, I know."

"Okay, but I'm coming with you again. We'll do the same as we did the last time. Drop me off when we get there, then pick me up after."

"But that's not fair on you Jai; you'll be walking around the shopping centre again."

"Is that what you call it? Looked more like a little market to me? Anyway don't worry about me. I quite enjoyed walking around the town and looking at some of the old Victorian shops and anyway, I enjoyed our last trip," and he raised his eyebrows at her. "I'm looking forward to our romp in the car," he laughed.

"Don't go getting any ideas," she smiled.

They travelled down a couple of weeks later and like the last time, Nikita dropped Jai into town. She pulled up into one of the parking spots and before Jai got out he leaned over and kissed her. "Good Luck," he said.

"Thanks," she replied.

Just as Jai got out of the car, Nikita's uncle, her dad's brother walked passed.

"Oh shit." Nikita's heart was in her stomach.

"What is it Nik?" Jai asked.

"Shit, shit, shit!"

"What?" he asked exasperated.

"It's my uncle, he's just walked passed and I don't know if he saw us. Shit, shit, shit, this is all I need."

"Calm down Nik, he might not have seen anything."

"Yes, but what if he did? He'll be on the phone as soon as he gets home." Nikita started to panic.

She took in a deep breath to calm herself. She thought for a moment. "I'll have to tell mum myself before she hears it from anyone else. This really will piss them off; I wasn't ready to tell them just yet."

"Don't panic, if he had seen, he probably would have stopped and said something, don't you think?" Jai asked.

"He wouldn't. You don't know him, he's like a woman. Actually when it comes to gossip, he's even worse than a woman. I'll have to tell mum, today, just in case he did see."

Jai placed his hands on her shoulder to calm her down. "Okay Nik, whatever you think is best."

She left Jai by the Arcadian and drove back to her mum's. Every time she drove down this road, she had the same weird sensation. It took her back to her childhood.

Mum was waiting in the window and opened the door before Nikita had knocked. Nikita tried to read her face to see if there was any anger in there, but it was calm. Mum held her as she walked in and dad was sitting there on his armchair as usual. The smell of fragrant scented incense sticks burning hit Nikita's nose. Jasmine and camomile and it escorted Nikita back to her life before marriage. She shook it off and walked into the living room. "Sat Shri Akal dad," Nikita greeted.

"Sat Shri Akal beta," he replied.

Her legs went weak at the knees and her eyes filled up with tears. This was the first time in years her dad had addressed her and she couldn't believe it. But even though he spoke to her, he wasn't his normal self, but that was okay, because it was going to take him some time. One step at a time, she thought to herself.

Mum went in the kitchen to make her some tea, Nikita followed in after her.

After exchanging pleasantries, Nikita had to tell her mum about Jai. "Mum, I need to talk to you about something," she grimaced. Nikita could tell her voice sounded tense. Her heart was in her stomach and her mouth went dry.

"What is it daughter?" Mum asked.

Nikita didn't know how to say it. How was her mum going to take it? It was really hard but she had to do it. She had to tell her mum about Jai, albeit she would give the toned down version of her story.

"Mum, I've met someone." There she'd said it. She waited for a reaction.

Her mum carried on pouring the tea but she didn't look at Nikita. She took a cup in for dad, and returned to the kitchen, quietly shutting the door behind her, her expression seething with anger.

"Who is he?" She asked quietly through gritted teeth. She didn't want dad to overhear. "What am I going to tell your dad? Is he black, is he white, oh God, this will be so shameful."

"Mum, he's Indian and I can talk to dad, you don't have to worry."

"He's Indian? What caste is he? You know that we only marry people of the same community."

"Hold on, wait. A minute ago you were worried about him being black or white and now you're talking about castes? Are you saying that it doesn't matter about the person? He can beat you as long as he's the same caste? Mum I didn't plan on meeting someone and it definitely wasn't written on his forehead what caste he was. The important point is that he's a very good man and he looks after me. He won't treat me the same as that other bastard did."

"But what will we tell our relatives? They will talk."

"I really don't care what they have to say. They never bothered with me when they found out what was going on, so why should I care about what they have to say?"

"What happened to you Nikita? You never used to speak this way."

"I grew up mum. I realised that life wasn't a game. I learnt that life can be such a miserable place. People hurt you and betray you and I realised when you discover something good, you have to grab it with both hands otherwise you'll regret it for the rest of your life."

Mum didn't say anything at first and then she took a deep breath. "I think you'd better leave," she said and Nikita's heart sank.

This was it. They were pushing her away again and it broke her heart. She wanted so much to be part of the family again, to be able to call her mum and tell her about Jai. Tell her how much he loved her, how he fussed over her, she wanted to share it all with her. But now it looked like she wasn't going to get this dream. Nikita brushed away the tears and straightened up. She wasn't doing anything wrong. If the price of happiness was that her family didn't want anything to do with her, then so be it. She was sick of people dictating to her. She needed to think about herself now, nobody else was going to.

"He's a good man mum and I love him. He's kind and loving and he will treat you and dad with respect, like his own mum and dad."

Mum didn't look at her.

Nikita walked through the living room. Dad was watching his Panjabi channel.

Nikita knew she had to tell him, it was now or never. She took a deep breath. "Dad, I need to speak to you." He didn't look up. Her stomach twisted and her throat seemed to close up. The pressure started to build in her head but she knew she had to do this. "Dad, I've met someone." No response. "He's kind and caring and he wants to meet you. His name is Jai." Dad's face dropped. He still didn't say anything. Her head felt pressurised with the stress and she forced herself to take a deep breath.

It was time for her to leave. She turned around and walked away. She looked back for a moment but nobody stopped her. Both mum and dad sat with their faces looking in the opposite direction to her. She had known what to expect from her dad, but it still broke her heart. She felt tears prickle at the back of her eyes and it took all her will power not to break down.

Nikita called Jai when she got in the car and told him she was coming to pick him up. When she got there he had a few carrier bags, which he placed in the boot. He handed Nikita a bag which had a box of Thornton's chocolates and a romantic fictional novel, 'Always in my heart,' by Catherine Anderson, another of Nikita's favourite authors. God, she loved him.

He opened the driver seat door. "I'll drive back," he smiled. Nikita pushed her leg over the handbrake and shifted her bum into the passenger seat. When he looked at her face, he saw the all too familiar sad expression. "I take it, it didn't go to plan?" he asked.

"Not quite, but I told them about you, so now anyone can say what they want. At least I'm not hiding anything."

"What did they say about us living together?"

"Oh, I left that part out."

"Are you alright?"

"I'm okay Jai. Better than I thought I would be. I told dad as well."

"Oh God, did you? You're brave; I have to give you that."

"I had to, I didn't want to leave mum in a predicament on whether to tell him or not and I knew that she would be worried about his reaction. So, I told him myself. If he is angry, he'll be angry with me."

Jai grabbed her hand and kissed it. He lowered it onto the gear stick with his hand on top. They were home in an hour and half, traffic was quite light.

Jai handed Nikita the box of chocolates urging her to open them. Nikita loved Thornton's chocolates, they were her guilty pleasure. Needing to feel better, she opened the ribbon bow, taking off the lid, looking for something to cheer her up. "Would you like some?" she shouted as Jai headed towards the bedroom.

"I'm okay, you go for it babe, I'll be out in just a minute."

She sat on the sofa and lifted the protective paper layer off the chocolates. "Mmmm, which one shall I have first," she mumbled. Her favourite were the nutty ones. She also loved the strawberry creams. As she run her finger across the rows of chocolate, something shiny caught her eye. It was placed in one of the little moulds in the plastic where a chocolate should have sat. She looked at it more closely and then realised what it was. It was simple but beautiful. She felt a little giddy, she couldn't catch her breath. Was she imagining this? She lifted the ring out and placed the box on the coffee table. "Jai," she tried to call but it came out more of a quiet murmur.

"Yes my Angel," he said leaning right over her. She hadn't realised when he had come back and stood by the sofa. Her eyes welled up.

Holding it in her thumb and forefinger she mumbled, "It's beautiful Jai."

He walked round the sofa and sat next to her, taking the ring from her. He took her hand and placed his hand on top of it. He was as nervous as hell, but he had wanted to do this for a while. If his mum was still around he would have taken Nikita to see her and introduced her. Deep down Jai felt his mum would have quickly fallen in love with Nikita, just as he had done. She had that effect on people.

He looked deep into her eyes, as though he was looking into her soul.

She knew what was coming and it made her feel so nervous, yet so happy and warm inside. She could feel her emotions running out of control, but she didn't want to ruin the moment by crying.

"Do you love me?" Jai asked.

"More than anything," she replied.

"Do you trust me?"

"More than I trust myself," Nikita replied quietly.

"I love you Nik," he said in a low husky voice. "You've quickly become my best friend, my family and my love. I want to spend the rest of my life with you and I want you to be my wife. Nikita Heer, will you marry me?"

Nikita gazed into Jai's eyes; she didn't know what to say. Well, she knew what she wanted to say but she was so shocked and she knew that if she tried to speak she would break.

Jai looked at her in anticipation.

She didn't want him to think she had to think about this. How could she? He was the most perfect person she had ever met. He was beautiful, caring, loving and had made her feel pleasures she had only ever dreamt about.

"Yes," was all she could say. He placed the ring on the third finger of her left hand and slid it up. She threw her arms around him and gave him the biggest hug ever, lifting herself up, until her legs were locked around his hips. She whispered in his ear, "It fits."

That was it, she couldn't control it anymore. The tears started streaming down her face and onto his shoulders. He had made her the happiest woman in the world.

A year ago she would never have dreamt that this would have happened to her. Maybe this was a dream. Maybe all of this was a dream and she would wake up any minute.

Jai pulled her back and wiped her tears.

"I'm sorry babe," she sniffed. "I'm just so happy, I can't control myself."

He just smiled and leant in and kissed her long and hard.

It excited her. Nikita wanted to show him how much she loved him. She realised she didn't feel the need to shy away anymore, so she stood taking his hand and led him to the bedroom. She sat him down onto the mattress, placing her arms around him in a desperate embrace to be close to him, her mouth was on his once again, delving deep, urging him for a response.

Jai liked the fact that she took the lead.

They kissed each other like nothing could pry them apart and before long they were fighting to get each other's clothes off. Nikita was sure she had popped a couple of the buttons on his shirt.

He stood next to her, pressing his body against her. She looked at his broad chest and run her hands across it.

Her breath caught.

Jai lifted her up in his arms and kissed her passionately on the mouth. He lay her down on the bed without breaking the kiss and climbed on top of her. His body aligned with hers.

Her hands were in his hair pulling him in deeper. They made love for a long while, slowly and passionately. It was out of this world. They were made for each other, they fit.

She lay on his chest holding her hand up and staring at her ring. It was beautiful. Jai fiddled with her finger as well, admiring the ring on her hand. It sparkled outrageously. She loved it and so did he.

Nikita was so taken aback by the sentiment. Jai could have bought the ring from anywhere, but he chose to buy it from her home town. Now she would always have the memory of her home with her all the time. Jai was so thoughtful and she believed he loved her unconditionally.

***

The following day her mobile started ringing. It was a number Nikita didn't recognise. Normally she didn't anonymous calls but she answered this one anyway.

"Hello."

"Hi Nikita, it's me Ria."

Nikita was shocked and she rocked back on her toes. She hadn't spoken to her sister for probably eighteen months if not two years. Ria didn't want anything to do with Nikita. She was just one other person in Nikita's life that Sam had managed to manipulate. Ria thought the sun shone out of Sam's backside and she was so busy with her own life at university that she didn't have time for anyone else.

"Hi Ria," Nikita said with a hint of sarcasm. "I'm surprised you remember who I am."

"I'm really sorry Nikita; I know you must hate me. You went through a tough time and I wasn't there for you."

Nikita laughed sarcastically. "Tough time, is that what you would call it?"

"I don't understand?" Ria said.

Nikita felt anger rise up inside her and she was unable to control her response.

"Well, if you call being forced to have sex, a tough time, then it was a tough time. If you call being strangled until you're unconscious a tough time, then it was a tough time. If you call having to live in a hostel for six months without any family or friends to support you a tough time, then it was a tough time."

Ria fell silent for a short while and then she let out a heavy sigh. "I'm so sorry Nikita, I had no idea."

"How could you know? You never even tried to contact me."

"I know I didn't and I don't know what to say. I'm sorry. I feel ashamed I didn't support you. I thought that Sam was a good guy and I believed him over you. I feel terrible about it."

"So why call now?" Nikita asked coldly.

"I spoke to mum yesterday and she told me that you visited. She told me that you've met someone and I just wanted to wish you all the best."

"Just like that?"

"Well yes. Actually mum told me about the incident that happened when you visited before and she told me the whole story as you told her. You have to believe me Nikita, I had no idea he was violent. Who'd have thought that someone so well educated could behave like such an animal?"

Nikita felt relieved that her sister had at least acknowledged what was going on. Mum must believe her also, otherwise why would she tell Ria? Nikita felt like heavy weights had been lifted off her shoulders.

"Well it's all in the past now. I don't care about him anymore. Tell me about you. How's Uni?"

"I've finished. I got a 2:1."

"Well, that's great, well done."

"Thanks. Mum told me about Jai. Are you sure about him?" Ria asked bringing the conversation back.

"Ria, just because I had one failing relationship doesn't mean they are all going to be like that," Nikita snapped back.

"I didn't mean it like that. I just meant is he the one for you?"

"He is," Nikita replied absolutely sure.

"Tell me something about him."

"Well he's an actor, he's my best friend, he's gorgeous, he's a wonderful person and he loves me and guess what?" Nikita couldn't help herself.

"What?"

"He proposed to me yesterday."

"Wow, congratulations. He sounds like a fantastic person. If he makes you happy Nikita, you should go for it. You know that mum isn't actually that against the idea, she's just worried about what dad will say. Deep down I think that she's relieved that you have found someone. She really worries about you."

"I know she does. Maybe you could come up some time and we'll go for a meal or something. Mum can come too and you can both meet Jai."

"I'd like that. I'll give you a call once I have sorted a weekend out."

"Okay, great. I'll see you soon."

"Bye." And then she was gone.

Nikita couldn't believe that Ria had called her. After the way mum had reacted yesterday, having been told about Jai, Nikita was surprised at what Ria had said. Maybe things would work out. If mum was coming round to the idea, may be dad would too, in time. Nikita recognised that may be she was being overly optimistic but a girl could dream couldn't she? Miracles still existed, Jai was testimony of that.

When Jai got home Nikita told him about Ria had calling that afternoon. Jai was as shocked as Nikita.

"It's great she called, sounds like she really is sorry," he said.

"I hope you don't mind, I've invited her and mum, if she'll come, over for dinner and to meet you but I'm not sure when that will be. Ria said she will let me know."

"That's fine babe, this is as much your home as it is mine."

Jai proved to Nikita once again what a wonderful person he was.

"Babe, Michael came to see me. He handed me this envelope and asked me to give it to you."

"What is it?"

"I don't know, open it and have a look."

Nikita ripped open the big A4 size brown envelope. It had a number of papers in it which she pulled out. She read them carefully. She couldn't breathe. She couldn't believe it. Finally.

"What is it Nik?"

"It's my divorce papers. It's all gone through. I can't believe it, it's finally over. Oh Jai," she screamed and she threw her arms around him. "I'm free, I'm finally free," she laughed heartedly. "Let's drink to it. Tea?"

Jai smiled with relief.

"But I don't understand, how did Michael pull it off so easily? I expected that low life would have made it as difficult as possible for me."

"Michael just knows which strings to pull. He called him and told him that if he resisted, he'd take it to court and he would call witnesses to the incident in Bradford. Michael told him that it was in his best interest to co-operate with him, otherwise his reputation would be dragged through the mud. So he signed the papers."

Nikita looked at Jai. She felt so much respect for him, so much love for him, it seeped through from every part of her body. It was too much. How could someone love another person this much? It was crazy.

"Jai, I don't know what to say to you. How can I ever show you how grateful I am for everything you've done for me?"

Jai brought his hands up and cupped Nikita's face.

"Just love me, that's all I ask."

"I love you more than anything."

Jai kissed her lips tenderly.

He'd been doing some thinking too. Nikita had taken the step and told her family about him. It was time he showed his commitment by doing the same.

"I've decided I'm going to tell uncle about us," he said.

"Are you sure?" Nikita asked. "What if they're not happy about it all?" What if they don't like me, she thought.

"I really don't care what they have to say. I'm just telling them because I know that's what mum would have wanted and if they're happy for me, then great and if they're not then I really don't care. I've made my own decisions for a long time without them and I will continue making them."

Nikita intertwined her fingers with his and pulled his hand up and kissed it. She would kiss him all day if she could. She always felt compelled to touch him, kiss him, hug him and make love to him. It was like someone had cast a spell on her, but she knew that was impossible. She knew that it was only her heart that compelled her to do all these things and she had no control over herself.

"It's up to you babe. When are you going to call him? Do you want me to be around?" She sounded a little nervous.

"Call him? I'm not going to call him. We're going to visit them."

"We? What do you mean we?"

"We, as in you and me. I'm going to take you down there so that they can meet you."

"I'm not sure that's a good idea. What if they don't like me?"

"They're going to love you. And if they don't, they probably need their heads testing but like I said, I really don't give a shit."

"Okay, but if they say something you're not happy with, I don't want you to start anything, we'll just leave. Is that okay?"

"Okay. Like I said before, mum always looked up to uncle and I'm only doing this for her."

Chapter 28 - Who is she?

Jai had called ahead and told his uncle and aunt he was coming down to visit and that he had a surprise for them. They seemed really happy that he was visiting. He hadn't been to visit since the funeral and it had been years since he had visited before then.

Nikita was so nervous; she didn't know how she was going to handle this. She didn't know what to wear and she was so worried. She knew the fact that she had been divorced was going to be a sore point and they would probably be unhappy with Jai for that reason. But then again, they may just think she wasn't good enough for him. What if they ask her about her education, what will she tell them? Their nephew is an up and coming superstar and she's a secretary. She didn't think that would go down very well either. Then she shook her head. Stop shredding your self esteem, she told herself. He loves you and that's all that matters.

Nikita decided to wear a baby pink Indian suit. She thought it would make a good impression. She kept it simple, not too much makeup and when she came out of Jai's bedroom, he liked what he saw and smiled.

"When I see you in those clothes, it really does something to me. You look beautiful."

"Thanks," she said smiling.

"Do you think uncle and auntie will like it?"

"Mum would have loved it."

"Do you think so?"

"She would have come over to you, put both hands on your face and kissed you on your forehead. Then she would have placed her hand on your head and given you her blessing." Jai spoke as he demonstrated the actions.

Nikita knew Jai missed his mum immensely, but there was nothing anyone could do about that. She wished she could, she hated to see him in pain like this.

It wasn't a long drive to his uncle's house. Jai pulled up outside. It was a big detached house, with a huge drive which had space enough for five cars. Uncle must be doing well for himself, she thought. She got out of the car and Jai walked round and grabbed her hand. He led her to the front door and rang the bell. The bell sounded and it chimed Sikh hymns. Nikita's dad had one of these door bells on his house in Punjab in India. They must be a religious family, Nikita thought. Was that a good thing or a bad thing? She couldn't make her mind up. Then she heard someone coming to the door and Jai squeezed her hand. She took a deep breath and the door opened. Auntie stood smiling on the doorstep. She was a big lady with a fair complexion and her hair was tied back in a bun. She wore an Indian suit with the scarf draped around her neck. She had a big gleaming smile, which made Nikita feel at ease. Maybe Nikita didn't have anything to worry about after all. Nikita put her hand out and she bent down to touch auntie's feet out of respect. Auntie put her hand on Nikita's head and then placed her hands on Nikita's shoulders and pulled her back up. She gave Nikita a big warm hug and her blessings.

"God bless you," she said.

Jai seemed very comfortable. Auntie walked them into the lounge and asked Jai and Nikita to sit down. She said that she was going to get the tea from the kitchen.

The house was big and beautiful. The wall between the living room and lounge had been knocked through to make an open plan lounge. They had beautiful leather sofas and with cream walls and laminate floors, the interior had a contemporary feel.

Nikita could smell the aroma of fennel seeds and cardamoms wafting through the house. She loved spiced tea.

Then Nikita heard a deeper voice and her stomach turned. It must be Jai's uncle. Jai squeezed her hand again reassuringly, just as uncle walked in.

"Hi uncle," Jai said.

"Hello putt."

It was nice the way uncle addressed Jai as son.

"Sat Shri Akal Uncle," Nikita said as she got up and touched his feet.

"It's okay, you don't have to do that," he said in a cold voice.

Uncle stared down at her and the little bit of confidence she had built up since she had met auntie in the last five minutes, suddenly sank away. She could tell this wasn't going to go well.

"So, this is your surprise." he said.

Doesn't beat around the bush does he? Nikita thought, but she didn't look up at him.

Jai introduced Nikita to him.

"Where are your parents from?" he asked

"They're from Punjab, India," she replied.

"Which part?"

"Phagwara."

"What caste are you?"

This question shook Nikita. These people were just as bad as her parents. This family obviously had issues with class and caste, how backwards.

"Uncle, what has that got to do with anything?" Jai asked quickly.

Nikita could tell he wasn't happy with the line of questioning.

Auntie walked in with the tea and placed it on the coffee table in front of them.

"I need to know," he snapped. "We have a status to uphold in society, so I need to know her caste."

He was talking as though Nikita wasn't even there and she decided she didn't like him. He sounded like an arrogant bastard but Nikita didn't want Jai to know how she was feeling. She knew he would set all his family aside for her, but she didn't want that. He had lost too much already. Jai's voice jerked Nikita's thoughts back to the living room.

"What sort of crap is this? All you need to know is that we are happy together and we are getting married, either with or without your blessing." Jai's voice was firm.

Nikita tugged on his hand, to remind him of their agreement. She didn't want Jai to argue with his family for her. Nikita looked over to auntie, who just stood in the corner, not saying anything. Same old story, Nikita thought. She was standing with her shoulders sagged, her face contorted and every now and then, Nikita thought she noticed her wanting to say something but then lowering her eyes again.

Nikita knew the caste difference would be an issue. She never understood why though. People believed themselves to be good Sikhs, yet they asked questions around caste. It went against the very basis of Sikhism and these practices shouldn't exist in society today, it was ridiculous.

Jai pulled Nikita up.

"We're leaving."

Nikita looked over at auntie but she couldn't meet her gaze, Auntie let her head hang. As they walked towards the front door, auntie followed.

She whispered in Jai's ear. "Meet me at the restaurant on the corner of the road in thirty minutes."

Jai looked at her confused.

"Please," she begged.

Nikita reached out and placed her hand on auntie's hand in reassurance, nodding in agreement.

Jai and Nikita got in the car and drove to the end of the road where there was a small bar and restaurant. Jai was very quiet. Nikita was glad they had stopped here. She felt parched. They hadn't had the chance to have any tea at the house before Jai's uncle started on them.

"Shall I get you a coke?" Jai asked quietly.

"Yes please, no ice."

Jai got himself half a pint of lager which he topped up with lemonade as he was driving and he sat down, still very quiet.

Nikita gave it a minute before she spoke. "Are you okay?"

"I'm okay," he sighed. "It just makes me so angry that in this day and age, people can still have such pathetic views."

"It's just the way that things are Jai. Your uncle isn't the only one that feels that way, many parents do. Even mine do."

"Yes but it's time things changed."

"And they will, with our generation. We will change things."

"I'm sorry I put you through that Nik, I should have realised these people were not going to accept this."

"I don't know Jai, auntie seemed to like me."

"But who's going to listen to her? She's just the silent minority in that house."

"Why do you think she asked to see us?"

"I'm not sure, but I guess we're about to find out." Auntie walked through the entrance door.

She came and sat down beside Jai. She was out of breath and Jai offered to buy her a drink.

"I'm really sorry about your uncle, Jai. He's just so old fashioned and no matter how hard anyone tries, he won't change his ways. And I'm sorry I couldn't do more to help you today. I can't speak against him."

She didn't look at them when she said this and she seemed to blush a little.

Nikita reached across Jai and placed her hand on auntie's hand to reassure her. "Don't worry auntie, we understand."

Auntie placed a hand on top of Nikita's. "You are so very dear Nikita, Jai has chosen well."

She took a deep breath. "Jai putt, I have something for you. Please hold out your hand."

Why on earth was she asking him to do that? He looked at Nikita and then looked back at his aunt, then opened his palm and held it out.

"You know that your mum and I were close." It was a statement rather than a question.

Jai nodded.

"Before she died, she gave me a couple of things for you. She didn't want these left with your dad because she knew he would sell them for cash and use the money for alcohol. So she left them with me and asked me to promise to give these to you when the time was right. I suppose that time is now."

Jai's face was like stone. Nobody ever spoke to him about his mum and for the first time someone had mentioned her, he felt like that little boy inside that wished his mum was still here.

She handed Jai a small red velvet pouch which had a gold draw string. Jai pulled the top of the pouch open and took out two gold bangles, studded with green and ruby stones and a gold cluster ring. He looked at his aunt in confusion.

She ran a hand over his head and placed it on his shoulder. "Your mum would have been so proud of your choice. When she was in hospital she asked me to pop round the house and she told me where she had hidden this bag. She asked me to bring it with me when I visited her the next time. I then went to your home and made an excuse about picking up some clothes for her and found the jewellery in her bedroom. I took it to the hospital with me and she told me she wanted to give these to her daughter in law herself, but when her health deteriorated, she knew she wasn't going to make it. So she gave them to me to look after. She said, 'when Jai decides to marry, give these to my daughter in law and give her my love and blessings. Tell her I'm sorry. I wanted to do so much more but I just haven't got the time now, but please accept these with my love'. She was a wonderful woman and my best friend for years. When she left this world, she took a piece of my heart with her. It's never been the same since she's been gone."

Auntie had looked after these gifts, all this time and never told anyone. Jai's aunt reached over and placed her hand on Nikita's head. "This is the blessing that she sent for you."

Nikita leaned in fighting back her tears and Jai's aunt kissed her temple.

Jai's forehead creased from the pain that was striking him in his heart. He never knew what his mum was planning, but it filled his heart with warmth to hear these words.

Jai stared at the jewellery in his hands.

"She always said to me, who ever Jai marries, will be an angel, because Jai himself is an angel. She asked me to tell you Jai, that she loves you and she will always love and watch over you."

Jai didn't know what to say. He was stunned. No one had ever told him this before. He didn't have anything that belonged to his mum and now all of a sudden he had all of this. He felt overwhelmed.

Nikita wanted to ask Jai if he was okay, but that was a stupid question. She placed her hand on his back and slowly stroked it. It was all she could do to comfort him.

Jai looked down at the bangles again. They looked very expensive.

"Your mum saved for a long time to get these made. She saved every pound she could. She always said she didn't want her daughter in law going without. She wanted me to give these to you Nikita, on your wedding day, but as I don't think that I will be able to attend, I thought it would be best that I give these to you now. It will be a weight off my shoulders."

Nikita gave auntie a hug and with that, Auntie left the restaurant. She wanted to get back quickly; she had told her husband, she was only popping to the shops.

Jai still looked stunned. He sat for some time holding the jewellery in his hand.

Nikita didn't say anything either.

After a few moments, Jai grabbed her hand, opened the bangle from the little screw fastening and then placed it around her wrist. Then he did the same with the other.

"Jai, I can't have these. This is your mums memory."

"No, she wanted for you to have them. Please wear them."

There was so much anguish in his voice; Nikita didn't have the heart to contest.

Jai fiddled with the bangles on Nikita's wrists and then he pulled her hands up and kissed them one by one. Then, as he let go of one hand, he placed the cluster ring on her finger. It was beautiful. Nikita wanted to argue with him, she didn't think it was fair. He had only just come into the possession of his mum's legacy and he was giving it away. To her.

Nikita adored this man sitting in front of her and couldn't bring herself to offend him or his mother's wishes.

When they got home Jai went straight to his bedroom. Nikita was torn between wanting to give him space and feeling he shouldn't be left on his own. She followed him in after a few moments and she could tell he was very upset and overwhelmed. She held him for a while. He lay between her legs, with his head on her chest as she sat leaning up against the bed headboard. Jai fell asleep in the comfort of Nikita's arms. She didn't want to disturb him so she sat there for an hour or so, before he started to stir.

Jai felt so comfortable where he lay, never wanting to get up. He felt such warmth and love for this woman and the notion that he could do anything for her, didn't surprise him. Jai had never felt such love before, it almost overwhelmed him. He knew at that point he had to marry her and make Nikita his wife. He could wait no longer.

Nikita thought about Jai's mum and wished she was still here. Nikita would have done everything to make her happy; she could feel it in her heart that they would have got along. She sounded like such a sweet lady and for one selfish second, Nikita felt cheated that she would never have a relationship with her. Nikita knew that her thoughts were silly. She had never met the lady and was sad, for Jai. His mum was everything to him and he had lost her in such a terrible way. No one deserved to go through that.

Jai's voice brought Nikita back from her thoughts.

"I love you," he said.

"I love you too," she smiled.

"Let's do it, let's get married. We don't need anyone there, just you and me. We'll find some witnesses."

Nikita looked at Jai startled. Oh my God, did he really mean this? Was he serious? Nikita wanted nothing more than to be tied to this beautiful, intelligent man. Her heart beat quickened in excitement.

"Are you sure you want to do this?"

"Do you doubt me?" he asked.

"No, no Jai, of course I don't."

"Then let's do it. My film is going to be launching next month and on the back of that, fingers crossed, I will get lots more work and I want you by my side, all the way."

Nikita felt a shudder of exhilaration run through her body. "But how and when? I'll have to buy something to wear."

Jai sat up. "Okay, let's go shopping."

"What now?" She couldn't hide the gleam in her eyes.

"No time like the present," he smiled. "We'll book a date at the register office as soon as they have a slot available. I don't want to wait anymore."

"Okay, but you have to promise me one thing."

"What?"

Holding his face in her hands, she kissed him. "You have to come to the Gurdwara with me afterwards to get blessed. Agreed?"

"Anything for you my baby. Anything."

Nikita lay in his arms and thought about forever. She couldn't believe how her life had changed and all because an angel had been sent to save her and set her free.

My angel, my life

You give me things I can only dream of
You protect me and love me
And share everything with me
If you hadn't been sent for me
I don't know where I would be
My prayers have been answered
Someone must have heard me
Sometimes I pinch myself to ensure I'm not dreaming
And if this is a dream, I pray I never awake
I feel like a bird, spreading my wings wide
Warming myself in the rays of your sunshine
You've showed me the way, to live my life for me
Because of you, I've learnt to be free